UNLOCKING THE TORAH TEXT

AN IN-DEPTH JOURNEY INTO THE WEEKLY PARSHA

BEREISHIT

SHMUEL GOLDIN

Typesetting: Raphaël Freeman, Renana Typesetting
Cover Design: S. Kim Glassman

ISBN 978-965-229-412-8

Edition 3 5 7 9 8 6 4

Gefen Publishing House Ltd.
6 Hatzvi Street, Jerusalem 94386, Israel
972-2-538-0247 • orders@gefenpublishing.com

Gefen Books
11 Edison Place, Springfield, NJ 07081
516-593-1234 • orders@gefenpublishing.com

www.gefenpublishing.com

Printed in Israel

Send for our free catalogue

Dedicated to the Memory of My Two Grandfathers

Rabbi Hyman E. Goldin, a true religious Renaissance man, Judaic scholar and groundbreaking author of English Jewish literature. My grandfather wrote over fifty works including: the English translation of the *Kitzur Shulchan Aruch* (the Code of Jewish Law), *Hamadrich* (the Rabbi's Guide), *The Case of the Nazarene Reopened* (an acclaimed scholarly text based upon sources in the Gospels in which he put the Jewish people on trial for the killing of Christ and legally proved their innocence), numerous Jewish histories, anthologies and texts.

During his life journey from Eishyshok, Lithuania, to Brooklyn, New York, to the Adirondack Mountains (where he established the boys' and girls' camps Nahar and Naomi and, later, the Blue Sky Lodge Hotel), his fertile mind found intellectual challenge every stop along the way (collaborating for example, as chaplain of Comstock Prison, with two convicts in the writing of the *Dictionary of American Underworld Lingo*).

His contribution to the scholarly growth of the American Jewish community was immeasurable.

Rabbi Avraham "Alter" Poplack, a Talmudic scholar, close associate of great Jewish luminaries (including Rabbi Yaakov Kamenetsky, Rabbi Aharon Kotler, Rabbi Yitzchak Hutner and many others) and pioneering teacher of rabbis and community leaders.

A product of the famed Slobodka Yeshiva, my grandfather carried that institution's living legacy with him throughout his life travels from Slobodka, Lithuania, to Seattle, Washington, to Brooklyn, New York, and finally to Bnei Brak, Israel. His traditional observance and values never wavered in the face of great challenge and adversity. With warmth and love, he successfully transmitted those traditions and values to countless students and, above all, to his own family.

I remember him always with a *sefer* (religious text) in his hand and warm words of Torah on his lips.

The balance of their combined legacies has helped shape not only my religious vision but my life path.

This set, *Unlocking the Torah Text*,
is lovingly dedicated to the memory of

my parents

Naftali and Lola Goldman
נפתלי בן יוסף הכהן
לאה בת חנניא יום טוב ליפא הלוי

who exemplified love of
תורה, ארץ ישראל ועם ישראל

and my grandparents, aunts and uncles, and great-grandparents
who perished in the Shoah

Josef (Yussel) and Bayla Goldman
Avrum, Ascher and Gittel

Leopold (Lipa) and Rose Weinfeld
Ascher Weinfeld

Yosef and Bina Korn

Shiya and Miriam Weinfeld

and to the memory of

David (Dudek) Fink
אריה דוד בן משה מאיר הכהן

stepfather and *bompa* extraordinaire

JOSEPH (YOSSI) AND GAIL GOLDMAN
NEIL, DANIEL AND MICHAEL

Contents

Acknowledgments

I could not have asked for a warmer welcome or more professional assistance than I received from the management and staff at Gefen Publishing House.

Ilan Greenfield, the publisher at Gefen, embraced the project from the outset with excitement and innovative skill.

Smadar Belilty, Gefen's projects coordinator, shepherded me with patience through the detailed steps of the publishing process.

Kezia Raffel Pride edited the manuscript with wisdom, clarity, professionalism and humor. Her direction, advice and friendship proved invaluable throughout.

* * *

Raphael and Linda Benaroya, Kenneth and Ruthann Eckstein, Daniel and Thalia Federbush, David and Jodi Goldberg, Mark and Anita Sarna and Seena Flechner (on behalf of the Eve Flechner Institute, where many of the studies in this book were first presented) provided material assistance and encouragement at a critical point in the development of this project. I deeply appreciate their support and friendship.

My dedicated administrative assistant, Eileen Gorlyn, helps manage my professional life on a daily basis. Without her steadfast service this project would not have been possible.

* * *

I have been blessed with the opportunity to serve for the past twenty-three years as Rabbi of Congregation Ahavath Torah in Englewood, New Jersey, one of the most extraordinary congregations in the Jewish world today. This book reflects the many lessons I have learned with and from my congregants as we have searched, studied and learned together. Mirrored, as well, are the probing questions and insights raised by my students at Yeshiva

University and in other settings. I am thankful for the countless hours of mutual exploration.

* * *

I owe everything to my family. My father, Isaac Goldin, of blessed memory, set an example of personal responsibility, fidelity, and commitment that continues to inform every day of my life. My mother, Pearl Goldin, teaches me daily through her exuberant love of learning, religious devotion, deep commitment to Torah ideals and love of family.

My children, Avi and Rena, Yossi and Shifra, Yehuda, Donny and Rivka, and my grandchildren, Isaac and Benjamin, are the light of my life and the inspiration for all that I do. Their suggestions, comments and gentle (and not so gentle) teasing helped me maintain my sanity during some difficult points in this project.

Special thanks to Yossi, my mother and my cousin Laura for the hours they spent in proofreading the text.

* * *

Finally, and most importantly, none of this (or much else, for that matter) would be possible without the love, support and wisdom of my wife, Barbara. Knowing me better than I do myself, she saw how critical a sabbatical year in Israel would be to my dream of writing, and she created – and insisted (over my shortsighted objections) upon taking advantage of – the opportunity for me to write this book. Through our years of partnership she has kept me on the straight and narrow, always helping me regain perspective on the important things in life when I begin to lose my way. I love her deeply and appreciate all that she does. Rabbi Akiva's admonition to his students concerning his own wife could not be more appropriate: What is mine and what is yours, we owe to her…

Introduction

I have wanted to write this book for years. Now that a sabbatical year in Israel provides me with the opportunity, I find the task both easier and harder than I thought it would be.

On the one hand, the necessary material is readily at hand. The studies in this volume are based on over three decades of classes and lectures, delivered to varied audiences ranging from those encountering the biblical text for the first time to those who have spent countless hours exploring its pages.

Clearly, the problem is not what to write.

The challenge instead stems from my desire to convey something deeper.

I want the reader to experience the sense of excitement and discovery that I feel when a familiar Torah passage finally gives up its treasures – age-old wisdom with uncanny relevance to our lives. I hope to convey the growing wonder that I have seen in the eyes of countless students when the full significance of texts they thought they knew suddenly becomes evident.

My teaching experience has convinced me that the wealth of the Torah text is accessible to all who seek it in earnest, regardless of their prior level of knowledge, educational background or religious affiliation. I have found that, when properly approached, the weekly reading of the Torah never fails to yield timely substance that can serve as the basis for challenging family study, meaningful discussion, deep philosophical debate and more.

Teaching Chumash has become, for me, a passionate journey – a passage shaped by timeless lessons emerging from an eternal text. My goal is to share that journey with you.

To succeed we must overcome two related obstacles.

1. *We will have to approach familiar texts with total openness, as if we have never seen them before.*

This is harder than it sounds. We first learn sections of the Torah – particularly sections of Bereishit – either within the text or in story form, as young children in grade school. Many of us never really return to these passages, in critical fashion, as adults. Our perception of their contents remains rooted at fourth- or fifth-grade levels. The well-known characters of the narrative attain a fairytale-like quality, so that neither they nor the experiences that surround their lives seem truly real.

The treasures of the text can only be uncovered when the narrative itself is seen as the truth, comprised of real events that happened to real people. The story of Noach is not a fable; the patriarchs and matriarchs lived, loved and struggled; Yosef truly journeyed from slavery to power in Egypt. They, together with other personalities whom we will meet as we travel through Bereishit, have much to teach us about ourselves.

When we break through the preconceived notions that color our approach to Torah text, we will find ourselves confronting rich, complex stories that can inform our own lives significantly.

2. *We will have to distinguish between what is written in the text and what is not.*

I have deep misgivings about the way Chumash is taught in our day schools and in other educational settings. Simply put, we constantly confuse *pshat* with *drash*.

As we will learn in greater depth (see Bereishit 5, *Approaches* B), *pshat* refers to the straightforward explanation of the text, while *drash* refers to rabbinic commentary serving as a vehicle for the transmission of lessons and ideas beyond the literal narrative. Proper understanding of *pshat* reveals deep, unexpected meaning within the text itself, while the lessons conveyed through *drash* provide an all-important glimpse into the hierarchy of values and concepts in rabbinic thought.

When we ignore the *pshat* and instead offer *drash* as the literal interpretation of the text, we end up understanding neither of these interpretive realms. This phenomenon is not only unfortunate but, in these times of intellectual searching, potentially dangerous.

A case in point might prove instructive.

A number of years ago, I challenged my students at Yeshiva University with the following sentence, describing God's actions on the fourth day of creation: "And God made *the two great luminaries*, the *greater luminary* to dominate the day and the *lesser luminary* to dominate the night…."[1]

---

1. Bereishit 1:16.

I asked the class: "The phrase 'And God made the two great luminaries' seems not only superfluous but incorrect. Why would the text first refer to the sun and the moon as if they are of comparable size and only afterwards distinguish between the *greater luminary* and the *lesser luminary*?"

Immediately a flurry of hands shot up.

"Rabbi, the answer is simple: God originally created the sun and the moon the same size (thus, the textual reference to 'the two great luminaries'). The moon, however, complained that it would be impossible for two luminaries of equal size to coexist. To punish the moon for its jealousy, God diminished the moon's size."

My students, many of whom had day school backgrounds, were accurately quoting a well-known Midrash cited in the Talmud.[2] They had obviously learned this Midrash years earlier in grade school, as explanation for the text.

I was unwilling, however, to let the matter rest.

"Tell me something," I challenged. "Do you really think that the Torah is informing us that the moon can talk? Is belief in a talking moon essential to the faith system of the Orthodox Jew?"

My students were dumbstruck. They had never before been forced to question their own acceptance of the Midrash as the literal interpretation of the text. Nor had anyone, for that matter, ever offered them an alternative explanation for the passage. Now, challenged to revisit their understanding of the text as adults, they found themselves suddenly searching for answers.

Carefully, I told the class that the Midrash in question was not necessarily meant to be understood literally. When we enter the realm of Midrash, I explained, the key question is not "*Is the Midrash literally true?*" but, rather, "*What are the rabbis trying to teach us?*" In this case, for example, the rabbis use the text to symbolically convey the dangers of jealousy as well as other, deeper messages cryptically couched in parable form.

"What, then," I continued by asking, "is the *pshat* explanation for the apparent redundancy in the text? What does the passage literally mean?"

As a possible answer, I cited a remarkable fact noted by Professor Nathan Aviezer of Bar-Ilan University. From the perspective of man, *the apparent sizes of the sun and the moon are exactly the same*. This equality in

2. Talmud Bavli Chullin 60b.

apparent size becomes evident during a solar eclipse when the moon, from our standpoint, totally covers the sun.[3]

On a literal level, the text before us first underscores the remarkable precision of God's creation. God places in the heavens "two great luminaries," two celestial spheres of dramatically different size, so precisely, that from the earth they are viewed as equal. Once this miraculous physical reality has been referenced in the text, the Torah then goes on to explain that, in terms of illumination, one of these spheres is the "greater luminary" while the other is the "lesser luminary."

My students at Yeshiva, all intelligent young men, had, for years, accepted a one-dimensional approach to this Torah text. Originally presented with the Midrashic explanation of the text as the only alternative, they found no purpose in continued inquiry into the narrative. What, after all, is the sense of further exploration when you have learned the one interpretation that *must* be accepted, even if that approach seems divorced from reality? The sophistication they would have brought to the study of any other discipline was notably absent in their approach to Torah study.

What would have been the outcome, I ask myself years later, had my students been challenged, not in the safety of my classroom, but by fellow students on a secular college campus?

To avoid these pitfalls we will have to approach the text with "new eyes."

Each of our studies will raise a series of questions designed to strike to the core of a particular passage in Bereishit. No part of the text or its contents will be off-limits. We will examine the motives and actions of the patriarchs, matriarchs and other personalities who populate the pages of Bereishit. We will probe God's role in the unfolding narrative and attempt to discern what the Torah reveals about his Divine will. We will seek to understand why events took place as they did and how the narrative might inform our lives. And, we will explore the deep philosophical currents reflected in the events described to us.

Traditional Torah study is based upon a fundamental belief in the divine authorship of the text. God's will can only be reflected in the text if the text itself is "God's word." That does not mean, however, that we are

3. Nathan Aviezer, *In the Beginning: Biblical Creation and Science* (Hoboken, NJ: KTAV Publishing House, Inc., 1990).

not supposed to question. In fact, the opposite is true. Without question and challenge, God's word and God's will remain distant and unclear. The Torah remains a closed book.

Our search for answers will take us on a journey through traditional commentary and original thought. In each study, a sampling of rabbinic opinion on the issues raised will be reviewed. Clear distinction will be made between *pshat* and *drash*, and the lessons learned from each will be discussed. Original approaches will also be offered as we humbly continue the struggle with the text.

And if we do this right, the journey will be, for each of us, a passionate one, inspiring continued exploration and thought, sparking conversation, dialogue and debate each week – over the Shabbat table and beyond – as together we unlock the treasures of the Torah text.

Bereishit

בראשית

CHAPTER 1:1–6:8

פרק א:א–ו:ח

Parsha Summary

The beginning…

With broad and majestic strokes, the Torah opens by describing the six days of creation. During this period, God forms the universe through the imposition of order upon primordial chaos. On the seventh day God "rests" and the Shabbat comes into being.

The scope of the text then narrows as the Torah returns in greater detail to the creation of Adam and Chava.

Seduced by the serpent, Adam and Chava disobey God's commandment, eat from the Tree of Knowledge of Good and Evil and are exiled from the Garden of Eden.

The second generation of man is marked by tragedy as Adam and Chava's son Kayin murders his brother Hevel in a jealous rage. Kayin is punished with continual exile across the face of the land.

Adam and Chava give birth to another son, Shet, who serves as the progenitor of all mankind.

Over the course of the next ten generations man descends into sin and corruption. As a result, God determines that mankind must be destroyed.

1 "And God Saw That It Was Good"

Context

As God views His handiwork at various points during the process of creation, the Torah declares, "and God saw that it was good."[1]

This phrase is omitted entirely on the second day of creation,[2] mentioned twice on the third day,[3] and is conspicuously absent in association with the creation of man.[4]

Finally, at the end of the six days of physical creation, the Torah states, "and God saw all that He had created and behold it was *very good*."[5]

Questions

The Torah is neither a history book nor a novel. Each word is divinely chosen to convey an essential idea.

What, then, does the Torah mean to convey with the phrase "and God saw that it was good"?

When you or I create we have no way of knowing what the finished product will be. We often step back, therefore, to determine whether what we are producing matches our intentions. For an all-knowing God, however, this review is obviously unnecessary. God knows from the outset what will be built and how it will turn out. An all-perfect being cannot make mistakes. How can it be, therefore, that God first creates and only afterwards determines that his creation is "good"?

Compounding the problem is the fact that the phrase is not used consistently in the text. What do these variations signify?

1. Bereishit 1:4, 10, 12, 18, 21, 25.
2. Ibid., 1:6–8.
3. Ibid., 1:9–13.
4. Ibid., 1:26–30.
5. Ibid., 1:31.

Approaches

A

The Ramban offers a brilliant solution to the basic question before us. He distinguishes between two different actions attributed to God throughout the creational narrative. The Torah tells us that God "spoke" (e.g., "and God said let there be light") and that God "saw" ("and God saw that it was good").

When God "speaks" during the story of creation, says the Ramban, He brings something into being; He *creates*. When God "sees," on the other hand, He moves from the realm of creating to the realm of *sustaining*. This transition is marked by the phrase "and God saw that it was good." The phrase appears when God has completed an element of creation and desires to maintain its existence.

The Ramban, however, goes much further. He emphasizes that God continues to sustain each element of creation eternally. Were God to withdraw His involvement for even a moment all would revert to nothingness.[6]

Far from a gratuitous phrase, the words "and God saw that it was good" convey the concept of God's ongoing involvement in the world. Through this eternal involvement, the process of creation continues until the end of days.

Millennia later, the rabbis would reflect this idea in the blessings before the Shma, through the statement "you renew in your goodness, each day, constantly, the works of creation."[7]

Centuries after that, Rabbi Joseph Soloveitchik (known to his many followers as the Rav) explains the difficult biblical concept of *hester panim* (the hiding of God's face) in light of the creation narrative. The Torah prophesizes that at particular moments of history, God, in response to sin, will take the radical step of "hiding His face from the world."[8] During these tragic moments, such as the Holocaust, suggests the Rav, God simply suspends His involvement and the pattern of creation is reversed. As G-d backs away, the world reverts to *tohu va'vohu*, the primordial state

6. Ramban, Bereishit 1:4.
7. Morning prayers.
8. Devarim 31:18.

of chaos which existed before God began to create. *Tohu va'vohu*, says the Rav, was not destroyed but continues to exist beneath the surface of the order imposed by God during the six days of creation. Only God's constant involvement in maintaining that order – "and God saw that it was good" – saves us from destruction.[9]

B

Having explained the basic significance of the phrase "and God saw that it was good," we now must turn our attention to the variations that appear in the text. Why, for example, is the phrase totally omitted on the second day of creation and repeated twice on the third?

Rashi explains that the work of the second day of creation was incomplete at the end of that day. Something that is incomplete, says Rashi, cannot be referred to as "good." The work of the second day was actually finished on the third day and another phase of creation was begun and completed on that day as well. The Torah, therefore, repeats the phrase "and God saw that it was good" twice on the third day to mark the completion of both of these stages of creation.[10]

Rashi's explanation, however, raises a substantial problem. Once again, we are dealing with a perfect God, Who can accomplish anything He wishes. How could it be that the work of the second day was not completed by God within its designated span of time?

Perhaps God wishes to teach us that the point of a task's end is not always clear or uniform. Certain tasks, in human experience, can be completed on one level yet remain incomplete on another. God deliberately fashions the work of the second and third days of creation to convey this lesson. He ends the second day of creation with the work of that day in flux. On one level, the job is done; the separation between heaven and earth, performed on the second day of creation, is complete. On quite another level, however, the task of separation remains unfinished. Land and water must still be delineated and that will only happen on the third day.

By leaving the work of the second day of creation finished on one level yet unfinished on another, God reminds us to be aware of the complex tasks

9. Avraham R. Besdin, ed., *Reflections of the Rav* (Hoboken, NJ: KTAV Publishing House, 1993).
10. Rashi, Bereishit 1:7.

that confront us within our own lives. A job may appear to be finished and, in fact, may be finished on one level, yet work may still need to be done. Through the story of creation, the Torah challenges us not to be misled, but to carry each task before us to its true and full point of completion.

C

Although the phrase "and God saw that it was good" is mentioned on the sixth and final day of creation, its mention precedes, and therefore excludes, the creation of man. Why is man, according to the biblical text, not "good"?

Some commentaries explain this textual phenomenon as a reflection of man's responsibility as a partner in his own creation.[11] The jury is still out. Unlike the rest of creation, man cannot be considered good from the outset, simply by dint of his being created by God. Whether or not man is a creature of value depends upon his own choices and actions, upon the self-determined quality of his own life. As the Rambam declares: "The Creator neither decrees that a man will be good nor that he will be bad."[12]

The Torah's omission of the phrase "and God saw that it was good" in association with man is, thus, essentially a challenge. We are challenged to complete the story, to determine whether or not, in the final analysis, the creation of man will be considered "good."

D

A different, unified approach can be suggested to explain the absence of the phrase "and God saw that it was good" on the second day of creation and in association with the creation of man.

On the second day of creation God created the firmament, effectively separating the realms of heaven and earth.

Perhaps the omission of the phrase "and God saw that it was good" following this act of separation is to be understood at face value. The separation of heaven and earth was effectively *not* good and simply could not be labeled as such. God wants the realms of heaven and earth to be connected. He desires that the spiritual and physical worlds interact with each other.

11. Nehama Leibowitz, *Studies in Bereishit* (Jerusalem: World Zionist Organization, 1976), p. 9.
12. Rambam, *Mishneh Torah*, Hilchot Tshuva 5:2.

Why then does God separate these two realms? To challenge man to unite them through his efforts.

The rabbis note that man is the only creature forged *min ha'elyonim u'min hatachtonim*, "from both the upper and the lower spheres."[13] We are essentially creatures in conflict, shaped from the dust of the earth, into which God breathes "the spirit of life." Heaven and earth vie for supremacy within our souls. We are part of the animal kingdom, and share with all creatures of that kingdom basic urges and needs; at the same time, however, we are the only creatures in creation who aspire to poetry, spirituality and song.

While other religions preach that sanctity can only be obtained by denying the base instincts within us, by retreating from the earthly, Judaism preaches that man is meant to unite heaven and earth within his soul. We are enjoined to raise the earthbound heavenward through the performance of daily mitzvot and the sanctification of everyday life. We are, at the same time, challenged to bring heaven to this earth through study, prayer and immersion in Torah text.

On the second day of creation, out of necessity, God separates heaven and earth but then tells us, through the omission of the phrase "and God saw that it was good," that this separation is not truly desirable. When God creates man, and challenges him to reunite heaven and earth, the phrase is once again omitted. The two omissions are clearly connected. The determination of whether or not man is good will depend on how successfully he repairs the necessary breach of the second day. God asks: Will man reunite heaven and earth through his efforts and struggles?

E

As the sixth and final day of physical creation comes to an end, the Torah states, "and God saw all that He had made and behold it was *very good*."[14] What does it mean when the Torah tells us that something is "very good" in God's eyes?

Rabbi Ovadia Sforno offers a straightforward yet wonderful suggestion. The Torah is reminding us that, in the case of creation, the whole is so much more beautiful than the sum of its parts. While every specific piece

13. Midrash Rabba Bereishit 12:8.
14. Bereishit 1:31.

of God's handiwork could be labeled by the Torah as "good," the natural world as a whole, with all of its exquisite checks and balances, can only be described as "very good."[15] We should never lose sight of the wondrous nature of the world around us.

F

On the opposite end of the interpretive spectrum, a striking Midrashic approach to the words "and behold it was very good" is offered by the rabbis. The phrase "very good," they say, refers to man's *yetzer hara*, his evil inclination.[16]

At face value, this suggestion is astounding.

According to Jewish tradition, two opposite internal forces struggle to control our lives. The *yetzer hatov*, the good inclination, is the part of man that drives him to do right; while the *yetzer hara*, the evil inclination, leads us to sin. How, then, can the rabbis possibly suggest that the evil inclination is seen by God as "very good"?

The Midrash goes on to explain: without the evil inclination, man would not get married, he would not build cities, he would neither explore nor succeed.[17]

Urges we often see as evil, suggest the rabbis – lust, ambition, the drive for control and power – are not inherently evil but, instead, natural parts of our being. Our task is not only to control these urges and drives but to channel and direct them. Properly harnessed they can lead us to the greatest good and accomplishment.

How far ahead of their time, then, were the rabbinic authors of this Midrash and how psychologically sound is their approach!

We should, the rabbis admonish, be ashamed of nothing found within our souls. No aspect of our makeup is inherently evil. Our task is to acknowledge the natural instincts and urges that beat within our hearts and then channel those urges towards good. In this way, even an impulse that could have lead us to evil – even the *yetzer hara*, the evil inclination itself – becomes "very good."

15. Sforno, Bereishit 1:31.
16. Midrash Rabba Bereishit 9:7.
17. Ibid.

2 Not Good for Man to Be Alone

Context

God creates all creatures in pairs – male and female – except for Man. Only after Adam is created in isolation does God declare: "It is not good for Man to be alone. I will create for him an *eizer k'negdo* – a helpmate."[1]

God then brings the animals before Adam to be named. When, in the process, Adam fails to find personal companionship within the animal kingdom, God causes a deep sleep to fall upon Adam and fashions Chava from a portion of Adam's body. Upon awakening, Adam proclaims, "This time, bone of my bone and flesh of my flesh." The first man realizes that he has now found the companion he seeks.[2]

Questions

An all-powerful God cannot arrive at delayed realizations. God obviously knows from the beginning that man needs companionship. Why, then, doesn't God create Chava at the same time as Adam?

The phrase *eizer k'negdo*,[3] used to describe Adam's potential companion, is also deeply puzzling, even self-contradictory. The word *eizer* means "help," while the root word *neged* means "against." Why would God want to create a "help against" Adam? What message could this phrase possibly be conveying concerning the male-female partnership?

Finally, why does God parade the animals before Adam to be named at this particular juncture? God clearly knows that Adam will not find a companion from within the animal kingdom. What, then, is the purpose of this exercise?

1. Bereishit 2:18.
2. Ibid., 2:18–24.
3. Ibid., 2:18.

Approaches

A

Numerous approaches to the original isolation of Adam are suggested within classical rabbinic literature. One authority in the Talmud maintains that God originally created man *d'yo partzuf panim*, "with two faces." Imbedded within Adam were both a male and female human being. When God creates Chava, He effectively separates one dual being into two.[4]

As is often the case, the rabbis are conveying a profound idea in the form of what seems to be a simple tale.

Adam and Chava were originally one. When they reunite, they simply return to their original unified state. Each marriage, each union between man and woman from that point on, is effectively a return to what is meant to be. The natural sanctity of marriage thus emerges from the very story of creation.

One can also find within this rabbinic tradition a tantalizing allusion to the biological facts that will emerge millennia later.

Each human fetus carries both male and female traits, like the original Adam. In the natural course of events, one set of traits then becomes dominant, determining the sex of the child. The birth of each child thus mirrors the path of man's original creation by God as understood by the Talmud.

B

Another fascinating moral lesson is gleaned by the Mishna as it discusses the phenomenon of man's original aloneness.

Man is created alone to teach us that each individual is an *olam malei*, "an entire world."[5] At the point of Adam's creation, the whole human race consists of one individual. From that time on, each human being is to be seen as of inestimable value.

Thus, anyone who sustains one individual, maintain the rabbis, has sustained an entire world. And anyone, God forbid, who destroys one individual has destroyed an entire world.

No matter how many people may populate the globe, we are meant to

4. Talmud Bavli Eruvin 18a.
5. Mishna, Sanhedrin 4:5.

remember the time when the entire human race consisted of one solitary man. In that way, we will never take individual life for granted.

C

Other Talmudic approaches to man's solitary creation include:

1. God creates man alone to encourage peace and harmony within mankind. All of humanity is descended from one ancestor. No individual has the right, therefore, to claim greater lineage than another.

2. Man is created individually to reflect God's oneness in the heavens.

3. By creating one original man as the progenitor of many others, God demonstrates His greatness. When a coin-maker creates numerous coins out of one mold, they are all the same. God, however, crafts countless human beings, all in the mold of Adam. Nonetheless, each person is different and unique.[6]

D

A sobering psychological truth may also be reflected in the biblical narrative concerning the creation of Man. Man is created alone, because at base level, throughout his life, he remains alone. There is a core of "aloneness" that characterizes our existence.

We are born alone, and we face death alone. No matter how hard we may try to understand each other and no matter how deep our desire for closeness with others, no one can ever fully penetrate this core of aloneness that lies within our souls. We never fully understand ourselves. How can we hope to fully understand each other?

The Torah is also teaching us that we are each personally responsible for the quality of our lives. While others may accompany us, even aid us, during the course of our life journey, the quality of that journey remains our individual responsibility – alone.

E

Most importantly, however, the mode of Adam's creation can be understood as an educational process for Adam about himself and his relationship to others.

Unlike other creatures, man needs to learn the value of companionship.

6. Talmud Bavli Sanhedrin 37a.

This is so because the quality of human companionship potentially differs from the quality of all other relationships in the world around us.

This difference, however, is not automatically guaranteed.

Our relationships as human beings have the possibility for unparalleled depth. We have the ability to transcend the physical and to establish true emotional ties, which can enrich and transform our lives.

There is a catch, however. The establishment of these ties is based upon learning, sacrifice and risk.

Firstly, human relationships are based upon sharing, and sharing does not come naturally or easily. A child has to be taught to share, to give up a bit of his space and self.

To make matters more difficult, there is also vulnerability inherent in close human contact. The closer we become with others, the greater the potential for pain. No one can hurt us as deeply as those who know us best.

God creates Adam alone, as Adam needs to understand that his aloneness is not good. He needs to feel the emptiness caused by in his isolation. Only upon feeling that emptiness can he understand why it is necessary to share with another. Adam has to learn that the choice for human relationships, with all of its consequent sacrifice and pain, is a better choice than the isolation that he now experiences. Had God created Chava immediately, Adam would have been unwilling to give of himself or of his world.

God then brings the animals before Adam to be named. Naming requires an understanding of the intrinsic nature of the creature.

Adam sees that every animal has companionship with its own kind. He also perceives, however, that the companionship reflected before him is inadequate to suit his own needs. Adam is looking for something greater and deeper. Only when Adam arrives at that realization does God then proceed with the creation of Chava.

The narrative of Adam and Chava's creation stands as a monumental lesson concerning the nature of human closeness.

When we understand and are willing to accept the work and sacrifice necessary for the establishment of deep human relationships, when we create relationships based upon mutual trust, we achieve the companionship that is unique to mankind.

F

Finally, we address the contradiction embedded in the phrase *eizer k'negdo.*

Rashi immediately quotes the famous Midrashic observation that this phrase actually reflects a choice. The words *eizer* (assistance) and *k'negdo* (against) are indeed mutually exclusive. When a man and woman succeed in creating a relationship of trust they will then live in a world of *eizer* – assistance. If, on the other hand, they falter, their relationship will be characterized by the word *k'negdo* – against.[7]

This same sentiment is reflected in the incisive rabbinic observation concerning the very words *ish* (man) and *isha* (woman). These two words differ by two letters: a *yud* and a *hei*, letters that spell the name of God.

When God is present in a relationship, suggest the rabbis, man and woman are present, as well. If God is absent, the *yud* and *hei* disappear and we are left only with the letters *aleph* and *shin*, which spell the word *eish* (fire).[8] The man-woman relationship is potentially explosive, for good and for bad, with a surprisingly thin line often separating the paths before us.

We have all witnessed the beauty of relationships based upon trust and love. We have also witnessed, unfortunately, the deep pain and animosity that inevitably eventuate when a relationship falters.

Constant work is required to ensure that our relationships will be characterized by the term *eizer* rather than the term *k'negdo*.

G

An alternative approach to the phrase *eizer k'negdo* can be suggested, if we choose the realm of *pashut pshat* (the simple, literal meaning).

This phrase is actually one of a number of phrases in the Torah which at first appear contradictory but which, when properly understood, reflect significant philosophical dialectics.

We must not choose between *eizer* and *k'negdo*. Instead, the phrase, taken as a whole, brilliantly mirrors the delicate balance essential to a healthy marriage.

In marriage, each partner must remain intact as an individual, never totally subsumed by the other. Husband and wife must learn to assist each other and cooperate with each other, but not overwhelm each other. When each is an *eizer k'negdo*, a "help standing opposite," when each partner

7. Rashi, Bereishit 2:18.
8. Talmud Bavli Sota 17a; Rashi, Sota 17a.

assists the other from a perspective of independence, then the vibrancy essential for a healthy relationship is achieved.

Two simple, seemingly contradictory words, spoken by God to describe the first marriage, aptly summarize the delicate balance of healthy marriages across the ages.

3 Deliberate Misunderstanding: The Origins of Failure?

Context

Whenever the Torah text repeats a conversation or an event we should see a red flag. If nothing in the text is superfluous, why does the Torah repeat?

Inevitably, the answer can be found by comparing the two versions of the event. Subtle and not-so-subtle differences always emerge: differences that teach significant lessons and convey important messages.

The Torah records two versions of God's commandment concerning the fruit of the Tree of Knowledge of Good and Evil. We first encounter the commandment when God actually issues it to Adam.[1] The directive is then later repeated by Chava to the serpent.[2]

Questions

Why are these two versions recorded in full detail? Why doesn't the Torah simply say, "and Chava repeated God's commandment to the serpent"?

Approaches

A

When the two versions of the commandment are compared, a series of striking variations emerges.

1. Bereishit 2:16–17.
2. Ibid., 3:2–3.

	God	Chava
1.	"From all the trees of the garden you may certainly eat."[3]	"We may eat from the trees in the garden."[4]
2.	"And from the Tree of Knowledge of Good and Evil you shall not eat."[5]	"And from the fruit of the tree that is in the midst of the garden, God has said we shall not eat from it nor shall we touch it."[6]
3.	"For on the day and you eat from it you shall certainly die."[7]	"Lest we die."[8]

Before we go any further, and lest we be accused of unfair bias towards Chava, we must note that it is unclear where the breakdown in communication between God and man actually takes place.

God originally commands Adam concerning the Tree of Knowledge of Good and Evil, before Chava is created. One would assume that Adam then shares the commandment with Chava and that Chava then repeats it to the serpent.

The Torah seems to deliberately leave this process of communication vague. At what point do the mistakes occur? Does Adam misunderstand God's words? Does he understand properly but communicate mistakenly to Chava? Or is it Chava who fails to properly comprehend the commandment?

By leaving the point of breakdown unclear, the Torah conveys an additional lesson. We are reminded of the game of telephone we played as children. The task of communication is at once important and delicate. We should be most cautious with how we deliver and receive verbal messages.

B

Nehama Leibowitz, in her landmark work *Studies in Bereishit*, immediately

3. Ibid., 2:16.
4. Ibid., 3:2.
5. Ibid., 2:17.
6. Ibid., 3:3.
7. Ibid., 2:17.
8. Ibid., 3:3.

points out that Chava makes the tragic error of accentuating the negative and negating the positive.[9] God allows Adam and Chava to eat from all of the trees of the garden. He, in fact, encourages them to do so.

In Chava's eyes, however, this expansive permission is of little consequence. There is a tree "in the midst of the garden" that remains beyond her reach. Not only is she forbidden to eat from it but she is even forbidden to touch it (a prohibition that she or Adam apparently manufactures).

Man falters when he fails to fully appreciate and take advantage of the vast and beautiful world open to him. When we focus only on what is prohibited, on what remains beyond our reach, then we fall into the trap reflected in this text.

This sentiment is conveyed in sharp Midrashic fashion by the rabbis. The Midrash states that when Chava tells the serpent that she is forbidden to touch the tree, the serpent proceeds to push her against it. Upon seeing that nothing untoward happens to her, Chava then eats from the tree and falls into sin.[10] This event, continues the Midrash, supports the dictum stated by King Solomon: "Do not add upon His (God's) words."[11]

While God's law is demanding, He has provided us with a bountiful world to appreciate and enjoy.[12] If we focus only upon what is prohibited to us, even adding to it in our minds, we are bound to fail.

C

When we examine all of the differences between the two versions of the commandment concerning the Tree of Knowledge of Good and Evil, another, even more significant pattern begins to emerge. By the time the commandment is repeated by Chava, the very nature of the directive has changed. God's original intent seems lost in Chava's words to the serpent.

God specifically referred to the tree as "the Tree of Knowledge of Good and Evil." *There is a tree in the garden that has a specific nature and remains forbidden to you. I'm not telling you why. The explanation remains outside your realm. All that matters is that you follow my will.*

Chava expresses things differently. From her point of view, the tree is no longer "the Tree of Knowledge of Good and Evil," but simply "the tree

9. Leibowitz, *Studies in Bereishit*, p. 28.
10. Midrash Rabba Bereishit 19:3.
11. Mishlei 30:6.
12. Talmud Yerushalmi Kiddushin 4:66 (Tur 2, halacha 19); Talmud Bavli Nedarim 10a.

in the midst of the garden." *God has arbitrarily planted a dangerous tree in the garden of Eden. It appears as no different from all the other trees and yet its fruit is forbidden.*

Absent in Chava's words is any indication of the specific nature of this tree. By failing to refer to it as the "Tree of Knowledge of Good and Evil," Chava ignores that God may have His reasons for the prohibition. More importantly, she fails to understand that the thrust of the prohibition is a demand upon man's behavior, rather than a warning concerning a dangerous tree. She would rather believe that she is facing an arbitrary danger, created by a capricious god, than confront the reality of a thinking Deity, Who is making demands upon her behavior.

This attitude is further reflected by the two other major variations in Chava's version of the prohibition. *Not only can't we eat from the tree*, she says, *but we can't touch it*. The tree is so dangerous that it must be avoided at all costs. According to the Midrash, the serpent sees an opening. He pushes her against the tree, thereby demonstrating that it is not inherently dangerous.[13] Once the danger disappears in Chava's mind there is no longer any reason to avoid eating from the tree.

What began as a reasoned, moral commandment has become a superstitious fear. Once the fear disappears, for Chava, the prohibition dissipates as well.

Further evidence that Chava understood the tree as inherently dangerous can be seen, according to the Ramban, from the verse in the text immediately following the serpent's words. The Torah states, "and the woman saw that the tree was good to eat, and beautiful to behold, and lovely to discern."[14] Why, asks the Ramban, does the Torah need to tell me that Chava saw that the tree was beautiful on all these levels? What difference does it make?

The Torah is indicating that Chava originally thought that the fruit of the tree was poisonous. When she sees that it is apparently not – but instead beautiful – she proceeds to eat from it.[15]

Chava's description of the ramifications of eating from the tree is also significant.

13. Midrash Rabba Bereishit 19:3.

14. Bereishit 3:6.

15. Ramban, Bereishit 3:6.

God had said, "for the day on which you eat from it you shall certainly die." Chava states simply, "lest we die."

God defines death as a moral consequence of the act of eating from the tree. There is cause and effect, justice based upon man's obedience or disobedience to the divine will.

Chava sees death as a potential, possible danger rather than as a moral consequence of disobedience to God.

D

Rooted in the Garden of Eden, therefore, are the seeds of sin and failure. From the moment Chava speaks to the serpent, a struggle is joined: a struggle between religion and superstition; between thought-filled dedication to God's will and rote, unthinking ritual; between what God wants and what we are willing to give. This battle can be traced across the generations as time after time, man seems to deliberately misunderstand what it is that God desires from us.

God clearly tells us that what He wants from us is *ourselves*. Over and over again, frightened by that demand, we desperately try to offer Him anything and everything else.

To cite a few examples:

1. One generation beyond Eden, the story of Adam and Chava's children reminds us that as parents, we must be careful of our missteps because our children will take them one step further.

When Kayin and Hevel each bring offerings to God, the Torah states, "And God turned *to Hevel and to his offering*, but *to Kayin and to his offering* He did not turn."[16] The language seems superfluous. Why didn't the Torah simply say, "And God turned to Hevel's offering while to Kayin's offering He did not turn"?

Clearly, God was responding to the individuals themselves and not simply to their offerings.

This fact becomes abundantly clear in the next few passages of the text.

When Kayin reacts to God's rejection with anger and despair, God

16. Bereishit 4:4–5.

turns to him and proclaims: "If you do good will you not be accepted? And if you do not do good, sin crouches at the door."[17]

In this seminal passage, God tells Kayin: *My choices are not arbitrary, nor is my approval capricious. It's really all up to you. I will judge you by who you are and by what you do.*

Kayin, however, finds himself unable to hear God's words. This primitive man, buffeted by forces which he believes are beyond his control, facing a God Who he feels has irrevocably rejected him for no good reason, responds the only way that he can. He murders his brother, God's favorite.[18] With this act, he believes, he will leave God no choice. God will now be forced to accept Kayin.

Confronted with God's clear directive towards self-improvement, Kayin chooses a different path. He would rather commit murder; he would rather remove the competition than examine his own ways.

The reality of a thinking God, Who demands compliance to His will, is too frightening to Kayin. It's easier to believe in a Deity Who chooses favorites by whim than to deal with the burden of God's true demands.

2. Towards the end of Parshat Noach, the Torah tells the story of the *dor haflaga*, the generation of dispersion. The sin of this generation, which builds the Tower of Bavel, however, is not made clear in the text.[19]

A variety of rabbinic suggestions are offered to explain their failure.

One particular suggestion captures our attention. Rashi, quoting the Midrash, explains that the people of this generation remembered the flood of Noach's time with fear. Further, they believed that once every 1,656 years God would again visit destruction upon the world, as He did in Noach's day. In order to protect themselves from the impending catastrophe, they built the Tower of Bavel.[20]

This approach to the sin seems abundantly strange. What's wrong with building earthquake-proof buildings? Why not protect yourself from impending disaster? Wherein, according to this Midrash, lies the sin of this generation?

Upon consideration, the answer becomes clear. The message of the flood was a moral message. God destroyed the world not upon a whim, but

17. Ibid., 4:7.
18. Ibid., 4:8.
19. Ibid., 11:1–9.
20. Midrash Rabba Bereishit 38:6.

because of the sinfulness of the time. Protection from a similar event is to be gained not through the search for physical safety, but through spiritual self-improvement.

By the time we reach the generation of the Tower of Bavel, according to this Midrash, the meaning of the flood has been lost. What God meant as a moral message is now perceived as a warning of arbitrary danger. Those who live in the time of the Tower of Bavel would rather build buildings to protect themselves from a capricious god than examine their own behavior.

3. Centuries later, the newborn Jewish nation stands at the foot of Mount Sinai. The grandeur of revelation, however, is marred by the sin of the golden calf.[21]

The behavior of the nation seems difficult to understand. How could a people standing in the presence of God's majesty and power commit such a brazen act of idolatry?

While a fuller explanation of the sin of the golden calf will be reserved for elsewhere, a brief examination of the events at Sinai can help us begin to understand the nature of the nation's failure.

The sin of the golden calf does not occur in a vacuum. It is, instead, part of a pervasive pattern of behavior established the moment revelation begins.

When God reveals Himself to His people, they respond in emphatic and unified fashion – *with retreat!*

The Torah states: "And the nation saw the thunder and lightning and the sound of the Shofar and the Mountain enveloped in smoke; and they trembled and stood from afar. And they said to Moshe: you speak with us and we will hear and let not God speak with us, lest we die."[22] (Note that the phrase *pen namut*, "lest we die," is exactly the same phrase used earlier by Chava in describing the potential ramifications of eating from the Tree of Knowledge of Good and Evil. This phrase, as we have noted, indicates a fear of impending arbitrary danger.)

The reaction of the nation stands in stark contrast to their response just a few weeks earlier after the destruction of the Egyptian army in the Red Sea. There, on the banks of the Red Sea, the revelation of God's power

21. Shmot 22:1–6.
22. Ibid., 20:15–16.

was greeted with song and with dance – not with fear and retreat.[23] Why do the people react so differently now?

The answer lies in the monumental difference between the two events.

The message at the Red Sea is "God will take care of you."

The message of Sinai is "God demands from you."

Faced with demands upon their behavior from a thinking God, the people opt for personal comfort rather than self-confrontation. They desperately seek distance from God and from His demands by insisting that Moshe speak in their stead.

And when Moshe disappears, failing to return from Sinai at the expected time, the nation's desire for distance from God becomes an overwhelming fear. The golden calf is created to replace Moshe, to serve as the intermediary between the nation and God, so that the burdens of a direct, close communication with the divine can be avoided.

Once again, God calls to man, this time at the moment of the birth of the Jewish nation. *Approach me*, He says. *Come close enough to feel the heat, to learn what I desire from you. Be willing to offer yourselves to this relationship. For what I desire is you, and nothing else.*

Tragically, the Jewish nation falls into the trap first established in the Garden of Eden. Frightened by the demands which a close relationship with God will create, the people instead choose retreat and distance, ultimately sinning through the creation of the golden calf.

Points to Ponder

Over and over again, God clearly tells us that what He wants from us is ourselves. He desires that we dedicate our lives and our behavior to the fulfillment of His will and His law, and He wants us to devote our energy towards an understanding of His ways and of our role in the world.

Too often we run away from these frightening demands. We choose *comfortable* rather than *confrontational* Judaism. As we hide behind the safety of rote ritual, religion fails to challenge us, to move us or to change us. We find ourselves mimicking Chava's approach in the Garden of Eden. Judaism becomes superstition, rather than a thought-filled, challenging enterprise.

---

23. Ibid., 15:1–21.

As a case in point, consider the one mitzva often focused upon when a family experiences moments of difficulty or tragedy – the mitzva of mezuza.

Frantically we check the parchments of the mezuzot on our door posts. We feel that perhaps a missing letter, a mistaken word might be found – something that could account for the apparent temporary suspension of God's protection.

Certainly mezuzot should be checked, as halachically mandated, twice in seven years. The focus on this mitzva alone at moments of tragedy, however, is particularly troubling.

Firstly, what does it say to us about our belief in God? Is God so arbitrary that He would strike us down simply because a letter is missing from the parchment of our mezuza scroll?

Even more problematic: Are we checking the mezuzot because we are afraid to "check" things that might challenge us more? Should we not examine our observance of kashrut, Shabbat, or the way that we treat our fellow man? Certainly a thinking God would want us to explore all aspects of our lives when we reassess our position in the world.

While we can never know with certainty why particular events occur within our lives, each of those events should move us towards self-examination and personal growth. Our Judaism must never be reduced to the performance of rote ritual and habitual observance. We must instead come close to God and to His law, close enough that we are challenged each day.

From the time of Adam and Chava until our own, God's message to us has been clear. He wants us to confront Him and to confront ourselves. We must find the strength to rise to the challenge.

4 Good and Evil: Who Decides?

Context

God places Adam in the beautiful Garden of Eden, surrounded by a bounty of natural sustenance. Two exceptional trees are also planted in the garden: the Tree of Life and the Tree of Knowledge of Good and Evil. God exhorts man to enjoy all the fruits of the garden, but specifically prohibits the fruit of the Tree of Knowledge of Good and Evil.[1]

Seduced by the serpent, Chava consumes the fruit of the Tree of Knowledge of Good and Evil and convinces Adam to do so as well. Adam and Chava are punished and exiled from the Garden of Eden.[2]

Questions

Questions abound concerning this familiar story: What "knowledge" is represented by the fruit of the Tree of Knowledge of Good and Evil? Why are the consumption of that fruit and the attainment of that knowledge prohibited? Why does God plant the tree in the first place? What kind of knowledge did Adam and Chava possess before eating of the tree? Can free will exist without knowledge? If not, how can Adam and Chava be held culpable for the crime?

Finally, the whole episode seems to be a recipe for predetermined failure – a setup. Take a child and place him in a room surrounded by an array of attractive toys. Place in that room as well a sealed package with the instructions that all the toys may be used with the exception of the object in the sealed package. It won't take long before the child gravitates to that one sealed package.

1. Bereishit 2:15–17.
2. Ibid., 3:1–24.

How could God expect Adam and Chava to ignore the lure of the one prohibited tree in the garden?

Compounding the problem, of course, is the fact of God's omniscience. God knows from the outset what will occur. Why doom man to predetermined failure?

Approaches

A

The relationship between prescience, preordination and free will has occupied the attention of philosophers and scholars across the centuries. While a full examination of their conclusions remains outside the scope of our discussion, a few observations must be made.

We believe in three philosophical concepts:

1. Prescience, God's knowledge of the future.

2. Free will, man's inherent ability and responsibility to choose the path his life will take.

3. Preordination, the predetermination by God of specific aspects of our lives.

In simple terms, the complex relationship between these three concepts can be summarized as follows: God's knowledge of the future does not control our present actions. Each step of the way we choose the path we wish to take. God's knowledge potentially affects our choice only on the rare occasions when He informs us of the future before it happens. Such exceptional occasions (for example, God's prediction to Avraham that his children will, centuries later, become strangers in a land not their own) must be examined on a case-by-case basis.

As a rule, free will remains an essential component of our lives. Without personal choice, we cannot be held responsible for what we do – for better or for worse.

There are, however, elements of our existence that remain outside of our control and are thus preordained. When we are born, to whom we are born, our personal gene pool, etc., are all elements of our lives that are predetermined by God. Each of us is born into a set of defined circumstances that comprise the box in which we live. Our responsibility is to make the most of those circumstances, to determine the quality of our lives. Our task is to push our personal envelope as far as it can be pushed.

Who we are as people and what we accomplish in life remains our choice.

The Talmud underscores this reality with a beautiful description of the inception of life:[3]

> The angel appointed over birth brings each potential soul before God and says: 'Master of the universe, what shall be with this drop [of life]? Will he be strong or weak? Will he be wise or foolish? Will he be rich or poor?'
>
> Will he be good or evil, however, is not asked.

That determination remains in the hands of the individual about to be born.

B

From time to time, the Torah will speak of tests administered by God upon man. Given our belief in prescience, the purpose of these tests cannot be the determination of information by God. God already knows from the outset whether man will "pass" or "fail" each test.

Why, then, are the tests administered at all?

Two fundamental approaches can be found in the classical commentaries. These approaches are not mutually exclusive and will be discussed in greater detail at a later point (see Vayeira 4):

1. God tests man so that man can gain information about himself and actualize his potential.[4]

2. God tests man so that future generations can learn from his success or failure.[5]

Each of these approaches can be applied to the story of Adam and Chava in the Garden of Eden.

C

While the above discussions help define the general parameters of the story of Adam and Chava, the specifics of the tale remain perplexing. At the core

3. Talmud Bavli Nidda 15b.
4. Ramban, Bereishit 22:1.
5. Rambam, *Moreh Nevuchim* 3:33.

of the narrative lies the mystery of the Tree of Knowledge of Good and Evil and the nature of its forbidden fruit.

Across the ages, a variety of approaches are suggested by the rabbis in their attempt to unravel this ancient puzzle.

D

The Abravanel, for example, suggests that the knowledge represented by the forbidden fruit is not the basic moral knowledge of good and evil. Moral awareness, he maintains, is essential for free will, and has existed from the moment that God created man "in His image."

Instead, suggests the Abravanel, the fruit of the tree represents the quest for physical pleasure and material gain.

When Adam and Chava eat from the tree, they turn their back on man's original, God-ordained mission. They leave behind the search for spiritual perfection and begin to immerse themselves in worldly indulgence. The biblical narrative of the sin of Adam and Chava challenges us, according to the Abravanel, to maintain proper perspective within our own lives by resisting the temptations of the physical world and by dedicating ourselves to spiritual perfection.[6]

Following in the footsteps of the Abravanel, the Malbim offers a fascinating insight into the biblical text.

Man, he says, was created of body and soul. The soul was meant to be central, while the body was created to serve as protection, or "clothing," for the soul. When Adam and Chava eat from the forbidden tree, they turn their bodies, rather than their souls, into the central component of their lives. In the aftermath of the sin, the Torah tells us that Adam and Chava recognize their physical nakedness. Now the body, originally meant to be "clothing" for the soul, has itself become central and must be clothed.[7]

E

Other scholars, such as the Ramban[8] and Rabbeinu Bachya,[9] take a totally different approach. They suggest that free will first enters human experience when Adam and Chava eat of the forbidden fruit. Before that fateful

6. Abravanel, Bereishit 2:4–24, question 14.
7. Malbim, Bereishit 2:25.
8. Ramban, Bereishit 2:9.
9. Rabbeinu Bachya, Bereishit 2:9.

act, maintains the Ramban, "Man, by his very nature, simply did what was right, as do the heavens and all of their hosts."[10] With the consumption from the tree, desire and free will are born. Man no longer automatically follows the will of God.

This approach, however, leaves open a series of serious questions.

How can Adam and Chava be held culpable for their actions if they did not possess free will before eating from the tree? How, for that matter, could they have disobeyed God's command if it was in their very nature to blindly follow God's will?

Numerous scholars attempt to explain the approach of the Ramban.

Harav Chaim of Volozhin, for example, suggests that man did indeed possess a degree of free will before eating of the Tree of Knowledge. Before the sin, however, evil remained external to man. To sin, Adam had to first make the decision to "enter evil," consciously, as one might enter fire. After the sin, however, the propensity for evil becomes a part of man, and his ability to discriminate between right and wrong is severely weakened.[11]

F

Finally, it is the Rambam who, with a comment in his *Guide to the Perplexed*, suggests what may be the most meaningful and relevant approach to the story of the Tree of Knowledge of Good and Evil.

Maimonides maintains that, before eating from the tree, man existed in the realm of "Truth and Falsehood." After the sin man enters the realm of "Good and Evil."[12]

These two worlds are very different.

Truth and falsehood are objective terms. Good and Evil can be seen as subjective phenomena.

God turns to man as He plants him in the Garden of Eden and says: *Your task is to follow my Will. Good and evil remain my prerogative. I will determine what is right, and what is wrong.*

The serpent attacks this divinely ordained structure and tempts Chava by saying: *If you eat from the tree, then you will be as God. You will decide, you will determine good and evil.*

10. Ramban, Bereishit 2:9
11. Nefesh Hachaim 1:6.
12. Rambam, *Moreh Nevuchim* 1:2.

From that moment on, a struggle is joined which in many ways defines the course of human history. At the core of this struggle lies a simple question: Are good and evil to be determined objectively or subjectively? Or to put it somewhat differently: Does each society have the right to define good and evil for its own citizens and within its own parameters?

Let us postulate for a moment an ancient civilization which determines that weak newborns should be put to death because they cannot contribute to the community and will instead be a drain upon precious resources. Is that determination moral or not? Do we have the right, looking in from the outside, to criticize the morals of any civilization?

What if a particular community determines that the elderly should be executed at a specific age, because they will no longer be contributing members of society? Is that decision moral or not?

And, of course, once we embark upon that slippery slope…

If the Nazis determine that the weak and the infirm shall be put to death as a prelude to the extermination of whole ethnic groups, can we criticize a decision considered moral within the context of the Nazi world? What gives world society the right to conduct the Nuremberg Trials, to define "crimes against humanity"?

Once we accept that each society can determine its own morality – define good and evil within the context of its physical and philosophical borders – morality no longer effectively exists. There is no objective standard for good and evil. Everything is subjective.

Judaism maintains that an objective morality was determined and mandated by God at the dawn of human history.

God creates the Tree of Knowledge of Good and Evil but forbids its fruit to man. By doing so, God reminds Adam and Chava and all of their descendents that the determination of Good and Evil must remain within divine control.

The problems emerge, whether in the Garden of Eden or across the face of history, when man attempts to usurp God's prerogative.

How much pain has been perpetrated across the ages, because we have claimed the right to define Good and Evil?

5 And Kayin Said to Hevel, His Brother...

Context

The tragic story of mankind's second generation unfolds as Kayin and Hevel, the sons of Adam and Chava, each bring an offering to God. God accepts Hevel and his offering but rejects Kayin and his efforts.

Unable to accept a divine rejection which he feels is both without reason and unreasonable (see Bereishit 3, *Approaches* D), a despondent and enraged Kayin lashes out. He murders his brother, forever eliminating his perceived rival.

God decrees, in response to this horrific act of fratricide, that Kayin will spend the remainder of his life in exile.[1]

Questions

A glaring textual omission emerges at the climactic moment of the Kayin and Hevel story.

The Torah states, "And Kayin said to Hevel his brother, and it was when they were in the field, and Kayin rose up upon Hevel his brother and killed him."[2]

What did Kayin say? Why does the Torah introduce a conversation which it then fails to record?

[Note: Had the Torah used the word *va'yedaber*, "spoke," as opposed to *va'yomer*, "said," to describe Kayin's communication with his brother, we might have argued that God simply wanted to indicate that a conversation took place. *Va'yomer*, however, always refers to a specific verbal communication, and is invariably followed in the Torah by the text of that communication.]

1. Bereishit 4:1–12.
2. Ibid., 4:8.

Approaches

A

The rabbis in the Midrash Rabba suggest three possible conversations which might have led to the fateful physical confrontation between Kayin and Hevel.

1. The brothers determined to divide the world. One of them took possession of the land while the other claimed all movable items. As soon as the division took effect, one said to the other, "You are standing upon my land!" while the other replied, "You are wearing my clothes!"

A struggle ensued, and Kayin killed Hevel.

2. Their dispute did not center upon material possessions at all but, instead, upon the Beit Hamikdash, the Holy Temple (which would be built by the Jewish nation millennia later). After they divided both the land and the movables equally, Kayin and Hevel both claimed dominion over the Temple, each arguing that it should be built in his domain.

A struggle ensued, and Kayin killed Hevel.

3. The battle centered upon neither of the above. Kayin and Hevel actually fought over their mother Chava (or alternatively, one of their sisters).

A struggle ensued, and Kayin killed Hevel.[3]

B

The Midrash seems to raise more questions than answers.

Can the rabbis suggest that they know the content of a conversation concerning which the biblical text is completely silent? Are we to assume that the Midrash reflects prophetic vision or that the rabbis were somehow personally present at the scene of Hevel's murder?

Further, each of the rabbinic suggestions seems more bizarre than the next. How can we seriously consider, for example, that Kayin and Hevel actually argued about the Temple? The very concept of the Beit Hamikdash would not be introduced into human experience until centuries after their death. Similarly, no clue is found in the biblical text to support the contention that Kayin and Hevel argued either about material wealth or about a woman.

---

3. Midrash Rabba Bereishit 22:16.

Simply put, how are we to understand the Midrashic approach to the struggle between Kayin and Hevel?

This seemingly strange rabbinic passage actually provides us with a perfect entrée into the world of Midrash.

There is a vast difference between *pashut pshat* (straightforward explanation of biblical text) and Midrash (rabbinical exegesis).

When we operate within the world of *pashut pshat*, we search for the direct meaning of the text before us. In this realm, everything is literal and concrete.

When we enter the world of Midrash, however, the rules change completely. Midrashim are vehicles through which the rabbis, using the Torah text as a point of departure, transmit significant messages and lessons. As such, Midrashim are not necessarily meant to be taken literally; nor are they are to be seen as attempts to explain the factual meaning of a specific Torah passage.

By using the vehicle of Midrash to convey eternal lessons and values, the rabbis connect these values to the Torah text itself. They also ensure that the lessons will not be lost and will always be perceived as flowing directly from the Torah.

Our task, therefore, when we enter the world of Midrash, is to determine the global lessons that the rabbis intend to convey.

C

In the Midrash before us the rabbis are not simply explaining the Kayin and Hevel story. They are, instead, viewing this first violent event in human history as the prototype of physical confrontation across the ages. True to Midrashic style, they express significant global observations in concrete, story-like terms.

Fundamentally, the rabbis make the following statement in this Midrash: *We were not present when Kayin killed Hevel. Nor can we glean any information directly from the biblical text concerning the source of their dispute. Were you to ask us, however, what these brothers were struggling about, we would be forced to suggest one of three options. Over the course of human history, man has killed his brother for material gain, over religion, and because of lust. All bloodshed and warfare can be traced to these three basic primary sources. We are, therefore, certain that one of these issues served as the basis of the confrontation between Kayin and Hevel at the dawn of human history.*

This rabbinic commentary serves as a sobering reminder that mankind has not moved one inch off the killing field of Hevel's murder. In spite of perceived social progress, nothing has fundamentally changed. The causes of human conflict have remained remarkably constant across the face of time.

The Midrash remains sadly relevant, centuries after its authorship.

If the twentieth century gave lie to any assumption at all, it was to the assumption that scientific and technological progress would automatically be accompanied by moral advancement as well.

The century that gave us the Holocaust serves to remind us that in many ways we have simply gotten better at killing each other.

So far, as we confront the pandemic of Muslim fundamentalism, the twenty-first century isn't looking much better.

D

As perceptive and as fascinating as the Midrash may be, however, it fails to answer the original textual question that we raised. Once again, why doesn't the Torah tell us what Kayin said to Hevel? Why introduce a conversation and then deliberately leave its content unrecorded?

On one level, we could simply answer that God wants us to fill in the blanks. Sometimes, a portion of the Torah is left unfinished in order to make us partners in the text. God challenges us to read into that text the myriad of possible lessons that are relevant to our lives.

Had the Torah told us the content of Kayin's dialogue with Hevel, the questions would not have been asked, the Midrash would not have been written and its fundamental lessons would have never been conveyed.

E

There may, however, be an even deeper and more powerful reason for the Torah's omission in the text before us.

The Torah edits out the content of Kayin's words to Hevel because God wants us to understand that those words, whatever they might have been, were of no ultimate consequence. Sometimes an act is so depraved that its cause and motivation is unimportant; no valid excuse can be offered.

Perhaps Kayin had justifiable grievances against his brother. We, however, will never know. Kayin loses all claims upon our empathy and understanding the moment he murders his brother. Nothing can explain that heinous act, and certainly nothing can justify it.

Once again, the eternal Torah text, this time through omission, delivers a message that is frighteningly applicable to our time. No matter what their cause, acts of terror, mayhem and murder perpetrated against innocent victims are inexcusable. The perpetrators of these crimes, through their very actions, render their own potential grievances irrelevant.

God wants us to know that Kayin said something to Hevel. He also wants to us to know, however, that what Kayin said ultimately doesn't matter. The text conveys this lesson in the most powerful way that it can. We are told that a conversation took place, but we are not told the content of that conversation.

Sometimes the Torah teaches us not by what is included in the text, but by what is left out.

Noach

נח

CHAPTER 6:9–11:32

פרק ו:ט–יא:לב

Parsha Summary

Cataclysmic events…

God plans the destruction and the rebuilding of the world in response to man's sinfulness.

God warns Noach of the impending flood and instructs him to build an ark in which to secure salvation for himself, his family and representatives of each species of the animal kingdom. Noach obeys.

Floodwaters cover the earth, as Noach and his fellow travelers ride out the cataclysm.

After Noach sends a series of birds from the ark to determine whether the flood waters have receded, God commands Noach to exit the ark. Noach and his family emerge to a scene of total devastation.

God appears to Noach with promises and instructions concerning the future of mankind.

Noach plants a vineyard and becomes drunk, which leads to family tragedy.

Generations after the flood, mankind converges on the plane of Shinar and determines to build the Tower of Bavel. God responds by confounding the language of all involved and man is dispersed across the face of the globe.

After listing a series of subsequent generations, the Torah records the lineage and birth of Avraham.

1 Between Individual and Community: Societal Balance

Context

In Parshat Noach two doomed societies are presented for our attention: the generation of the flood and the generation of dispersion (the Tower of Bavel).

In response to sin, God destroys the first of these generations through a flood which encompasses the entire world. The only survivors are Noach, his family and the animals that Noach, upon God's command, brings into the ark.[1]

The second generation is punished through divinely decreed linguistic confusion. In response to the building of the Tower of Bavel, God creates a myriad of languages. The builders of the tower, unable to communicate with each other, disperse across the face of the earth.[2]

Questions

How are we to understand the concept of trial and error as applied to God's creation of the world? Why did a perfect God create two societies that He then felt compelled to destroy?

The Torah states that, upon seeing the evil of the generation of the flood, "God regretted that He had created man in the land, and He was saddened unto His heart." How could God regret the creation of man when He knew from the outset that man was destined to sin?

The Torah cites violent theft as the crime that seals the fate of the generation of the flood. The sin of the generation of dispersion, however, is not clearly defined in the text. What was wrong with building the Tower

1. Bereishit 6:9–8, 14.
2. Ibid., 11:1–9.

of Bavel? Why did God feel compelled to destroy this second society, as well?

Why did the punishment of the two generations differ and how did the "punishment fit the crime" in each case?

Approaches

A

As a first step, we must understand that the "trial and error" implicit in the stories of the flood and the Tower of Bavel does not exist on God's part but on man's.

God creates a world based upon free will, and the existence of free will is predicated on the possibility of human failure. God knows from the very beginning that man will sin, but He does not interfere. He, instead, retreats to allow man room to succeed or fail on his own.

As indicated in our earlier discussion concerning prescience, predestination and free will (see Bereishit 4, *Approaches* A), God's knowledge of the future does not affect man's ability to choose.

B

God's regret upon the occasion of man's failure at the time of the flood is explained in a famous conversation between Rabbi Yehoshua the son of Korcha and an Epicurean.

The Epicurean questioned how God could possibly regret a tragedy that He knew was bound to occur.

Rabbi Yehoshua responded by asking, "Did you ever have a child and, if so, did you celebrate his birth?"

"Of course! I rejoiced and encouraged others to rejoice!" answered his adversary.

"How could you celebrate the child's birth?" asked Rabbi Yehoshua. "Did you not know that he would eventually die?"

"So, too," continued Rabbi Yehoshua, "God celebrated the creation of man in its time and mourned the pain of man's failure in its time."[3]

3. Rashi, Bereishit 6:6.

C

Granted free will, civilization, in its infancy, stumbles and falls. The Torah apparently details the initial tragic missteps of man in order to ensure that we learn from the errors of the two earliest societies whose story it records.

What societal lesson, then, is the Torah conveying through the contrasting stories of the generation of the flood and the generation of the Tower of Bavel?

D

The answer lies in a clearer understanding of the failure of each of these two civilizations.

While the generation of the flood was, according to tradition, guilty of a multitude of heinous crimes,[4] the sin that actually sealed the fate of that society was *hamas*, violent theft.[5]

It remains, however, for the rabbis in the Talmud to fully describe the nature of the theft that characterized the generation of the flood.

"Rav Acha asked, 'What did they steal? A merchant would walk through the marketplace with a container filled with grapes and each passerby would reach forth and steal a small amount, less than he could be called to judgment for.'"[6]

From the rabbinic perspective, the sin of the generation of the flood lay in their mocking of societal norms and laws. Driven by personal greed, each individual steals from his neighbor. He does so in such a way, however, as to escape the reach of the law. By the time the merchant reaches the end of the marketplace he has no grapes left. No one, however, can be taken to court. Societal rules have been rendered ineffective in the face of personal greed.

The sin of the generation of the Tower of Bavel, in contrast, is more difficult to ascertain. As indicated earlier, the Torah does not clearly delineate the crime of this generation.

To fill the gaps in the story of the generation of dispersion, a variety of approaches are offered within rabbinic literature. Many suggest that the

---

4. Talmud Bavli Sanhedrin 108a.
5. Bereishit 6:13.
6. Talmud Yerushalmi Bava Metzia 4:2.

tower was built as a direct attack upon God's authority.[7] Others maintain that the sin of this generation lay in their attempt to stay together in one place as one people instead of populating the world in fulfillment of God's command.[8] Yet others suggest that the people of the time were simply trying to protect themselves from a calamity similar to the flood of Noach's era. According to this interpretation, the builders of the tower ignored the moral lessons of the flood (see Bereishit 3, *Approaches* D2).[9]

Among all of the approaches offered, however, one specific Midrashic interpretation is particularly telling. The Midrash describes the following scene: "Seven levels were created to the tower from the East and seven to the West. The bricks would be brought up from one direction while the descent was from the other. If a man fell down and died during the process of construction, no attention was paid to him at all. If one brick fell, however, all would sit down and weep: 'Woe to us! When will we find another to take its place?'"[10]

This Midrash (clearly based upon hints in the text which describe the driving force behind the creation of the tower as the desire to create a societal name) details a frightening civilization in which communal need takes total precedence over individual value. Those working on the Tower of Bavel cared not at all about the lives of their neighbors. All that mattered was the creation of the tower and the society that it represented.

E

In the eyes of the rabbis, the two civilizations described in Parshat Noach reflected polar extremes. The society of Noach's time was characterized by individual greed at the expense of communal structure. The generation of dispersion, on the other hand, was willing to sacrifice individual life to the creation of society.

The ultimate punishments inflicted by God upon each of these generations perfectly fit their crimes. The generation of Noach, which was marked by individual greed and corruption, could only be addressed through total destruction. None of the individuals, other than Noach and his family, could remain. When it came to the builders of the Tower of Bavel, however,

7. Talmud Bavli Sanhedrin 109a; Rashi, Bereishit 11:1.
8. Rabbeinu Bachya, Bereishit 11:4; Ohr Hachaim, Bereishit 11:1.
9. Midrash Rabba Bereishit 38:6; Rashi, Bereishit 11:1.
10. Pirkei D'Rabi Eliezer 24.

the problem was with the society, not the individuals. In this case, therefore, only the society is destroyed.

F

In each era, man struggles to strike a balance between two opposing forces: the needs of the individual and the needs of the community. Each of these forces, by definition, impinges upon the other.

In order to create and maintain the rules necessary for communal governance, a society must, of necessity, place limits upon personal freedoms (you cannot, to cite the well-known example, allow someone to yell fire in a crowded theater with impunity). On the other hand, a society must limit the restrictions it places upon its citizens in order to allow for individual freedom of expression and action.

The particular balance that a society creates between these two forces determines the very nature of the society itself. The difference between Communist Russia and the United States of America lay in the vastly different ways these two societies chose to strike this very balance.

Far from fairy tales, the two major narratives found in Parshat Noach inform us concerning the development of our race. At the dawn of history, two generations fail in their attempts to create an equilibrium between individual and community, with the failures occurring at opposite ends of the spectrum.

The cautionary tales of Parshat Noach remind us of the difficult task that confronts any society as it attempts to address these potentially conflicting needs. Only those civilizations which succeed will eventually endure.

How appropriate that Parshat Noach ends with the introduction of Avraham Avinu and with the launching of Jewish history.

In the aftermath of the failures of both the generations of the flood and dispersion, a new society emerges: one that will successfully create a delicate balance between the needs of the community and the needs of the individual. This society, the Jewish nation guided by its Torah, is therefore destined to endure across the ages.

2 Avraham and Noach: Why Compare?

Context

The first sentence of Parshat Noach describes Noach as "righteous, complete in his generations." The Torah goes on to say, "Noach walked with God."[1]

These two statements serve as the foundation for the following well-known rabbinic observations:

1. "Righteous, complete in his generations."

Rabbi Yochanan said: The qualification "in his generations" indicates that Noach can be considered righteous only when judged against members of his own evil generation. Had he lived at another time, however, he would not have been considered righteous.

Reish Lakish said: The qualification "in his generations" indicates that Noach was righteous in spite of his generation. Had he lived at another time, however, he would have been even more virtuous.[2]

Rabbi Mordechai Yaffe in his commentary *Levush Haora* notes that both Rabbi Yochanan and Reish Lakish agree upon the mediocre nature of Noach's righteousness. Even Reish Lakish, who interprets the text to Noach's benefit, believes that this biblical hero could have been better. Noach, according to Reish Lakish, failed to live up to his potential because of the evil influence that surrounded him.[3]

2. "Noach walked with God."

Avraham, however, describes his relationship with God as follows: "the Lord before whom I walked."[4] Avraham walked before God; Noach only walked with God. This textual contrast indicates that

1. Bereishit 6:9.
2. Talmud Bavli Sanhedrin 108a.
3. Mordechai Yaffe, *Levush Haora*, Bereishit 6:9.
4. Bereishit 24:40.

Noach needed assistance and support while Avraham strengthened himself and walked in righteousness on his own.[5]

Questions

What force compels the rabbis to view Noach as mediocre and limited? Why do they insist upon comparing Noach to Avraham, invariably to Noach's detriment?

As a rule, each hero of the Torah is viewed in his own right and not in contrast with another.

The question is compounded by the fact that other passages in the text might have led us to a different conclusion. Noach, for example, is described as *tamim*, "complete,"[6] while concerning Avraham God says, "Walk before me *v'heyei tamim*, and become complete."[7] Are we to assume that Noach had attained a degree of completeness towards which Avraham could only strive?

Finally, the contrast drawn by the rabbis between Avraham and Noach potentially acquires greater significance in light of the fact that these biblical figures ultimately become the progenitors of two very different populations. Avraham, of course, is the father of the Jewish people. The nations of the world, on the other hand, are referred to, in rabbinic literature, as B'nai Noach – the sons of Noach.

Are the rabbis simply comparing Noach to Avraham or are they conveying a message concerning the worldviews of their descendents?

Approaches

A

The most obvious behavioral contrast between Noach and Avraham lies in their vastly differing responses to the calamities that are about to visit their worlds. When God informs Noach concerning the impending flood, destined to destroy all of creation, Noach is tellingly silent. He does not plead for God's mercy nor does he argue for justice. Accepting the impending

5. Rashi, Bereishit 6:9.
6. Bereishit 6:9.
7. Ibid, 17:1.

destruction of the world as inevitable, Noach sets himself to the fulfillment of God's instructions. Without a word, with no apparent thought given to the fate of those around him, he builds the ark to ensure the survival of his own family and the animals that he will bring onto that ark.

In stark contrast stands Avraham's dramatic reaction to the news of the impending destruction of the cities of Sodom and Amora.

Although he is well aware of the evil perpetrated by the inhabitants of these cities, Avraham enters into dramatic debate with his Creator on their behalf. With strength and, one might argue, with a degree of chutzpa, he refuses to accept God's judgment. He does not rest until God agrees that the inhabitants of the cities will be spared if ten righteous *tzadikim* are found among them.

Here then, one obvious reason for the rabbinic rejection of Noach in favor of Avraham. One simply cannot remain silent in the face of other people's pain. Noach's submissive acceptance of such pain dooms him to mediocrity. Avraham's struggle, on the other hand, even on behalf of people he knows to be evil, marks him for greatness.

B

There is, however, an even broader behavioral contrast that can be drawn between Avraham and Noach as their stories emerge in the Torah. This contrast carries theological implications of profound proportions.

Noach excels at following orders. He listens to God's commandments completely and responds submissively and to the letter. As the Torah states, and then repeats, "And Noach did all that God commanded him, so he did."[8]

God says, "Build an ark," and Noach builds an ark. God says, "Enter the ark," and Noach enters the ark. Even after determining that the flood has ended, Noach will not exit the ark until God commands him to do so.[9]

Avraham, on the other hand, is constantly struggling with his destiny even when it means that he must actively confront his Creator. This confrontation is not limited to the debate concerning Sodom and Amora but, instead, characterizes Avraham's relationship with God at all times.

8. Ibid., 6:22, 7:6.

9. Ibid., 8:11–16.

Examples abound. To name a few:

When famine strikes the land of Canaan shortly after Avraham's arrival, Avraham saves his family by descending into Egypt. He does not wait for God to tell him what to do.[10]

When Avraham hears that his nephew Lot has been taken captive in battle, he immediately responds. Without waiting for instructions, Avraham pursues the enemies and frees his nephew.[11]

When God turns to Avraham and proclaims, "Your reward will be very great," Avraham argues, "My Lord God, what can you give me as long as I remain childless?"[12]

When God promises, "I am the Lord, Who took you out of Ur Casdim to give you this land to inherit," Avraham responds, "My Lord God, how do I know that I will inherit this land?"[13]

Clearly, Avraham is active while Noach is reactive. Noach accepts the world and God's will as it is. Avraham, on the other hand, struggles, even when his struggle takes him to the very throne of God.

C

Our tradition's choice of Avraham over Noach was not a foregone conclusion. One could argue that, theologically, the model represented by Noach is the preferable one. After all, isn't it our task to follow God's will, to respond to His wishes without question?

And yet, we choose Avraham.

While other faith traditions might preach a stoic acquiescence to divine will, Judaism mandates active engagement and struggle. Our relationship with God is one of partnership, a partnership that permeates every element of our existence. We have the right – no, the obligation – to pray, to plead, even to wrestle with our Creator. And while we will ultimately accept God's will at the end of the struggle, who knows what the struggle itself will have achieved? Who knows whether or not, on some level, our efforts have resulted in the bending of God's will in our direction? Who can assess how the process has fundamentally changed us, thereby transforming God's verdict concerning our destiny?

10. Ibid., 12:10.
11. Ibid., 14:14.
12. Ibid., 15:1–2.
13. Ibid., 15:7–8.

The rabbis reject Noach and embrace Avraham. In doing so they remind us that God prefers active engagement over passive submission.

D

We can now understand the Torah's reference to Noach as "complete" while God speaks of Avraham as "becoming complete."

To Noach, life was a destination potentially reached. Completeness could be attained through the fulfillment of God's desires, the straightforward adherence to God's commandments.

To Avraham, on the other hand, life was a journey without end. Completeness could never be fully attained, for as long as there remained breath, there remained potential challenge and growth.

The greatest blessing, therefore, that God could give to Avraham was "Walk before me and become complete."[14]

Partner with me, God says to Avraham and to us. *Never rest, never stop, meet the challenge of each day, and travel towards completeness.*

14. Ibid., 17:1.

3 Boys and Girls Together: Or Not?

Context

A series of slight textual variations appear in the flow of the Noach story.

The Torah describes the entry of Noach's family into the ark by stating, "*Noach and his sons and his wife and his sons' wives* entered the ark, because of the waters of the flood."[1]

When God commands Noach to exit the ark after the flood has ended He states, "Go out from the ark: *you and your wife and your sons and your sons' wives* with you."[2]

Finally, when Noach actually leaves the ark, the text reads as follows: "And *Noach went out and his sons and his wife, and his sons' wives* with him."[3]

Questions

Why is the Torah inconsistent in its description of the order of entry into and exit from the ark? Why is it that when Noach enters the ark, husbands and wives are listed separately; when God commands the departure from the ark, husbands and wives are listed together; and, finally, when the actual departure from the ark takes place, husbands and wives are again listed separately?

Approaches

These seemingly unimportant variations serve as a reminder that, when it

1. Ibid., 7:7.
2. Ibid., 8:16.
3. Ibid., 8:18.

comes to the Torah, nothing should be taken for granted. Each subtle nuance of the text carries significant lessons and ideas which are too easily missed in a less than careful reading.

B

Commenting on the separation of the men and women as Noach's family enters the ark, Rashi immediately states, "The men separately, and the women separately: marital relations were prohibited during a time when the world was engulfed in sorrow and tragedy."[4]

It would have been totally inappropriate, the Torah hints, for Noach and his family to carry on life as normal, complete with the pleasures of intimate relations, at a time when destruction literally rained down upon the world. In spite of the inevitability of the flood, and in spite of the unimaginable evil that caused it, Noach and his family members are forbidden to ignore the pain and suffering outside the ark. The Torah indeed often indicates (as it does here through nuance) that it is immoral for man to live in a vacuum. We are forbidden to ignore the pain and suffering of others.

We can now also understand why God switches the familial order when He instructs Noach's family to exit the ark at the end of the flood: "You and your wife, and your sons and their wives," God commands Noach, "men and women together." The flood is over. Rebuilding civilization and repopulating the world have become the order of the day. The resumption of family relations is not only a right, God states, but an obligation.

C

At this point, however, the logical pattern seems to break down.

The Torah indicates that as Noach's family departs the ark, men and women remain separate, in apparent defiance of God's wishes. Why is this gender separation consciously maintained by Noach's family even now that the flood has ended?

This apparent problem actually provides a key to the final phases of Noach's story. We must, however, read the story in human terms.

Imagine the scene of total devastation that greets the members of Noach's family as they begin to exit the ark. How deep their despair must have been and how overwhelming their sense of aloneness. In the face of such

4. Rashi, Bereishit 7:7.

tragedy and destruction how can one possibly trust in the future? How can one even contemplate the thought of rebuilding, of beginning again?

Noach and his children are paralyzed by the scene before them. They trust neither God nor themselves. They do not believe that they can be successful in building a new world; and they are unable to imagine the benevolent protection of a God Who could visit such destruction upon mankind.

Men and women leave the ark separately, because they simply cannot contemplate the future.

D

A careful reading of the continuing text shows that God feels compelled to respond in a number of ways:

He promises that He will never again curse the earth because of man's actions.[5]

He blesses Noach and his sons and commands them, not once but twice, to be fruitful and to multiply.[6]

He constructs and commands a series of laws, establishing a basic morality for mankind. Hopefully, these laws will ensure that the kind of evil that characterized the generation of the flood will never again mark civilization.[7]

He establishes a visible covenant with mankind, symbolized by the rainbow, and promises that He will remember that covenant and never again destroy the world through flood.[8]

God directly responds to the paralysis Noach and his family are experiencing. He urges, encourages and cajoles them to move beyond the moment, to realize that the future can and must be built.

Everything hinges upon how Noach and his family respond at this juncture. The world that God intends to create will depend on this last human remnant's ability to move forward.

E

The results are mixed. On the one hand, civilization continues. Noach's

5. Bereishit 8:21–22.
6. Ibid., 9:1, 7.
7. Ibid., 9:2–6.
8. Ibid., 9:8–17.

children have children, and the world is populated in the aftermath of the flood.

On the other hand, on a personal level, Noach never moves past the tragedy of the world's destruction. The text chronicles his spiritual descent as he plants a vineyard, drinks from its wine and falls into a drunken stupor. Unable to face what the world has become, Noach apparently escapes in the only way that he can.

The man who has saved the world at God's command is transformed into a tragic figure right before our eyes.

Points to Ponder

Noach's struggle and failure in the aftermath of the flood should move us to consider the spiritual heroism of a generation of our own time.

In the aftermath of World War II, survivors of the Shoah emerged, one by one, from ghettos, concentration camps, forests and other places of hiding, to face a world similar to Noach's after the flood. These survivors had witnessed unspeakable cruelty and horror. Their world had been totally destroyed, their families murdered.

Who could have blamed these survivors had they given up on the world? Who would have called them to task had they said, "We have lost faith: lost faith in the world, in our God, even in ourselves."

How understandable it would have been had they been paralyzed, like Noach, unable to continue.

Almost to a one, however, that was not their response. With unimaginable strength and indomitable spirit, these survivors rebuilt their worlds. They married, had children and grandchildren, and successfully created professions and careers. They refused to succumb to hatred and bitterness, all the while courageously living decent, moral lives.

The contributions made by this generation to the Jewish community at large, and to the State of Israel, in particular, are immeasurable; and the families that they built, in the aftermath of their own indescribable personal tragedies, will continue to shape the story of our people for generations to come.

Where Noach failed, they succeeded.

4 Across the Great Divide: Between Jew and Non-Jew

Context

A monumental shift in focus takes place as the Torah moves from Parshat Noach to Parshat Lech Lecha.

Until this point, the narrative has been universal in scope, as the text has chronicled the world's creation and man's early generations. Now, however, the Torah's range narrows as it begins to tell the story of Avraham and his descendents, the chosen Jewish nation.

Before this shift takes place, however, a universal moral code for the world is laid out by God. This code, referred to in rabbinic literature as *Sheva Mitzvot B'nai Noach* (the seven mitzvot of the children of Noach), or the Noachide code, is derived from a passage found at the end of the Noach narrative and consists of seven basic commandments.[1] Taken together, these commandments form a moral blueprint for all civilizations.

The seven Noachide laws are the following: do not steal, do not kill, do not eat the limb of a living animal, do not commit acts of sexual immorality, do not practice idolatry, do not blaspheme God, and establish courts of law.[2]

Questions

How can the existence of the Noachide code inform our understanding of and our relationship with the non-Jewish world? How does God relate with the non-Jewish nations after He "chooses" the Jewish people? Can we

1. Ibid., 9:2–6.
2. Talmud Bavli Sanhedrin 56a–b.

morally defend a two-tiered system in God's relationship with the nations of the world?

Approaches

A

The seminal nature of the Noachide code can be seen in the rabbinic tradition that Midrashically roots these laws in the commandment concerning the Tree of Knowledge of Good and Evil, the very first commandment given by God to man.[3] According to the rabbis, God would not have created the human race without simultaneously producing a moral code of behavior.

Once commanded, these laws remain in force for the entire non-Jewish world even after God chooses the Jewish nation. God's relationship with all of humanity is clearly eternal and His expectation of moral behavior from all never diminishes. After Avraham begins his journey, God's relationship with the Jewish nation may be unique but it is certainly not exclusive.

A dramatic reference to the nonexclusive nature of God's bond with the Jewish people can be found in a powerful sentence in the *Brit bein Habetarim*, "the Covenant between the Pieces" contracted between God and Avraham in Parshat Lech Lecha.

In this covenant God predicts that Avraham's descendents will be strangers in a land not their own, where they will be made to work and to suffer for four hundred years.[4] God then proceeds to tell Avraham, "And the fourth generation will return here (to the land of Canaan) for the iniquity of the Emorites will not be complete until then."[5]

At the dawn of Jewish history, God delivers a clear and sobering message to Avraham and his descendents: *I do not relate to you alone and, therefore, your fate will be determined not only by your merit but by the legitimate rights of other nations as well. You will not return to this land until its inhabitants have become so corrupt that they deserve to be expelled. Until that time, their rights to the land will trump yours.*

Even if the Jewish nation has to pay the price, God will not overlook the rights of others.

3. Ibid.
4. Bereishit 15:13.
5. Ibid., 15:16.

All peoples and nations potentially have independent value and validity in the eyes of God. The retention of that value will depend upon their own moral behavior.

B

If "chosenness" does not connote exclusivity, what, then, does it mean? From the beginning of time, the answer is made clear. The Jewish people are *chosen for obligation*. In the aftermath of the failures of both the generation of the flood and the generation of dispersion, God selects a nation of teachers. The Jewish people, designated at Sinai as "a kingdom of priests and a holy people,"[6] are enjoined to teach through example by setting the standard for human behavior and achievement.

The very nature of this arrangement indicates an inherent value to those whom we are meant to "teach." The role of the Jewish nation is only meaningful if we acknowledge the intrinsic worth and moral potential of the non-Jewish world. This point is underscored immediately to Avraham at the very start of his journey when God commands: "And all the nations of the world will be blessed through you."[7]

C

Is there not, however, a degree of hubris in the contention that we are a "chosen" people? Doesn't the existence of two moral standards, the Torah for the Jewish people and the Noachide code for the rest of the world, create a theological structure that is prejudicial at its very core? How are we to defend ourselves against the accusation heaped upon us, generation after generation, that the very idea that we are the "Chosen People" reflects an inexcusable sense of superiority on our part?

D

As is often the case, the truth lies not in lofty theological concepts, but in the practical facts on the ground. Jewish tradition actually chooses the most broad-minded and tolerant of all possible approaches in determining its attitude towards others.

To prove this point, one need simply review the three potential options

6. Shmot 19:6.
7. Bereishit 12:3.

available to any faith tradition when defining its attitude towards those outside of its circle of belief.

1. A tradition can preach that its adherents have a lock on the ultimate truth and that all who dare to believe differently are doomed to distance from their Creator. The task of all those within the tradition is to somehow convince "outsiders" of the error of their ways.

This choice, historically made by the Catholic Church in its dealings with the Jewish people, has led to all sorts of seemingly logical, yet horrific excesses. After all, if I believe that I am right and you are wrong, if I believe that you are damned and I have the ability to save you, then I am doing you a favor as I attempt to convince you, through any means possible, of the one singular truth. Physical torture and pain is a small price for you to pay if I ultimately succeed in persuading you to "see the light."

How much torment has been inflicted across the ages by those who have ostensibly only had the best interests of their victims at heart?

2. A tradition can preach that its adherents have a lock on the ultimate truth and that no one else can join. Once again, there is only one true way. In this case, however, anyone outside of the circle is doomed and beyond salvation.

3. Finally, there is a third path. This path, chosen by Jewish tradition, is philosophically the most complex and difficult, yet ultimately the most tolerant and open-minded.

Judaism, unlike other faith traditions, preaches that there is more than one way to reach God, that what is right for one individual is not right for someone else. Each human being has his own personal potential, and his own learned traditions. As long as that potential is used for good, and as long as those traditions are moral at their core (in consonance with divinely ordained standards), that individual can develop a personal relationship with God.

While the Jewish nation has its own particular mission, other nations have their valuable missions as well. Our task as Jews is to follow the laws of the Torah and to serve as an example to the nations of the world. Other peoples are challenged to define their own tasks. In the process, however, they can never deviate from a basic set of God-given moral principles: the Noachide code.

Our challenge, as Jews, is not to make everyone else Jewish but to convince the world of the benefit of moral behavior and of the beauty of a relationship with the Creator. If people wish to convert to Judaism (for the right reasons) they are, of course, to be welcomed. We do not, however, consider such conversion to be a prerequisite to the attainment of a relationship with God.

Points to Ponder

Partially as a result of our turbulent history and of the torment that we have received at the hands of others, we have lost sight of the true traditional Jewish attitude towards the non-Jew. Too often, prejudiced and intolerant views are inaccurately presented as "authentic Judaism"; comments derogatory towards others are regularly heard on the Jewish "street." Such views only degrade us as a people and distance us from the very moral behavior we are meant to teach.

A return to classical Jewish sources allows us to regain our footing in our approach to those outside the circle of our belief.

Lech Lecha

לך לך

CHAPTER 12:1–17:27

פרק יב:א–יז:כז

Parsha Summary

Our story begins…

God appears to Avraham and launches his career by commanding him to leave his home and "travel to the land that I will show you." Avraham obeys and journeys to the land of Canaan.

Shortly after Avraham's arrival in Canaan, famine strikes the land. The patriarch responds by descending with his family to Egypt where he asks Sara to masquerade as his sister. Sara is abducted to the palace of the king and only released when God intervenes.

Avraham and his nephew, Lot, part ways and Lot chooses to settle on the border of the evil city of Sodom.

God appears to Avraham and promises him that he and his descendents will acquire the land of Canaan and that his children will be as plentiful as the dust of the earth.

Lot is taken captive in war and Avraham immediately responds by rushing into battle to save his nephew.

In response to Avraham's complaint that he and his wife Sara remain childless, God again promises the patriarch that his children will be as numerous as the stars of the heavens and that they will acquire the land of Canaan. When Avraham expresses doubts concerning the acquisition of the land, God executes the Brit bein Habetarim, *"Covenant between the Pieces," within which He predicts the exile and persecution of Avraham's descendents as well as their eventual return to the land of Canaan.*

Concerned by her continued childlessness, Sara convinces Avraham to take her servant, Hagar, as a concubine. As a result of this union, Hagar conceives.

Friction develops between Sara and Hagar, and Hagar is forced to temporarily flee. An angel appears to Hagar and informs her that she will give birth to a son, Yishmael, who will be the ancestor of many descendents.

God again appears to Avraham, changes his name from Avram to Avraham and his wife Sarai's name to Sara. He again promises the patriarch that Sara will give birth to a son Yitzchak, who will be the progenitor of a great nation. God then commands Avraham to circumcise every male member of his household. Avraham complies.

1 Finished and Unfinished Journeys

Context

God appears to Avraham and launches Jewish history with the commandment: *Lech lecha mei'artzecha...*, "Go for yourself from your land, from your birthplace and from the home of your father to the land that I will show you."

Avraham responds by journeying to the land of Canaan; and the story of our nation begins.[1]

Questions

God did not specify the destination of Avraham's journey. The text, however, indicates that Avraham left his home "to go to the land of Canaan."

How did Avraham know where to go?

Approaches

A

Some authorities, including the Ohr Hachaim, suggest that the question is simply not pertinent. From the outset, God increases Avraham's challenge by deliberately omitting the journey's intended destination. Once the patriarch responds and begins to travel to the unknown, however, "it is self-understood" that God then informs him that his ultimate objective is to be Canaan.[2]

B

Other commentaries, such as the Sforno, claim that the land of Canaan was the natural choice for Avraham to make, on his own, in response to God's

1. Bereishit 12:1–5.
2. Ohr Hachaim, Bereishit 12:1–4.

instructions. Canaan was "well known to them (the people of Avraham's time) as a land prepared for contemplation and the worship of God."

The Sforno goes on to say, however, that although Avraham left for Canaan on his own, he did not stop traveling until God appeared to him in the city of Elon Moreh (also identified as Shechem). That appearance fulfilled God's promise: "The land that I will show you."[3]

C

The most intriguing of all possibilities, however, is actually suggested by the Torah text itself.

At the end of Parshat Noach, Avraham's father, Terach, embarks upon a mysterious journey with his entire family. Without indicating why, the Torah simply states, "And they [Terach's family, including Avraham and his family] left from Ur Casdim to travel to the land of Canaan."[4]

This journey was aborted, however, short of its destination, as the Torah indicates: "And they came to Charan and they settled there.... And Terach died in Charan."[5]

What was the catalyst for Terach's journey towards Canaan and what was the purpose of the expedition? Why did it end in Charan?

The answers are shrouded in the mists of history. The Torah gives no indication as to why Terach begins this journey. Nor does the text tell us why the journey ended prematurely.

Perhaps the very fact of Terach's travels is proof of the Sforno's suggestion that the land of Canaan was well known for its holiness. Perhaps, as well, the Torah is suggesting that Terach, a man identified within Midrashic literature as a purveyor of idolatry, might have been searching for a greater truth. Could it be that Avraham's father was not irredeemable, but actually showed a spark of the spirit that would eventually burn full force in his son's heart?

We will never know for sure.

What we do know is that Avraham's journey emerges from the text as *a continuation of his father's original quest.* The difference between father

3. Sforno, Bereishit 12:5.
4. Bereishit 11:31.
5. Ibid., 11:31–32.

and son, from this perspective, lies in their ability and in their willingness to stay the course, to complete the journey.

Terach may well have begun with high hopes, but his journey is tragically and prematurely aborted; he is sidetracked by whatever attracts him in Charan. There Terach remains, only to disappear into the mists of history. Avraham picks up where Terach leaves off, completes his father's journey and changes history forever.

D

The Torah's message is clear. Success in life depends not only on originality and inventiveness but also upon the often overlooked qualities of persistence and constancy. What separates Avraham from Terach, on one level, is that Avraham finishes the journey while Terach does not. How many individuals across the face of history have made a real difference simply because they have been willing and able to finish the task?

Points to Ponder

The Torah chooses to teach us the important lesson of "staying the course" within the context of Avraham's journey to the land of Israel. This confluence of themes is hardly coincidental; the message created could not be more pertinent to our times.

Today's diaspora Jewish community exists at a time when return to the land of Israel is possible. And yet, for a variety of reasons, some more compelling than others, our personal journeys to our homeland have been voluntary aborted. Like Terach we have decided to remain in Charan at a time when other choices exist.

At the very least, our decisions should create a fundamental tension that courses through our lives. There should be an ever-present dissonance created by the fact that we have decided to remain on the periphery of our nation's history, while others, in its center, fight our battles for us.

Living with dissonance is not easy, and that might explain why one can currently observe, even within the affiliated Jewish community, a growing apathy to the miracle that is the State of Israel. We care about Israelis; we are concerned for their safety; but in our eyes the State of Israel has, to a great extent, lost its luster. Israel's existence no longer moves us as it once did.

This growing apathy is reflected in the ambivalence of the "Yeshiva world" towards the state, in the declining spirit of the organized Religious

Zionist community in America, and in our growing tendency to make our support of the State of Israel conditional upon its adherence to our political positions.

Perhaps we feel that if we can dismiss the importance of the State of Israel, we can't be so wrong for living in the diaspora. If Israel isn't a miracle, then we are not blind for ignoring her.

Time is precious, and we cannot afford the luxury of avoidance. Tension can be productive if it moves us towards positive action.

Perhaps some of us will find the dissonance of diaspora existence today so great that we will resolve it the only real way possible – by making aliya; or, at least, by encouraging our children to do so. Short of this dramatic step, however, other opportunities exist as we strive to play a role, however small, in the central Jewish drama of our time.

Political action, missions to Israel, making certain that the State of Israel remains a featured element of day school curricula and other steps must be taken to ensure that we do not sink into the elusive comfort that can be gained through avoidance. We must remember and our children must learn that we live in a time when the dreams of thousands of years are being realized.

Not all of us have the strength or the ability to be an Avraham, but, at least, we must avoid being a Terach. We cannot afford to be comfortable in the diaspora.

By recognizing that the journey is not yet over and that we are not yet home, we will play a role in ensuring that our people finish the journey.

2 Reckless Endangerment: Did the Patriarchs and Matriarchs Make Mistakes?

Context

Soon after Avraham's arrival to Canaan, famine strikes the land. Avraham responds to the danger by moving his household to Egypt. As they approach this strange land, Avraham becomes fearful that the inhabitants will kill him and take his wife, Sara, for themselves. He therefore asks Sara to masquerade as his sister.

As soon as the patriarch and matriarch arrive in Egypt, the Egyptians take note of Sara's beauty and she is abducted and taken to Pharaoh's palace. Sara is released only after God afflicts Pharaoh and his household with disease in punishment for her abduction. Pharaoh admonishes Avraham for concealing Sara's true identity and exiles Avraham and Sara from Egypt.[1]

Questions

Avraham's actions are deeply disturbing on numerous levels. Firstly, is he right or wrong when he leaves the land of Canaan in response to famine? After all, God commanded him to come to Canaan and has not now told him to leave. Should he have stayed and relied upon God's miraculous intervention?

Even more troubling, of course, is Avraham's behavior concerning his wife. If he knew that the descent to Egypt was fraught with inevitable danger, particularly for Sara, then what right did he have to go there? Above all, how could he endanger Sara's life by suggesting that she masquerade as his sister?

Compounding the problem, similar events occur when Avraham and

1. Bereishit 12:10–20.

Sara, later in their lives, travel to the kingdom of the Philistines and, yet again, in the next generation, when Yitzchak and Rivka travel to that same location. On each of these later occasions the patriarchs once again attempt to present their wives to the surrounding society as their sisters.

Approaches

Our discussion concerning these and similar issues will reflect the spectrum of opinion within rabbinic thought concerning the potential fallibility of biblical heroes. At one end of the spectrum are those authorities who refuse to see any possible failing on the part of the patriarchs, matriarchs and other heroes of the Torah and Tanach (an acronym for the Biblical canon – Torah, Nevi'im, Ketuvim: the five books of Moses, the Prophets and the Writings). According to these scholars, our heroic ancestors loom larger than life and are beyond any possible reproach. Any failings that we might attribute to them actually stem from our inability to understand the text properly.

At the opposite end of the spectrum are those rabbinic authorities who insist upon seeing the heroes of the Torah as human beings. From the perspective of these scholars, the greatness of our ancestors stems from their very humanity and from their ability to reach lofty spiritual heights in spite of the human frailties that we all share.

These rabbis recognize that whereas pagans deified their heroes, and Christians returned to such deification, Judaism insists upon seeing its heroes as human beings. When your heroes are gods you can worship them, but *you cannot emulate them*. As long as we see the characters of our Torah as human beings, their greatness may be beyond our reach, but we can, nonetheless, aspire to that greatness.

As is always the case when approaching rabbinic debate: *Eilu va'eilu divrei Elokim chaim*, "These and these are the words of the living God." We need not take sides. We can, instead, learn from every position along the spectrum of rabbinic opinion.

A

By failing to record a verdict concerning Avraham's descent into Egypt, the Torah opens debate concerning an issue that will span the generations until our time: At what point does trust in God's involvement end and our own efforts to secure our destiny begin?

B

Some scholars, among them the Ramban and Rabbeinu Bachya,[2] do not hesitate to take Avraham to task for his decision to leave Canaan: "His leaving the land, to which he was commanded from the outset," says the Ramban, "was a sin that he transgressed. Even in a famine, God will redeem one from death."[3]

Avraham, according to these scholars, fails this test through a lapse in belief in God's Providence.

The Ramban goes on to say that because of this sin and the events that followed, the exile of Avraham's descendents to Egypt was decreed.[4] (For a discussion concerning the effect of parents' actions upon the fate of their children see Lech Lecha 4, *Approaches* A.)

C

Many other classical commentaries are conspicuously silent on the issue, accepting, perhaps, that Avraham had no choice but to act to save his family.

Particularly noteworthy is the Sforno's brief comment that the Torah uses the term *lagur,* "to dwell," when it describes Avraham's sojourn into Egypt. This word invariably appears in the text when a temporary rather than a permanent residence is being established. The Torah wants us to know, says the Sforno, that Avraham did not intend to stay in Egypt for an extended period of time. After the famine passed, he fully anticipated a return to the land of Canaan.[5]

D

While debate rages concerning the propriety of Avraham's descent into Egypt, the verdict concerning his behavior towards Sara would seem, at first glance, to be more clear-cut. The Ramban, for example, minces no words in his assessment of Avraham's actions: "And know that our Father Avraham sinned a great sin in error by placing his righteous wife in a situation of potential transgression because of the fear that he might have been

2. Ramban, Bereishit 12:10; Rabbeinu Bachya, Bereishit 12:13.
3. Ramban, Bereishit 12:10.
4. Ibid.
5. Sforno, Bereishit 12:10.

killed. He should have trusted in God to save him, his life and all that was his; for God has the power to help and to save."[6]

The Ramban even goes on to suggest that Sara never actually agreed to Avraham's request. Instead, when the patriarchal family arrived in Egypt, the "evil and sinful" Egyptians did not even bother to ask who Sara was before abducting her to Pharaoh's house. Sara remained silent while Avraham, on his own, told the Egyptians that she was his sister.[7]

Rabbeinu Bachya and others follow the Ramban's lead and view Avraham's behavior in critical fashion.[8]

E

Even concerning the episode of Sara's abduction, however, some commentaries quickly rise to Avraham's defense. The Sforno, for example, who had limited himself to a brief comment concerning Avraham's descent into Egypt, now develops an intricate theory concerning Avraham's behavior towards Sara. Basing himself upon clear textual indicators, this scholar paints a picture of an emergency plan gone awry.

Avraham, according to the Sforno, simply wanted to buy time. He suggested to Sara that she masquerade as his sister so that each of the Egyptians would vie for her hand. "If you say that you are my sister, each one will hope that I will give to him your hand in marriage, and none of them will consider killing me. They will, instead, bargain and ply me with gifts as is the custom of the time."[9]

While the citizens of Egypt haggled for Sara's hand, Avraham intended to quickly purchase provisions and leave.[10]

When the patriarchal family arrived in Egypt, however, the plan quickly fell apart. For although the Torah testifies that the citizens of Egypt immediately perceived Sara's beauty, before they could act, "The officers of Pharaoh saw her and praised her before the king; and the woman was abducted to the house of Pharaoh."[11]

According to the Sforno, Sara's immediate abduction to the house of

6. Ramban, Bereishit 12:10.
7. Ibid., 12:11–13.
8. Rabbeinu Bachya, Bereishit 12:13.
9. Sforno, Bereishit 12:13.
10. Ibid.
11. Bereishit 12:14–15.

Pharaoh, at the hands of the king's servants, preempted Avraham's delaying tactics. The patriarch had fully intended to leave Egypt before Sara entered any real danger.[12]

Points to Ponder

The rabbinic debate concerning Avraham's actions during this difficult episode reflects a refreshing honesty concerning the stories of the Torah. Rather than engage in apologetics concerning Avraham's behavior, the scholars cited above and others wrestle with the facts.

Some, such as the Ramban and Rabbeinu Bachya, come to the conclusion that Avraham's actions reflected unintended sin and error. Avraham's descendents, continues the Ramban, will ultimately pay the price for these errors through their own descent into Egypt.

Other scholars, such as the Sforno, defend Avraham's behavior in intelligent, thoughtful fashion.

In the final analysis, of course, it is not the ultimate verdict that is important but, rather, the debate and discussion. We are not meant to judge Avraham's behavior from the safety of our own lives but to learn from it.

Like the patriarch, we will, in every era, struggle with the age-old question: At what point does God's Providence end and our efforts begin? For us as for the patriarch, the answers will be complex.

12. Sforno, Bereishit 12:13.

3 Too Much Information?

Context

At a dramatic juncture in Avraham's career a strange, unwieldy sentence is found in the biblical text.

Avraham's nephew, Lot, is taken captive in battle and the Torah states, "And the survivor came and told Avraham the Ivri [the Hebrew]; and he was dwelling in the plains belonging to Mamreh the Emorite, the brother of Eshkol and the brother of Aner, and they were the holders of a covenant with Avraham."[1]

Questions

Why does the Torah give us all of this information?

Why, for example, is it important for us to know, specifically at this juncture, that Avraham is an "Ivri"? The root of the Hebrew word *Ivri* is *la'avor*, which means "to cross over." Avraham is referred to as an *Ivri*, either because he crossed to Canaan from the other side of the Jordan or because he stands *mei'eiver*: across the philosophical divide from the rest of the world.[2]

This is the one and only time that the Torah uses this term in reference to Avraham. The word does not again appear until the story of Yosef, three generations later.[3]

Why, in addition, do we need to be informed that Avraham is dwelling on the property of a man by the name of Mamreh the Emorite? Why do we need to know that Mamreh's brothers are Eshkol and Aner? And, finally, why do we need to know that these brothers hold a covenant with Avraham?

None of this information seems relevant.

---

1. Bereishit 14:13.
2. Midrash Rabba Bereishit 42:8.
3. Bereishit 39:14, 17; 41:12.

Approaches

A

The Sforno offers a straightforward approach to this sentence, rooted in the realm of *pshat.*

According to the Sforno, Avraham is referred to as an Ivri to explain why he is being informed about Lot's capture. Although the "survivor" did not know that Avraham and Lot were related, he did know that they were both "Ivrim." He therefore assumed that Avraham would be interested in Lot's fate.

The Torah draws a connection between Avraham, Mamreh, Eshkol and Aner, continues the Sforno, to indicate that these allies will now go into battle together. Their partnership is later indicated in the text after victory is achieved. Avraham refuses to benefit from the battle but says to the king of Sodom, "Aner, Eshkol and Mamreh shall receive their portion."[4]

B

Perhaps, however, a simple rereading of this sentence reveals another, deeper message. The Torah is, in the clearest of terms, describing the delicate nature of Avraham's position at this critical juncture of his life.

Avraham is an Ivri, a vulnerable stranger in the land in which he now dwells. He is surrounded by potential enemies. He parted with his nephew Lot earlier, under less than pleasant circumstances, and Lot made the choice of going to the evil city of Sodom.[5] Finally, Avraham has achieved a degree of safety and stability in that he now quietly lives on the property of his friend Mamreh, and also enjoys an alliance with Mamreh's two brothers, Eshkol and Aner.

The Torah is telling us that Avraham has every reason not to get involved. This battle is not his own; Lot has made his decisions and determined his own fate. Avraham is generally vulnerable and yet, is, at this moment, safe. Why should he risk everything by becoming involved in a conflict that has nothing to do with him?

Nonetheless…

---

4. Ibid., 15:24.
5. Ibid., 13:5–13.

As soon as Avraham hears that Lot has been taken captive he springs into action, without hesitation.

As the very next sentence in the Torah records, "And Avraham heard that his brother had been taken captive; and he armed the members of his household, eight hundred thirteen strong, and he pursued [the enemy] until Dan."[6]

From Avraham's perspective, Lot is not his nephew, but his brother. Their disputes of the past are now of no consequence. In fact, Avraham's own safety and security is immaterial.

When your "brother" is in danger, nothing can stand in your way.

—C—

The Torah never provides us with "too much information."

Instead, the passages before us describe Avraham's eloquent, wordless response to Kayin's protest at the time of Hevel's murder: "Am I my brother's keeper?"[7]

Through his actions Avraham informs us that we are all "our brothers' keepers." Whatever the cost, whatever the complications, when our brothers are in need nothing should stand in our way.

6. Ibid., 14:14.
7. Ibid., 4:9.

4 What Kind of Answer Is This?

Context

Towards the end of Parshat Lech Lecha God delivers two dramatic promises to Avraham. The patriarch reacts to each in vastly different ways.

God first states, "Look up to the heavens and count the stars if you can; thus will be your children." Faced with this prediction, Avraham responds with unquestioning belief. God then continues, "I am the Lord Who took you out of Ur Casdim to give you this land to inherit." Here, Avraham objects, "O Lord God, how do I know that I will inherit?"

In response to Avraham's objection, God commands the patriarch to slaughter a series of animals, divide some of the carcasses in half and place each half opposite the other. God causes a deep sleep to fall on Avraham and appears to him in a dramatic vision. "Know full well," God proclaims, "that your children will be strangers in a land not their own, where they will be tormented and enslaved for four hundred years.... And the fourth generation will return here..."

God's presence then passes between the divided animals and a covenant between God and Avraham is struck, known as the *Brit bein Habetarim*, the "Covenant between the Pieces."[1]

Questions

Why does Avraham believe God's promise concerning progeny, yet question the inheritance of the land? If it is within God's power to bless Avraham and Sara with children after so many years of barrenness, He is certainly capable of ensuring that the Jewish nation will inherit its homeland. Compounding the problem is the fact that on two previous occasions

1. Bereishit 15:5–21.

God has already clearly promised that the land of Canaan will be given to Avraham's descendents.[2] Avraham, for some reason, does not question that promise until now.

On the flip side, God's response to Avraham's doubts seems abundantly strange. How is the prediction of Egyptian slavery meant to allay Avraham's fears or answer his questions? Is there a message of reassurance hidden in the dark vision of exile and slavery? Or is this simply God's way of saying that "all will be well that ends well"? Further, what is the significance of the ritual accompanying the Covenant between the Pieces?

Finally, on a deeper level, how does this entire episode affect the delicate balance existing between prescience (God's knowledge of the future; see Bereishit 4, *Approaches* A) and man's free will? Once God informs us of the future, is He not, then, predetermining it? Are Joseph and his brothers, the biblical characters whose actions will lead to the descent of the Jewish people into Egypt, simply actors playing out predetermined roles on a predefined stage?

Approaches

A

The scholars of the Talmud and Midrash draw two direct yet vastly different connections between Avraham's question and God's response at the Covenant between the Pieces.

The first approach perceives the patriarch's question as the catalyst for God's dire prophecy. The very descent of the nation into Egyptian slavery will be a direct result of Avraham's doubts. "Shmuel said: 'Why was our forefather Avraham punished through the enslavement of his children in Egypt for 210 years? Because he questioned the powers of God, by saying, 'how do I know that I will inherit?'"[3]

In Shmuel's eyes, God's message at this moment is not one of reassurance but punishment. *You have doubted my power, and as a result your children will suffer through enslavement at the hands of strangers. Then, and only then, will they inherit the land.*

Shmuel fails to explain why Avraham suddenly doubts God. He also

2. Ibid., 12:7; 13:15.
3. Talmud Bavli Nedarim 32a.

raises the serious philosophical question of why children should be punished for a sin committed by their ancestor.

The question as to whether or not children are affected by the sins of their parents is dealt with on a number of occasions within rabbinic literature. The most well-known iteration of the issue is found in a Talmudic passage in the tractate of Brachot. The Talmud notes an apparent discrepancy between the following two biblical passages:

1. "He Who visits the iniquity of fathers on children and children's children until the third and fourth generation."[4]

2. "Fathers shall not die because of their children, nor shall children die because of their fathers. Each individual will die in his own sin."[5]

The Talmud resolves the contradiction by suggesting that God will indeed punish children for their parents' sins but only if the children persist in continuing in their parents' ways.[6]

Based upon this Talmudic passage, the following balance can be suggested.

Judaism absolutely rejects the Christian concept of "original sin" (the idea that all generations of mankind continue to bear guilt for the original sin of Adam and Chava). We are not responsible for the sins of others. We are each responsible for our own fate.

Judaism cannot deny the idea, however, of "intergenerational reverberation." Our actions help shape our children's lives, just as we are, in large measure, a product of our ancestors' decisions and deeds.

We are not guilty of the sin committed by Adam and Chava. We do, however, still pay the price. This is not punishment, but, rather, a reality of life. Had Adam and Chava not sinned, we would now be living a very different existence in the Garden of Eden. We are still affected by the actions of our primal ancestors.

Similarly, such overarching life issues as where we are born, to whom, into what environment, and, in fact, whether or not we are born at all, are determined not by us and not only by God, but also by our parents and those who came before them as well.

If, as we have said before, the box that defines our lives is, in large

---

4. Shmot 34:7.
5. Devarim 24:16.
6. Talmud Bavli Brachot 7a.

measure, predetermined by God (see Bereishit 4, *Approaches* A), it is also partially created by those who precede us.

The Talmud warns that parents and grandparents should be careful of their decisions and actions, for they help shape the lives of generations to come. Their children will build upon what they have built, reaping the rewards or paying the price.

In the episode before us, for example, Avraham's descendents are neither guilty of nor punished for his failings. They are, however, affected by his decisions and by his actions – either because they will learn from his example and make the same mistakes in their time, or because Avraham's actions themselves will create a given set of circumstances that will reverberate across the ages and influence generations to come.

B

The second Midrashic approach focuses not on the substance of God's prophecy but on the ritual that accompanies it.

"Rabbi Hiyya Bar Hanina said: [Avraham did not question] as an accuser but, rather, he asked, 'By what merit [will my children inherit the land]?' God responded, 'By the atonements that I will give to Israel.'"[7] Rabbi Hiyya goes on to explain that the animals used in the covenant ritual represented specific sacrifices that would be brought by the Jewish people as atonements throughout the ages.[8]

Rashi summarizes Rabbi Hiyya's approach as follows: "Avraham asked, 'In what merit?' and God responded, 'In the merit of the sacrifices.'"[9]

According to this approach, Avraham is not questioning God's power at all. He is instead questioning his own merit and that of his progeny. He believes in God's ability but he doubts his own.

Textual support for Rabbi Hiyya's position can be found in the seemingly superfluous word *lerishta*, "to inherit," found at the end of God's promise to Avraham concerning the land. In its active conjugation, this word does not mean to inherit but to conquer and acquire.[10] God is informing Avraham that the land will not be given to his children as a gift. They will have to actively acquire the land when the time comes.

7. Midrash Rabba Bereishit 44:14.
8. Ibid.
9. Rashi, Bereishit 15:8.
10. Rabbi Shimshon Raphael Hirsch, Bereishit 15:8.

When the patriarch hears that his children will have to participate in the conquest of Canaan, he realizes, for the first time, that the acquisition of the land is not a foregone conclusion. He therefore asks: "How do I know that they will do their part? How do I know that they will inherit the land?"

God responds by reassuring Avraham that his children will indeed merit a return to their homeland. The source of that merit will be their religious devotion, represented by the sacrifices they will offer across the years. This reassurance is then driven home through the symbolic ritual of the covenant itself.

C

While Rabbi Hiyya focuses on the ritual of the covenant as a response to Avraham's self-doubts, perhaps the prophecy of exile itself contains an element of reassurance. God is saying to Avraham that his children will inherit the land because when the time comes to leave Egypt, they will rise to the challenge. After centuries of slavery, they will still be a recognizable people and they will respond to God's call.

In that merit, they will inherit the land.

Interpreted this way, the Covenant between the Pieces can also be seen as a harbinger of exiles to come. Throughout our turbulent history, we will be challenged, against great odds, to retain our integrity as a people and to keep the dream of return to our Homeland alive. How much greater is the challenge in our own day when the possibility of such return is real.

D

Finally, there are those commentaries, Rabbi Shimshon Raphael Hirsch among them, who see no element of doubt at all in Avraham's reaction. They claim that the patriarch, hearing for the first time that his children will have to actively conquer the land, simply asks, *Ba'ma eida? How will I know when the time is right?*

God responds: *It will not happen in your time, or in your children's time, or in their children's time. Only after generations, only after exile, will your descendents conquer the land.*[11]

11. Ibid.

Points to Ponder

The tension between God's foreknowledge of events and our own free will comes to a head when we encounter an event such as the Covenant between the Pieces (for a brief discussion of the concepts of free will, prescience and predestination see Bereishit 4, *Approaches* A). For while God's prescience does not normally affect our actions in any way, the moment He shares a prediction of the future with us the equation changes dramatically. How much choice can we have if we know that events are already predetermined? How much choice, for that matter, did Joseph and his brothers have concerning Joseph's sale, the catalyst for our exile in Egypt?

While a full discussion of the issues raised by this question is well beyond the scope of our text, the following brief comment can be made.

God will often paint the broad brushstrokes of history but allow us to fill in the details. We are told, for example, that the Mashiach (Messiah) is destined to come, bringing with him the culmination of our nation's story. How he comes, when he comes, how much difficulty or ease will precede his arrival, and which of us will be there to greet him are all issues that are determined by our actions. Similarly, while God predicted in general fashion that the Jewish people would experience hardship and exile in a strange land, the details of how those events came to fruition were determined by the actions of the personalities at the time. (For a more complete discussion of these issues see Vayeishev 3, *Approaches* A.)

Vayeira

וירא

CHAPTER 18:1–22:24

פרק יח:א–כב:כד

Parsha Summary

Visits and trials...

Three angels visit Avraham and Sara and are greeted with warm hospitality. During the course of the visit, the patriarch and matriarch are informed of the impending birth of a son.

God decides to inform Avraham of His decision to destroy the evil cities of Sodom and Amora. The patriarch courageously responds by arguing in the cities' defense based upon the possible presence of righteous individuals. God agrees not to destroy the cities if ten righteous individuals are found.

Two of the three angels arrive at the gates of Sodom where they are greeted by Lot, who offers them hospitality. After being threatened by the residents of the city, the angels warn Lot to leave with his family in order to escape the coming cataclysm. Lot and his family escape. Lot's wife, however, disobeys God's command not to look back and turns into a pillar of salt.

Believing that the entire world has been destroyed, Lot's daughters seduce their father, conceive and give birth to the progenitors of the nations of Moav and Amon.

Avraham and Sara travel to the territory of the Philistines, where Avraham again asks his wife to masquerade as his sister. Sara is abducted to the palace of the king and only released when God intervenes.

After many years of childlessness, Sara gives birth to Yitzchak.

Sara perceives the danger to Yitzchak presented by Yishmael and prevails upon Avraham to exile the older son and his mother, Hagar, from the family home. An angel appears to Hagar and promises her that Yishmael will be the father of a great nation.

Avraham and Avimelech, king of the Philistines, contract a covenant.

God tests Avraham through Akeidat Yitzchak, *"the Binding of Isaac," as He commands Avraham to take Yitzchak and raise him as an offering at a designated site. Avraham complies. Father and son ascend Mount Moriah together only to have the intended sacrifice stopped at the last moment through divine intervention in the form of an angel. Avraham sacrifices a ram in Yitzchak's stead and the angel blesses the patriarch in God's name.*

1 When God Talks to Himself

Context

As God prepares to destroy the sinful cities of Sodom and Amora, He apparently opens a dialogue with Himself:

> And God said: 'Will I hide from Avraham what I am about to do? And Avraham is destined to be a great and powerful nation and all of the nations will be blessed through him. For I know of him that he will command his children, and his household after him, and they will guard the way of God to do righteousness and justice, so that God may bring upon Avraham all that He has said concerning him.[1]

Questions

Why, at this juncture, does the Torah take the unusual step of recording a conversation between God and himself? What are we meant to learn from this dialogue?

What is the connection between God's dilemma and its resolution? The text seems unclear. Why does God feel compelled to reveal His plans to the patriarch?

Approaches

A

As we have noted before, each word of the Torah is purposeful and divinely chosen. The anthropomorphic, heavenly self-addressed dialogue before us, therefore, must be seen as the Torah's way of providing us with a glimpse into "God's mind."

---

1. Bereishit 18:17–19.

God is telling us that He sees a fundamental connection between Avraham's mission to the world and the impending destruction of the cities of Sodom and Amora. So deep is that link that Avraham must be "brought into the loop" before God can continue.

While the connection is clear, however, the substance is not. What aspect of Avraham's mission moves God to reveal His intentions to the patriarch?

B

Two global approaches are suggested within Midrashic literature and by the commentaries that follow:

1. Avraham's rights stem from the new role that he now assumes at this critical juncture of world history.[2] Avraham rises to the level of prophecy as, for the first time, God invites a mortal into what Nehama Leibowitz refers to as "the intimate counsels of the divine."[3]

From this point onward, in each generation, a few chosen spiritual heirs to Avraham will receive that divine invitation. Serving as prophets, they will partner with God and play a major role in bringing His message to the Jewish nation and, at times, to the world. As the Prophet Amos declares, "For the Lord God will not do anything until He has revealed His counsel to his servants, the prophets."[4]

Prophecy will continue across the generations, according to the rabbis, until the time of the Babylonian exile. During that period (the authorities disagree as to the exact moment), man enters the non-prophetic era,[5] and God's will must be determined without direct communication.

2. Avraham's rights at this point stem from his ownership of the land of Canaan.

The situation can be compared to a king who had an orchard which he gave to his beloved friend as a gift. After a period of time, however, the king found it necessary to cut down some of the orchard's trees. The king decided that although the orchard had originally been his and had only been given to his friend as a gift, he would not touch a tree without first consulting with that friend.

2. Midrash Tanchuma Bereishit 49.
3. Leibowitz, *Studies in Bereishit*, p. 165.
4. Amos 3:7.
5. Talmud Bavli Bava Batra 12a–b, Megilla 3a, Moed Katan 25a.

So, too, God gave the land of Canaan to Avraham and his descendents. He was, therefore, unwilling to destroy any part of that land without first consulting with Avraham.[6]

C

A third, entirely different explanation for God's decision to reveal His intentions to Avraham can be uncovered if we turn to the events that immediately follow in the Torah text. A study of these events reveals that God is forced to inform Avraham because failure to do so would have dealt a mortal blow to the patriarch's perception of his own mission to the world.

Consider the very next passages, which detail Avraham's well-known arguments in defense of the citizens of Sodom and Amora. A striking, fundamental flaw begins to emerge in the patriarch's logic as he argues passionately with his Creator.

Avraham's dramatic opening argument runs as follows: "Will you destroy the righteous with the wicked? Perhaps there are fifty righteous individuals in the midst of the city..."[7]

The logical extension of this argument should, of course, be: *When you destroy Sodom and Amora, spare the righteous individuals.*

In fact, Avraham later picks up exactly that thought: "It would be sacrilege were You to do such a thing, to destroy the righteous with the wicked and make the righteous like the wicked! It would be sacrilege were You to do this! Will the Judge of the land not do justice?"[8]

In the middle of this abundantly rational argument, however, Avraham suddenly takes an illogical argumentative leap and inserts the following demand: "Will You not forgive and spare *the entire place*, because of the fifty righteous men who are in its midst?"[9]

What gives Avraham the right to ask that the cities be entirely spared? His own argument, "Will You destroy the righteous with the wicked," would seem to defend the righteous alone yet allow for the destruction of the wicked.

---

6. Midrash Tanchuma Bereishit, Vayeira 5.
7. Bereishit 18:23–24.
8. Ibid., 18:25.
9. Ibid., 18:24.

D

The key to Avraham's debate with God on behalf of Sodom and Amora may well lie in God's earlier promises to the patriarch himself. Through the impending fate of these evil cities, and the relationship of the cities to righteous individuals who might be in their midst, Avraham is confronted with a microcosm of his own relationship to the world.

When God launched Avraham's career with the dramatic commandant of Lech Lecha, He actually delivered two promises to the patriarch:

1. He promised that Avraham's progeny would survive the evil of a surrounding world.[10]

2. He promised further that, if Avraham's descendents fulfill their righteous mission, they will have an effect on those around them. "All the nations of the world will be blessed through you."[11]

The entire episode of Sodom and Amora, therefore, presents a critical challenge to Avraham's own self-perception. If God had destroyed these evil cities without revealing the absence of any righteous individuals in their midst, Avraham's own world would have been severely threatened. He might then have wondered: *Perhaps righteous individuals perished in the conflagration. How, then, do I know that I and my own children will survive the evil world that surrounds us? Even further, what about the promise that God made to us that we could change that world, that humankind would be blessed through our efforts? If the righteous men of Sodom and Amora could not save their own cities how can we possibly affect the world?*

Thus Avraham argues on two levels – the very two levels reflected in God's promises to him.

E

We can now better understand God's conversation with Himself as a necessary prelude to His actions concerning the cities of Sodom and Amora.

God feels compelled to reveal His intentions to Avraham because He wants Avraham to understand that the destruction of the cities will not in any way contradict God's promises to the patriarch. Upon careful rereading, God's internal dialogue reflects exactly this point: "And God said: 'Will I hide from Avraham what I intend to do? And Avraham will be a

10. Ibid., 12:2.
11. Ibid., 12:3.

great and powerful nation, and all the nations of the world will be blessed through him.'"

Imbedded in this passage are the two fundamental promises given by God to the patriarch from the very start. "You will thrive and your actions will affect the world." The Torah tells us that God is now driven to inform Avraham of the impending fate of Sodom and Amora specifically because of those earlier promises.

The Torah, however, is not only telling us why God had to inform Avraham, but, also, why Avraham had to respond as he did. Faced with the impending destruction of Sodom and Amora, Avraham struggles with his own destiny as well. He argues that the righteous to be found in the cities should not only be saved themselves but that their actions should impact upon the fate of those around them. He desperately wants not only to save the cities but to preserve the integrity of his own mission to the world.

In the aftermath of Avraham's pleadings, he learns the tragic truth: there are not even ten righteous individuals within the cities of Sodom and Amora. There is no one to affect the destiny of these doomed cities.

Avraham's mission, however, remains intact. He and his descendents can and will change the world.

2 Lot's Frightening Journey

Context

One of the strangest and most disturbing episodes in the entire Torah is recorded immediately before the destruction of the city of Sodom. Two of the three angels who earlier visited Avraham now arrive at his nephew Lot's doorstep in Sodom. Lot showers them with hospitality as he invites them into the protection of his home. It does not take long, however, before the evil inhabitants of the city learn of the angels' presence and surround Lot's house demanding that the strangers be given up to them. Seeking to protect his guests from the danger confronting them, Lot reasons with the mob and offers his two unmarried daughters in their stead. The Sodomites refuse the offer, and prepare to storm the house. The angels miraculously afflict their potential attackers with blindness, and then inform Lot that to protect himself and his family he must now leave Sodom.[1]

Questions

How are we to understand Lot's bizarre behavior? He welcomes strangers into his home, but is then willing to sacrifice his own daughters to mob violence.

Does this episode provide us with any kind of window into Lot's personality and soul? If so, what does a glimpse through that window reveal?

Approaches

With the story of Lot, we are confronted with one of those occasions where a simple, careful, straightforward reading of the biblical text reveals easily

1. Ibid., 19:1–13.

missed significance. We must first, however, back up to gain an overview. When we do so, a tragic pattern begins to emerge. This pattern, spanning a number of chapters in the text, enables us to understand Lot and his frightening journey.

B

Our story begins in Parshat Lech Lecha at the point when Avraham and his nephew part ways.

Responding to a dispute that erupts between Avraham's and Lot's shepherds, the patriarch turns to his nephew and says: "Let there not be a dispute between you and me and between my shepherds and your shepherds, for we are brothers. Behold, all of the land is before you. Separate yourself from me. If you go left then I will go right, and if you go right I will go left."[2]

Given the opportunity to choose anywhere within the land of Canaan, Lot chooses the fertile Jordan plain and the Torah states, *Va'ye'ehal ad Sodom*, "And he tented until Sodom."[3]

C

Two elements of this phrase immediately catch our attention.

1. First of all, the Torah uses the verb *va'ye'ehal*, "and he tented," to describe Lot's relationship to the land near Sodom.

The two words normally used by the Torah to indicate residence in a particular location are *lashevet*, "to live," which connotes permanent residence, and *lagur*, "to dwell," which connotes impermanent residence.

Here, however, the Torah chooses to use an even more transient term – "tenting." Why?

2. Secondly, the word *ad*, "until," is an inherently ambiguous one and its use here seems strange.

The rabbis tell us that *ad* can mean one of two things depending upon context. The word sometimes means "up to and including," and sometimes means "up to but not including."[4] (For example, if Jewish law says that a certain object is acceptable *ad*, "up to," a height of forty *amot* [a halachic

2. Ibid., 13:8–9.
3. Ibid., 13:12.
4. Talmud Bavli Brachot 20b.

measurement], the rabbis will still have to define what that means. Is an object forty *amot* high acceptable, or must the object be, at most, 39.999 *amot* high?)

By stating that Lot tents "*ad* Sodom," the Torah deliberately leaves his situation vague. Is Lot in the city or outside the city? The facts are unclear.

The Torah goes out of its way to convey a sense of ambivalence on Lot's part as he considers his relationship to the city of Sodom. The reasons for this ambivalence are made abundantly clear in the Torah's very next sentence: "And the citizens of Sodom were greatly evil and sinful towards God."[5]

Lot is aware of the true nature of the city before him and consciously tents at its border. He literally has one foot in the city and one foot out. He believes that he can live on the edge of Sodom without being affected by its evil.

D

We next encounter Lot a chapter later, when he is taken captive during a war involving Sodom. The Torah states: "And they took Lot and all of his wealth, the son of Avraham's brother, and they went. *V'hu yoshev b'Sodom*, and he was living in Sodom."[6]

The seemingly superfluous phrase *v'hu yoshev b'Sodom*, "and he is living in Sodom," is actually chronicling an important transformation. By this point, Lot is no longer living at the edge of the city, but rather "in Sodom." At first ambivalent about his relationship with Sodom, Lot is now comfortable as a full citizen within its borders.

E

Finally, we meet Lot yet again, this time in Parshat Vayeira five chapters later. The occasion is the event with which we began: the visit of the angels to Sodom. The Torah introduces this event in the following fashion: "And the two angels came to Sodom in the evening; and Lot was sitting *b'sha'ar Sodom*, in the gates of Sodom."[7]

5. Bereishit 13:13.
6. Ibid., 14,12
7. Ibid., 19,1

You could easily miss it, but the Torah is conveying a very significant point with the two words *b'sha'ar Sodom*, "in the gates of Sodom."

Only specific people had the privilege of sitting in the gates of a city in biblical times: the elders and officials of that city. By now, Lot's transformation is complete. He has moved from the edge of the city to its center. Lot is now a respected elder of the evil city of Sodom. The man who felt that he would be able to withstand the lure of the city has fallen prey to its power.

F

With the pattern of Lot's personal transformation as a backdrop, we can now begin to understand his seemingly inexplicable behavior when confronted with the threatening mob outside his door.

Lot is not an evil, but, rather, a weak man. His most fatal flaw, in fact, is his failure to recognize his own vulnerability. He believes that he can withstand the temptations of Sodom. Without realizing it, however, he is sucked in and indelibly transformed by the city around him. The Torah testifies that you cannot live near Sodom and remain unchanged.

At the most critical juncture of his life, Lot displays the aberrant behavior of a man who is trying to reconcile the irreconcilable. On the one hand, he desperately attempts to hold true to the traditions he witnessed in his Uncle Avraham's tent. He welcomes guests and treats them royally. He is willing to go to any lengths to protect them. At the same time, however, he seamlessly crosses over into the horrific world of Sodom and offers to sacrifice his own daughters to a brutal fate. Lot fails because he believes that he can live in two worlds at once – in two worlds *which simply cannot coexist.*

Points to Ponder

Over the course of several chapters, the Torah clearly chronicles Lot's step-by-step transformation: an unwitting journey into the hell that is Sodom. Lot's story remains a cautionary tale concerning the effects of external environment on our lives. We must be ever aware of the world that surrounds us, and we must actively reject those elements of our surroundings that are incompatible with our own standards.

Through such vigilance, we will escape Lot's fate.

3 Avraham's Sudden Silence

Context

Two towering events serve as dramatic bookends within Parshat Vayeira: the destruction of the cities of Sodom and Amora and the *Akeida* (the aborted sacrifice of Yitzchak).

Avraham reacts to the first of these events true to expected form. Unable to accept an unacceptable reality, he argues, debates and struggles with his Creator. He is determined to change God's mind.[1]

When confronted with the commandment to sacrifice his son, however, Avraham is silent and obedient.[2]

Questions

Why does Avraham react to the challenge of the *Akeida* with deafening silence? Where is the Avraham that we have come to know – the man who is unwilling to accept the world as it is; the man who, unlike Noach before him, struggles with his Creator at every stage of his life (see Noach 2, *Approaches* B, C)?

Approaches

A

Clearly bothered by Avraham's apparent silence in the face of the *Akeida*, scholars across the ages, in the Midrash and beyond, fill in the blanks of the biblical text. They claim that, at least internally, Avraham was not silent at all. These scholars paint a picture of an Avraham terribly torn by the task that lies before him. He is not only a father moved beyond measure by compassion and love for his son, but also a patriarch unable to recon-

1. Bereishit, 18:23–33.
2. Ibid., 22:3.

cile God's previous promises to him – of a nation to be created through Yitzchak – with the current commandment to sacrifice that very son.

B

The Midrash, for example, presents a detailed narrative in which Satan appears to Avraham in the guise of an old man. Step after step, along the journey to Mount Moriah, this old man argues with the patriarch: "Where are you going? Old man! Have you lost your mind? A child is given to you after a hundred years, and you go to slaughter him? Tomorrow God will accuse you of murder, of shedding the blood of your own son!"

When Satan sees that Avraham is not dissuaded from his path, he creates physical obstacles blocking the patriarch's journey, to no avail. Avraham is determined to carry through with the sacrifice of Yitzchak in response to God's command.[3]

Using the beautiful picturesque method so characteristic of Midrashic literature, the rabbis detail the profound internal struggle that must have been taking place within Avraham's soul. The old man who appears before the patriarch is clearly Avraham's own alter ego as the patriarch wrestles with his powerful doubts: *After waiting so long for a son, am I now to lose him by my own hand? How could a God who promised me yesterday that Yitzchak will be the progenitor of a great nation now command Yitzchak's death? Will God change his mind again tomorrow?*

Neither these doubts nor any physical obstacles, however, sway Avraham from his path. Against all odds, he will carry out the will of God.

C

Rashi, for his part, sees Avraham's struggle reflected in the text itself as the *Akeida* begins. God's commandment reflects a series of unwritten responses on the part of the patriarch. God said, "Take your son, your only son, whom you love, Yitzchak"

At each stage of this commandment, claims Rashi, Avraham argued: When God said, "Take your son," Avraham responded, "I have two sons."

When God said, "Your only son," Avraham responded, "Each one of them is the only son born of his mother."

3. Midrash Tanchuma Bereishit, Vayeira 22.

When God said, "Whom you love," Avraham responded, "I love them both."

Only then does God say, "Yitzchak."

Rashi portrays Avraham fighting against the dawning realization that Yitzchak is to be the subject of God's command. Step-by-step, the darkness closes in, until, finally, God makes his intentions crystal clear.[4]

D

While the Midrash, Rashi, and other commentaries portray a complex picture of struggle on Avraham's part, however, our fundamental problem remains.

Why is it left to the rabbis to paint this picture? As we have noted, the Torah does not shy away from detailing other occasions when Avraham grapples with his destiny and with his world.

Why then, within our own parsha, does the Torah clearly chronicle Avraham's struggle concerning the evil cities of Sodom and Amora, yet leave him conspicuously silent as he confronts the *Akeida*?

E

The answer may lie in recognizing that the two events before us represent two separate realms within God's relationship to man.

When it comes to Sodom and Amora, God is operating within the realm of *din*, "judgment."

God's commandment concerning the *Akeida*, on the other hand, takes place squarely in the realm of *nissayon*, "trial."

When God relates to man in the realm of *din*, everything makes sense. There is clear cause and effect. God says, "The inhabitants of the cities of Sodom and Amora are evil; therefore they deserve to perish."

As long as we remain within the sphere of *din*, we can argue and struggle with our Creator. God is, in fact, inviting us to do so. Perhaps there is a logical argument to be made that can sway God from His intended path; perhaps one more prayer, one more plea will tip the balance of judgment in our favor.

That is why Avraham argues with God in defense of Sodom and Amora.

---

4. Rashi, Bereishit 22:2.

When God brings us into the world of *nissayon*, on the other hand, nothing makes sense. God Himself is hidden from view, and there is no perceptible logic to his actions.

Here, argument and struggle are futile. Everything that is happening is beyond our ken. There are certainly reasons for God's actions, but we cannot begin to understand them.

Our challenge within the realm of *nissayon* is solely to pass the trial, to respond to God's will with dignity as we remain constant in our faith and loyalty to Him.

That is why Avraham is silent in the face of the *Akeida*. He realizes that he has entered the world of *nissayon*, and that his challenges have changed.

F

A beautiful possible textual allusion to God's "hiddeness" at the time of the *Akeida* can be found in three words embedded within the text of the narrative itself. As Avraham approaches Mount Moriah, the site of the *Akeida*, the Torah states, *Va'ya'ar et hamakom mei'rachok*, "And he saw the place from afar."[5]

The rabbis wonder: How did Avraham know that he had reached his destination? God had never referred to Mount Moriah by name, but had simply said, "...raise him [Yitzchak] as an offering upon one of the mountains which I shall tell you."[6]

The Midrash responds that Avraham knew that he had reached his destination because he saw "a cloud tied to the mountain."[7]

The imagery of Mount Moriah enveloped in mist is particularly telling. God's appearance in a cloud, a phenomenon that occurs on a number of occasions within biblical literature, always reflects the hidden element of God's being, even at a time of revelation. By suggesting that Avraham is able to identify Mount Moriah by the cloud that surrounds it, the Midrash alludes to the hidden nature of God's presence at this difficult moment in Avraham's life.

An even more direct possibility lies in an alternative application of

5. Bereishit 22:4.
6. Ibid., 22:2.
7. Midrash Rabba Bereishit 56:1.

the word *makom* in this sentence. *Makom* is one of the titles given to God within our literature. This sentence may therefore read: *Va'ya'ar et HaMakom mei'rachok*, "And he saw God from afar." As Avraham approaches the site of the *Akeida*, God is hidden and distant.

In a similar vein, Jewish tradition mandates the formula of consolation recited at the home of a mourner: *HaMakom y'nachem etchem b'toch she'ar aveilei Tzion v'Yerushalayim*, "May God console you among the mourners of Zion and Jerusalem."[8]

God is, once again, referred to in this sorrowful ritual by the appellation *HaMakom*. We turn to the mourner and we say, "May God, who seems distant from you at this difficult time of your life, come closer and console you among the mourners of Zion and Jerusalem."

Points to Ponder

Avraham, through prophetic vision, was able to distinguish between the two realms of *din* and *nissayon*. He could clearly see the difference between God's logical decision concerning Sodom and Amora, and the inexplicable commandment of the *Akeida*. The patriarch was, therefore, able to react to each of these major events in Parshat Vayeira in appropriate fashion.

We, however, are unable to make this distinction. We never know whether a particular challenge facing us in life is a reflection of *din*, of *nissayon*, or of a combination of the two. We are, therefore, meant to react to all challenges of life on both levels at once. We struggle, pray, plead and argue for Justice. At the same time, when all the prayers have been recited and all our arguments have been offered, we turn to God, and we accept his will. We then pray again; but this time we pray that God grant us the strength to pass the test.

---

8. Responsa Shevut Yaakov 98.

4 Understanding a Test

Context

Our confrontation with *Akeidat Yitzchak*, the classical example of *nissayon* (a trial administered by God to test man) in biblical literature, provides us with a perfect opportunity to explore the concept of *nissayon* within Jewish thought as a whole.

The rabbis delineate ten separate tests administered by God to Avraham over the course of the patriarch's lifetime. Some are found in the biblical text, while others are only recorded in Midrashic literature. The most dramatic of these tests is *Akeidat Yitzchak* (the aborted sacrifice of Yitzchak).

The very concept of God testing man, however, is very difficult to comprehend. A test is usually administered for the purpose of gathering information. God, however, is all-knowing. He knows in advance whether Avraham will or will not "pass" a specific test. Why, then, are these tests necessary at all? Two distinct approaches are suggested by the classical commentaries:

1. God tests man to enable man to become aware of his own capabilities and actualize his own potential.

None of us knows before a moment of crisis exactly how we will respond. If a fire breaks out in a crowded theater, some of us will save our own lives without thought for anyone else, while others will be heroic. The quality of our actions, however, cannot be predicted in advance. Through the course of the tests that he experiences, man learns the full extent of his own capabilities.

Even further, after that moment of crisis, we are no longer the people we were before. The very experience, and our corresponding reaction, changes us. Our potential for good or for bad is actualized and concretely shapes our further actions.

An individual changes with each passing test.[1]

2. God tests an individual to proclaim that individual's capabilities to others. As Avraham undergoes each test his greatness is recorded as an example for the world. That is why the word *nissayon* (test) is derived from the word *nes* (banner).

A person's true nature is revealed in the quality of his responses to the tests that confront him.[2]

In every generation, God will test man, say the rabbis, for each and both of these reasons.

While these explanations help us understand the biblical concept of *nissayon* in general, a specific question emerges when we consider the text describing the *Akeida*. The answer to this question creates yet another layer in our understanding of this powerful test…

Questions

Avraham's most dramatic test, the *Akeida*, is introduced in the Torah by four seemingly superfluous words, which appear from time to time in the biblical text: *Va'yehi achar hadevarim ha'eileh*, "And it was after these things."[3]

These words seem unnecessary because, as a rule, the Torah follows chronological order. Unless we are told otherwise, by the text itself or by rabbinic interpretation, events occurred in their recorded sequence. [Note: Periodically, the rabbis will clarify a puzzling sequence of events in the text by explaining that the Torah is not written in chronological order. This leads to the common misconception that the whole Torah narrative is not generally sequential. As a rule, however, temporal order is maintained in the text except in unusual cases where the rabbis specifically note an exception – and, even in those cases, the issue is often subject to debate.]

Why then, if the text is generally sequential, does the Torah periodically find it necessary to introduce an event with the phrase "and it was after these things"?

In order, explain the rabbis, to draw a thematic connection between the event that just occurred and the event that is about to occur.

1. Ramban, Bereishit 22:1.
2. Rambam, *Moreh Nevuchim* 3:24; Rabbeinu Bachya, Bereishit 22:1; Abravanel, Bereishit 22:1.
3. Bereishit 22:1.

Therein, however, lies the problem. Immediately before the *Akeida*, the Torah relates that Avraham contracts a covenant with the king of the Philistines, Avimelech. This covenant is viewed in rabbinic tradition as a negative and dangerous step on Avraham's part.[4]

What possible connection could there be, however, between the aborted sacrifice of Yitzchak, one of the most well known and significant episodes in the Torah, and this ill-fated covenant?

Approaches

Some scholars, unable to find a connection between the two events, immediately turn to a Midrashic approach.

Rashi, for example, cites a Midrash quoted in the Talmud as his only explanation for the phrase in question. The Talmud interprets the introductory phrase of the *Akeida* to mean "And it was after these *words*" rather than "And it was after these *things*" (the root of the word *devarim* is considered in this case to be *diber*, "to speak," rather than *davar*, "thing").

Two possible sets of words, suggests the Talmud, set the *Akeida* in motion:

1. The words of Satan, who turns to God and argues, "During the entire party that Avraham made on the occasion of the birth of his son he did not offer you one sacrifice." To this accusation God responds: "Avraham's entire celebration was in honor of his son. Were I to command him to sacrifice that son, he would not refuse."

2. The words of Yishmael who mocks Yitzchak by saying, "I was willing to undergo circumcision at the age of thirteen years; at the time of your circumcision you were but an infant." Yitzchak responds: "You mock me on the basis of one limb? Were God to ask me to sacrifice myself entirely to him I would not refuse."[5]

B

Other scholars, such as the Ohr Hachaim, struggle to remain true to the flow of the text. They suggest that the phrase "and it was after these things"

4. Midrash Rabba Bereishit 54.
5. Talmud Bavli Sanhedrin 89b; Rashi, Bereishit 22:1.

connects the *Akeida* not to the covenant directly but to the series of events that preceded it. These events included: Avraham and Sara's long wait for a child, God's promise that Avraham's legacy would live on through Yitzchak, and Yitzchak's birth and growth into manhood. These events, says the Ohr Hachaim, create the setting for the *Akeida* – a setting rife with deep trauma, conflict and tribulation.[6]

C

A few other commentaries, however – Rashi's grandson the Rashbam prominently among them – are bold enough to suggest what to Rashi was apparently unthinkable. The *Akeida*, they say, was, at least on one level, the direct result of Avraham's covenant with Avimelech.

The Rashbam, a commentator who always adheres to the *pashut pshat* of the text, sees the connection between the two events as crystal clear. He points to one specific phrase in the narrative describing the covenant. The Philistine king turns to Avraham and states, "And now, swear to me by God if you will deal falsely with me or my son or my grandson."[7]

Avimelech is clearly suggesting a covenant in perpetuity. Avraham agrees.

The patriarch, says the Rashbam, endangers his progeny when he contracts an intergenerational covenant with the likes of Avimelech. While Avraham may make a personal agreement with Avimelech himself, he has no right to make a concrete covenant complete with commitments on behalf of his children and grandchildren. God is, therefore, moved to respond: "You were careless with the son I gave you. You contracted a covenant with them and with their children. Now take that son, offer him as a sacrifice and see what good the contracting of your covenant has done."[8]

The Rashbam's suggestion is nothing short of mind-boggling. The *Akeida*, Avraham's greatest test, emerges, at least in part, as a corrective for Avraham's own behavior. Through the *Akeida*, God lets Avraham know that he is failing to pay enough attention to the effects of his actions upon his own son.

Once this door is opened, other tantalizing clues within the text create

6. Ohr Hachaim, Bereishit 22:1.
7. Bereishit 21:23.
8. Rashbam, Bereishit 22:1.

a pattern that would seem to support this thesis. After the birth of Yitzchak, for example, Sara recognizes the danger posed to her son by Yishmael, Yitzchak's half-brother. She insists that Yishmael be exiled from the home. The text then testifies that Avraham, faced with this difficult decision, is "terribly troubled concerning *his son*."[9]

The Torah does not clearly specify which son; nor does the text tell us what actually troubles Avraham at this critical moment. Is the patriarch frightened by the danger posed to Yitzchak? Is he troubled by the idea of exiling Yishmael?

A surprising possibility is suggested by the Midrash Rabba and quoted by Rashi. What deeply troubled Avraham at this moment, says the Midrash, was that his son Yishmael had gone so far astray.[10]

Where was Avraham until now? Can the Midrash be suggesting that, for years, the patriarch was unaware of the behavior of his son, Yishmael?

Obviously what prompts the Midrash to make this suggestion is the textual evidence that Sara was aware of what was happening within the home while Avraham was not. Avraham's sights were on distant horizons, as he attempted to preach the word of God to a waiting world. He wanted to "save the world." It remained for his wife to recognize the dangerous drama unfolding within their own home and to take the initiative to save her son from that danger. It is no accident, therefore, that God responds to Avraham's hesitation by stating, "All that Sara says to you – heed her voice."[11]

Even more telling, perhaps, is the contrast in Avraham's own behavior before and after the *Akeida*. Prior to the *Akeida*, Avraham's activities are directed in the main towards an outside world. While he prays for a son and is clearly concerned about his familial legacy, on an active level his attention is overwhelmingly directed outward. He "creates souls" in Charan, interfaces with Pharaoh and Avimelech, contracts covenants, fights in a war to save Lot, welcomes guests and argues on behalf of Sodom and Amora. The very sentences prior to the *Akeida* describe Avraham planting a tree in Be'er Sheva and proselytizing "in the name of the Lord, God of the world."[12]

The Avraham who emerges following the *Akeida* is very different. His total focus turns inward, as in the next parsha, Chayei Sara, he occupies

9. Bereishit 21:11.
10. Midrash Rabba Devarim 4:5; Rashi, Bereishit 21:11.
11. Bereishit 21:12.
12. Ibid., 21:32.

himself with two primary tasks: burying Sara, and finding a wife for Yitzchak.[13] Past and future within his own family occupy his attention, and there is no mention of further preaching to the world.

Apparently Avraham, traumatized by the *Akeida*, learns the lesson that, according to the Rashbam, God wanted to convey. Avraham recognizes that his mission to the world remains of extreme significance and importance. His mission to his own family, however, and his responsibility to his nation's future, become primary.

At the end of the patriarch's life we do not know the fate of the many souls whom Avraham touched through his preaching to the world. We do know, however, that Avraham's legacy is narrowed down to the life of one individual: his son Yitzchak. Avraham realizes that success or failure will depend upon Yitzchak and Yitzchak alone. Perhaps it takes the *Akeida* to teach the patriarch this lesson.

Points to Ponder

The Rashbam's bold approach to the *Akeida* broadens the lessons that can be learned from this event.

On the one hand, we are reminded of the potential "covenants" that we make on a continual basis with an outside world. Particularly in our age, when that world invades our homes through television, computer and other venues, we must be ever vigilant concerning the environment that impinges upon our own as well as our children's lives. Elements of outside culture that are counterproductive to their well-being must be actively rejected while other aspects must be nurtured. Only such proactive parenting can positively shape our children's worlds and ensure the safety – both physical and spiritual – of generations to come.

Avraham's personal journey surrounding the *Akeida* also serves as a clear reminder of our need to focus on what happens within our families. History is replete with the stories of successful individuals who somehow were not successful within the context of their own homes. Our involvements in our communities and in the outside world, as important as they may be, can never become our sole or even primary focus. Time and effort must be spent on what is most important: the education and the development of our children.

---

13. Ibid., 23:1–24:67.

Chayei Sara — חיי שרה

CHAPTER 23:1–25:18 — פרק כג:א–כה:יח

Parsha Summary

Closing the past; looking towards the future…

Sara dies. After mourning her loss, Avraham successfully negotiates with the Hittites for the purchase of the Cave of Machpeila in Hevron as a burial site.

Avraham asks his servant to return to the patriarch's homeland to search for a wife for Yitzchak.

The servant's mission is successful as he meets Rivka, determines her worthiness and negotiates with her family. Rivka returns with the servant and marries Yitzchak.

Avraham marries again and has additional children.

Avraham dies and is buried by his two sons, Yitzchak and Yishmael, in the Cave of Machpeila, alongside Sara.

The text enumerates the children of Yishmael.

1 Ger V'Toshav

Context

Parshat Chayei Sara opens with the death of Sara and the purchase of the Cave of Machpeila by Avraham as a burial site.[1]

Questions

The Torah dedicates no less than twenty sentences to the negotiations between Avraham and the Hittites concerning the purchase of the Cave of Machpeila as a burial site for the patriarchal family. This is more text than was dedicated to the entire story of *Akeidat Yitzchak*.[2]

Recognizing that every word of the Torah is significant, why is this incident recorded in such seemingly unnecessary detail?

Approaches

A variety of approaches are suggested by the classical commentaries. The Talmud, in a passage echoed elsewhere in Midrashic literature, sees the entire story of the purchase of the Cave of Machpeila as a testament to Avraham's loyalty and fortitude. Even Satan has to admit: "I have traveled across the whole world and have found no one as faithful as your servant [Avraham]. You promised him, 'Arise, walk across the length and breadth of the land for I will give it to you.' Yet when the time came to bury Sara and he could not find a spot for her burial, he did not question your ways."[3]

Some authorities actually suggest that this episode is one of the ten

1. Bereishit 23:1–20.
2. Ibid., 22:1–19.
3. Talmud Bavli Bava Batra 15b.

tests administered to Avraham throughout his lifetime (see Vayeira 4, *Context*).[4]

B

Other sources see this narrative as one of a number of texts that record for perpetuity the clear claim of the Jewish nation to specific areas in the land of Israel. The details serve to underscore and cement the legal, contractual nature of our ownership.[5]

How ironic that in our time the city of Hevron and the Cave of Machpeila have once again become the flashpoints for violent dispute between Israel and its neighbors. The Torah's recordation of Avraham's purchase of this land remains frighteningly prophetic. We are being told that we will need, across the ages, every possible proof that the land of Israel belongs to the Jewish people.

C

Yet others understand this narrative as underscoring the deep respect that must be shown, according to Jewish law, towards the dead. With meticulous detail, the Torah records Avraham's extraordinary efforts to ensure a proper burial for Sara.

From that time onward, Avraham's descendents will continue to care for those who pass from this world with honor and dignity.

The Chatam Sofer goes so far as to learn from this episode the halachic requirement to purchase a burial plot, rather than simply receive it as a gift.[6]

D

A careful reading of the text, however, reveals another, deeper level to this episode.

Beneath the surface, a defining confrontation actually takes place between Avraham and his neighbors as he negotiates for the purchase of the Cave of Machpeila. This confrontation brings Avraham's career full circle and may well present him with the greatest challenge of his life.

---

4. Ramban, Bereishit 24:19.
5. Midrash Rabba Bereishit 79:7.
6. Responsa Chatam Sofer Yoreh Deah 332.

The key to the episode lies in a strange two-word phrase used by Avraham as he opens the dialogue with the Hittites dwelling in Hevron: *Ger v'toshav anochi imachem*, "I am a stranger and a citizen together with you."[7]

The word *ger*, "stranger," is derived from the verb *lagur*, "to dwell," whereas the term *toshav*, "citizen," emerges from the verb *lashevet*, "to live."

As we have noted before (see Vayeira 2, *Approaches* C), these two verbs describe very different relationships with the land: *lagur* connotes impermanent residence while *lashevet* speaks of permanent residence.

Avraham's self-description is, therefore, inherently self-contradictory. Is he a citizen or a stranger? It would seem that he cannot be both.

Rashi immediately notes the problem and offers two possible solutions:

On a *pashut pshat* level, Avraham is saying, "I am a stranger from a different land, who has come to live with you."

On a Midrashic level, Avraham is saying: "It is up to you. If you treat me well, I will deal with you as if I am but a stranger who has no rights to the land. If not, I will consider myself a citizen, and take this property by law."[8]

Each of these explanations is predicated on the assumption that the terms *ger* and *toshav* are, indeed, mutually exclusive. One simply cannot be a stranger and a citizen at the same time. Any explanation of the phrase containing both words must therefore resolve the internal conflict between the terms.

E

A totally different approach to the phrase *ger v'toshav*, however, can be suggested. Perhaps the inherent conflict between *ger* and *toshav* is not meant to be resolved at all. We are confronted, instead, with one of those phrases in the Torah which at first appear contradictory but which, when properly understood, reflect a significant philosophic dialectic (see Bereishit 2, *Approaches* G).

Avraham's two-word self-description summarizes, in uncanny fashion,

7. Bereishit 23:4.
8. Rashi, Bereishit 23:4.

not only his own place in society at this critical moment of his life but the place that his children will occupy in the world community across the ages. What better description of the Jew than "a stranger and a citizen"?

Throughout our history, in country after country, the Jew has maintained a delicate balance in order to survive and succeed. Given the opportunity, we have been "citizens" of every country we have lived in. We have participated in all facets of communal life, contributed well beyond our numbers to culture and technology, played a role in governance and risen to the top echelons of societal life. At the same time, however, we have always been "strangers." By choice, we have turned to an outside society and declared our difference. We have maintained our own laws and rituals, our own belief system and our own cherished traditions. We have been part of and apart from every civilization in which we have lived. Our ability to maintain the balance defined by the phrase *ger v'toshav* has determined our very survival in every generation, and how each Jewish community defines the balance for itself determines the very nature of that community.

This balance, so crucial to our nation's existence, is struck at the dawn of our history.

Towards the end of his life, Avraham turns to the society surrounding him and says: *Ger v'toshav anochi imachem*, "I am a stranger and a citizen together with you." Through this declaration Avraham announces: *This is who I am. I am, at once, a stranger and a citizen with you. I will participate with you, I will contribute to your culture and to your life; but I will always be separate and apart. This is the balance that I must maintain if I and my descendents are to survive and contribute as a people.*

How telling is the response of Avraham's neighbors in the very next sentences! *Nesi Elokim ata b'tocheinu*, "You are a prince of the Lord among us." *B'mivchar kvareinu kvor et meitecha*, "In the choicest of our graves bury your dead."[9] The message they convey is the following: *Avraham, why all the fuss? No need to struggle with the parameters of your identity. No need to remain separate. You are fully accepted among us without reservation or stipulation.*

From that moment the battle is joined. A battle that courses silently beneath the surface of Avraham's negotiations, first with the Hittites in general and then with Ephron (the owner of the field) in specific.

9. Bereishit 23:6.

It is noteworthy that even when Avraham negotiates privately with Ephron, the Torah goes out of its way to tell the reader repeatedly that the negotiations take place in full public view and hearing.[10] These are not simply private negotiations over the ownership of a field but a clash of two cultures.

Over and over again, the Hittites attempt to persuade Avraham to lower his guard, to join their community without conditions. Over and over again, Avraham refuses, insisting upon boundaries and separation, insisting that the grave for Sara be fully purchased and not received as a gift. Even after death the Jew must remain distinct, his unique identity fully preserved.

This is one of those quiet moments of history where everything hangs in the balance. If Avraham fails, God forbid, in his attempt to define his identity, Jewish history ends right here. He is assimilated into the Hittite community, the Jewish nation never forms, and all the contributions that the Jewish people are destined to make to the world are never made.

F

The event at *Machpeila* also brings Avraham's career full circle. The patriarch's mission to the world was launched with God's commandment: *Lech lecha mei'artzecha…*, Leave your land, your birthplace and the home of your father and go "to the land that I will show you."[11] (see Lech Lecha 1).

The rabbis understand this commandment as creating a twofold obligation. On the one hand, Avraham was instructed to separate himself from his background and from all within the world incompatible with his mission. On the other hand, the rabbis say, God commanded Avraham to journey from place to place, in order to actively spread God's word to a waiting world. The Midrash, in fact, compares the patriarch at the beginning of his career to a small jar of perfume. Left in one place, the perfume cannot be appreciated. If it is carried throughout the room, however, all can benefit from its aroma. So, too, Avraham was commanded by God to travel from his home so that others could benefit from his efforts.[12]

In short, the rabbis see the first commandment given by God to Avraham as a commandment to be part of the world and apart from the world at

10. Ibid., 23:10–20.
11. Ibid., 12:1.
12. Midrash Rabba Bereishit 39:10.

the same time. This dialectic is reiterated by Avraham decades later, when he faces Hittite society and proclaims: *Ger v'toshav anochi imachem*, "I am a stranger and a citizen together with you."

At the dawn of Avraham's journey, God openly delineates the balance that will define Jewish identity across the ages. When the patriarch negotiates for the Cave of Machpeila, however, God is silent. Alone and on his own, Avraham must discern the challenge that confronts him and respond appropriately. He looks back upon the lessons he has learned throughout his career and, facing a foreign society, carefully negotiates the equation that will preserve both his involvement in that society and his own individuality. Avraham's triumph at that lonely moment ensures the survival and success of his people.

2 Why Go Back?

Context

As Avraham's life draws near its end, he turns to his trusted servant (identified by the rabbis as Eliezer) and instructs him to return to his homeland, Aram Naharaim, in order to find a wife for Yitzchak. He specifies that he does not want Yitzchak to marry a woman from the Canaanite nations that surround him.[1] (Aram Naharaim is generally identified as the area bounded by the Tigris and Euphrates Rivers. Padan Aram, mentioned in the text as the birthplace of Rivka and the home of her extended family,[2] refers to a specific region within Aram Naharaim.)

Questions

Avraham's decision seems completely counterintuitive. Why does he send Eliezer back to Aram Naharaim to find a match for Yitzchak? After all, isn't this the very land that Avraham himself was commanded to leave at the dawn of his career? The patriarch's own journey was launched when God commanded him to separate himself from his homeland, his birthplace and the home of his father. What possible reason could there now be to return to that land?

Complicating matters is the fact that there would seem to be absolutely no moral difference between the inhabitants of Canaan and the inhabitants of Aram Naharaim. Both locations are populated by idol worshipers.

It cannot be said that Avraham does not want his son to intermarry; there are no Hebrews in either location.

1. Bereishit 24:1–9.
2. Ibid., 25:20.

Approaches

A

Some classical commentaries suggest that Avraham specifically wanted a wife to be chosen for Yitzchak from his own family.

The Midrash Hagadol suggests two reasons for this preference. Firstly, Avraham reasoned to himself, "The people I should first convert to Judaism are the members of my own family." Secondly, Avraham believed that the members of his family were "nearer to repentance."[3]

One possible problem with this interpretation lies in the fact that Avraham does not directly refer to his family in his instructions to Eliezer. He simply tells his servant to return to his land and his birthplace.[4]

Eliezer, on the other hand, during his negotiations with Lavan and Bethuel (Rivka's brother and father), does mention that Avraham wanted him to choose a wife from the patriarch's own family.[5] The commentaries note that this is one of a number of variations between Avraham's instructions and Eliezer's repetition of those instructions. These variations demonstrate Eliezer's diplomatic skill as he endears himself to Rivka's family (see Chayei Sara 3, *Approaches* C).[6]

B

A number of commentaries, among them Rabbeinu Nissim Ben Reuven (the Ran) do suggest a fundamental moral contrast between the inhabitants of Canaan and those of Aram Naharaim. While both cultures were idolatrous, Canaanite society was particularly marked by its evil practices.[7] Over and over again, the Torah speaks of the abominations perpetrated by the nations of Canaan. Rashi states, "The nations [of Canaan] conquered by the Israelites were more corrupt than any other."[8]

Forced to choose between two idolatrous societies as the source of a potential mate for his son, Avraham avoids the society marked by immoral behavior.

---

3. Midrash Hagadol Bereishit 24:4.
4. Bereishit 24:4.
5. Ibid., 24:38.
6. Abravanel, Bereishit 24:1–67, question 17; also numerous other commentaries.
7. Drashot HaRan 5.
8. Rashi, Vayikra 18:3.

Given the evil nature of Canaanite society, one might ask why God commanded Avraham to relocate specifically to Canaan. Two answers might be proposed:

1. The land itself embodied a special sanctity in spite of the evil nature of its inhabitants.

2. Avraham was safer in a society that was more clearly evil than in his homeland, where the danger was more subtle and the culture potentially more attractive.

C

Perhaps, however, a totally different explanation for Avraham's decision to send Eliezer back to Aram Naharaim might be proposed. This approach depends upon seeing Parshat Chayei Sara as a cohesive unit with one overarching theme that marks the culmination of Avraham's career.

Parshat Chayei Sara can be neatly divided into two major sections: the purchase of the Cave of Machpeila as a burial site for Sara and the selection of Rivka as Yitzchak's wife. As we have noted, however (see Chayei Sara 1, *Approaches* E), beneath the surface of the first section lies an even more important narrative: Avraham's dramatic negotiation for self-definition as a *ger v'toshav*, a stranger and a citizen.

We have also discussed how Avraham, through this two-word phrase, not only describes himself but also delineates the place his descendents will take in society throughout the ages. To survive and to succeed the Jew must be both a stranger and a citizen in in any country where he lives, participating in the culture that surrounds him while maintaining his own unique identity.

Having arrived at his own self-definition, perhaps Avraham now looks towards the future and begins to fear: "I have been able to strike the balance necessary for my survival because I began in this land as a stranger. I came from a foreign land, and have always been able to maintain my distance from those within Canaan. Yitzchak, however, is different. My son was born here. He is too close to those around him. He is familiar only with this culture, with this population and with this land. How do I know that he will learn to discern the dangers that surround him? How do I know that he will be able to distance himself from elements of this society counterproductive to his spiritual development? How do I know that he will maintain the appropriate balance and truly be a *ger v'toshav*?"

Avraham then sets about guaranteeing the continuation of his legacy. He determines that at least one member of the next generation must make the same journey that he made, from Aram Naharaim to Canaan. More important than the physical journey, however, will be the philosophical journey. Yitzchak's wife will, it is to be hoped, be able to see herself as a *ger v'toshav*. She will begin with a natural distance from the Canaanites surrounding her. Given her foreign background, she will have a head start in maintaining the perspective needed to discern and confront the dangers around them.

In short, Avraham does have a deep ulterior motive for sending Eliezer back to his birthplace to find a wife for Yitzchak. The patriarch hopes that his son's wife will ensure the survival of the Jewish people by maintaining the delicate balance of self-definition that he himself has achieved.

D

It comes as no surprise, therefore, that as the story of the second patriarchal generation unfolds, Rivka emerges as the more perceptive parent. She alone sees their two children, Yaakov and Esav, for who they really are, and she alone acts with strength to perpetuate Avraham's legacy through Yaakov.[9]

E

The next parsha, Toldot, opens the story of Yaakov and Esav by reintroducing their mother, Rivka, to us as "the daughter of Bethuel the Aramite from Padan Aram, the sister of Lavan the Aramite…" This description stands in stark contrast to that of her husband, Yitzchak, about whom the Torah says, "The son of Avraham; Avraham gave birth to Yitzchak."[10]

Why repeat information that we already know?

The Torah is telling us that Rivka's background, in contrast to Yitzchak's, specifically enables her to play the instrumental role within her family, to ensure the survival of our tradition.

Avraham's genius in orchestrating the selection of Rivka as a wife for Yitzchak guarantees the perpetuation of the patriarch's legacy to the next generation and beyond.

---

9. Bereishit 27:1–46.
10. Ibid., 25:19–20.

3 Be a Man

Context

Mystery surrounds the search for Yitzchak's wife.

Although the rabbis identify the servant sent by Avraham to Aram Naharaim as Eliezer, he is not mentioned by name in the text at all. Instead, two terms are used interchangeably throughout the narrative to describe the anonymous envoy: *eved*, "servant," and *ish*, "man."[1]

Questions

Why does the Torah fail to identify Eliezer in his central role in this pivotal event?

What is the significance of the seemingly interchangeable terms *eved* and *ish* in the narrative, and why does the Torah text fluctuate between the two?

Approaches

A

The mystery of Eliezer's "absence" from the text raises a series of tantalizing possibilities within rabbinic literature.

Some authorities actually suggest that the omission of Eliezer's name reflects a fundamental ambivalence on the servant's part concerning the possible success of his mission. At some level, Eliezer may well have hoped that he would fail.

Until the birth of Yishmael and Yitzchak, Eliezer was the heir apparent to Avraham's wealth and spiritual legacy. This fact is reflected in Avraham's

1. Bereishit, 24:1–67.

own complaint to God: "And the controller of my home is Eliezer of Damascus."[2]

Eliezer, say these scholars, still harbored a hope that he would somehow be Avraham's heir. He even believed that if his journey to find a wife for Yitzchak ended in failure Avraham would consider a marriage between Yitzchak and Eliezer's own daughter.[3]

The Midrashic tradition of Eliezer's ambivalence reminds us that the Torah narrative reflects the lives of real individuals in complex situations. Avraham's servant could well have patiently guarded his own personal aspirations over years of faithful service to his master, only to find those very aspirations now threatened by a mission in which he is to play the pivotal role. The Midrash thus adds a poignant and complex human twist to a familiar biblical tale.

Whatever the truth concerning Eliezer's intentions, however, the textual evidence is clear. This faithful servant responds to Avraham's wishes completely and without hesitation.

Perhaps the Torah omits Eliezer's name from the narrative to demonstrate the total sublimation of his personal aspirations as he fulfils his respected master's will. He is, in this tale, truly and completely the nameless servant of Avraham.

B

More significant, perhaps, than the omission of Eliezer's name in the narrative is the seemingly arbitrary alternation between two terms in the Torah's description of the messenger sent by Avraham. At times the envoy is referred to as an *eved*, "servant," and at times as an *ish*, "man."

While this linguistic fluctuation might seem inconsequential, a careful review of the narrative reveals, once again, that no word in the Torah text should ever be taken for granted. By alternating between these two terms, the Torah creates a subtle pattern which courses beneath the surface of this tale. Once revealed, this pattern chronicles significant changes in Eliezer's role as his mission progresses.

2. Ibid., 15:2.
3. Midrash Rabba Bereishit 59:9.

C

Eliezer's journey can be divided into three major sections. During the first, he receives instructions from Avraham, agrees to carry them out, travels to Aram Naharaim, prays to God for success and devises a test by which a wife will be chosen for Yitzchak. Throughout these steps he is consistently referred to as Avraham's *eved*, "servant."

Suddenly, however, Eliezer's efforts are blessed with success. Rivka appears and passes her test, and the second phase of Eliezer's mission begins. The servant is now in uncharted territory. He has come to the point where he no longer has clear instructions from his master telling him what to do. On-the-spot decisions now must made. Serious diplomatic skill will have to be brought to bear as he enters into active negotiations with Rivka's family. Personal initiative and inventiveness will be required if his delicate mission is to be blessed with success.

As Eliezer moves into this new, autonomous arena, the Torah no longer refers to him as an *eved*, "servant." He is now *ha'ish*, "the man." He has become an independent operator who must move beyond the instructions he has received if he is to succeed in fulfilling his mission.

Evidence of Eliezer's new role can be clearly seen in the text as the envoy repeats Avraham's messages to Rivka's family. The Abravanel enumerates no less than ten substantive changes between Avraham's instructions to Eliezer and the way the servant repeats those instructions to Rivka's family.[4] Other commentaries also illuminate additional variations.

This is one of a number of instances where the Torah repeats a conversation or an event. As we have noted before, such repetition serves as a red flag and challenges us to compare the two versions before us (see Bereishit 3, *Context*). The differences that emerge are invariably meaningful and instructive.

While each variation in Eliezer's dialogue warrants its own study and explanation, an overall pattern begins to surface. Eliezer changes his master's very words in order to make the messages more palatable to his audience. To cite a few examples:

4. Abravanel, Bereishit 24:1–67, question 17.

	Avraham	Eliezer
1.	"You shall not take a wife for my son from the daughters of the Canaanites *among whom I dwell*."[5]	"You shall not take a wife for my son from the daughters of the Canaanites *in whose land I dwell*."[6]
2.	"*Go to my land and to my birthplace* and take a wife for my son Yitzchak."[7]	"...*to the home of my father shall you go and to my family* and you shall take a wife for my son."[8]
3.	"He [God] shall send His angel before you and you shall take a wife for my son *from there*."[9]	"[God] shall send His angel with you...and you shall take a wife for my son *from my family and from the home of my father*."[10]

The differences between Eliezer's words and Avraham's words are extremely telling.

Avraham has successfully fulfilled God's commandment of Lech Lecha and has effectively severed his connection with his past. Canaan is now his land and he no longer refers to his family as his family at all.

Eliezer, on the other hand, correctly perceives Avraham's severance with the past as an insult to the patriarch's family. He therefore alters the text of Avraham's message to suit the situation.

Eliezer's diplomacy is revealed through his words as the Torah testifies not only to his loyalty but to his initiative, as well. He has truly been transformed from a servant into a man.

The tale, however, does not end there. As soon as Rivka's brother and father agree to her union with Yitzchak, the Torah states, "And the *servant* took out jewelry of silver and gold..."[11]

Eliezer's brief transformation into an *ish* has ended and from this point in the narrative onward he will be referred to once again as an *eved*. His

5. Bereishit 24:3.
6. Ibid., 24:37.
7. Ibid., 24:4.
8. Ibid., 24:38.
9. Ibid., 24:7.
10. Ibid., 24:40.
11. Ibid., 24:53.

diplomatic initiative behind him, he is again Avraham's servant, fulfilling the specific instructions of his master as he brings his mission to a close.

Points to Ponder

Through the use of specific words the Torah transforms the simple story of a servant on a mission into the poignant tale of a man with his own conflicting dreams and responsibilities.

On the one hand, Eliezer emerges as the most faithful of servants, enshrined in our history as an example of fealty and devotion. Living at a time when servitude was commonplace, he had the good fortune not only to serve a benevolent master but to play an important role in the unfolding story of the Jewish nation.

At the same time, however, who knows what personal dreams may have remained unrealized? For a moment, as his story unfolds, Eliezer reveals initiative and talents until this point unexplored.

In a different situation, at a different time, given other opportunities, who knows what kind of "man" this "servant" would have been?

A final possibility is hinted at by a Midrashic tradition which suggests that Eliezer was actually the son of the powerful and corrupt hunter and ruler, Nimrod.[12] One can only imagine the possibilities for personal advancement that must have confronted the heir to Nimrod's throne; and yet, Eliezer becomes Avraham's servant.

Is it possible that Eliezer's servitude is a matter of personal choice? Does this biblical figure make the conscious decision to live by the rabbinic dictum verbalized centuries later, "Be a tail to lions rather than a head to foxes?"[13] Faced with the possibility of ruling over an immoral domain, does Eliezer instead put personal ambition aside and deliberately choose servitude to a great man?

If so, Eliezer sets a quiet example of private sacrifice, nobility of service and dedication to society, concepts so sorely missing in our "me first" world.

12. Targum Yonatan Ben Uziel, Bereishit 14:14.
13. Pirkei Avot 4:20.

4 Establishing Balance: Avraham's Life Draws to a Close

This study is presented as an overview. Some of the sections that we have already examined will now be briefly reviewed as part of a cohesive textual flow. For greater detail on these sections please reference Vayeira 4, Chayei Sara 1 and Chayei Sara 2.

Context

A series of five seemingly unconnected events towards the end of Avraham's life actually establish a pattern designed to teach the patriarch the parameters and boundaries of his involvement with an outside world:

1. Avraham prays on behalf of the Philistine king, Avimelech. The king had been punished with illness after abducting Sara[1] (see Lech Lecha 2 for a discussion of a similar event).
2. Yitzchak is born.[2]
3. Avraham and Avimelech contract a covenant.[3]
4. The *Akeida* takes place.[4]
5. Avraham defines himself as a *ger v'toshav* in his negotiations with the Hittites for the Cave of Machpeila. The patriarch then sends Eliezer to Aram Naharaim to find a wife for Yitzchak.[5]

---

1. Bereishit 20:17–18.
2. Ibid., 21:1–3.
3. Ibid., 21:22–32.
4. Ibid., 22:1–19.
5. Ibid., 23:1–20.

Approaches

A careful look at events 1–4 reveals an alternating pattern between connecting "external" and "internal" events in the patriarch's life. One step forward, one step back, these events create a tension that helps Avraham arrive at a critical moment of self-definition.

A

Event 1 – External: Avraham prays on behalf of Avimelech after Sara is released from the king's palace.

B

Event 2 – Internal: Yitzchak is born.

Avrahams' prayers on behalf of Avimelech, according to the rabbis, affect not only the foreign king's destiny but the patriarch's own. The Talmud perceives a fundamental link between Avraham's supplications and the subsequent birth of Yitzchak: "The Torah records the birth of Yitzchak immediately after Avraham's prayers on behalf of Avimelech to teach us that if one asks for mercy for his friend and is himself in similar need, he is answered first."[6]

Avraham thus learns that his prayers on behalf of another allow his own dreams to be fulfilled. The intertwining of the patriarch's personal fate with his global mission to the world is underscored.

Avraham and his family cannot live in a vacuum. Their personal success depends on their active involvement in the lives of those around them.

C

Event 3 – External: At Avimelech's request, Avraham and the king of the Philistines contract a covenant.

This covenant is viewed within rabbinic thought as a dangerous error on Avraham's part (see Vayeira 4, *Approaches* C).

Emboldened, perhaps, by the positive results of his previous encounter with Avimelech, Avraham oversteps his bounds in his desire to interface with the outside world. He fails to recognize the dangers of unfettered involvement with those around him.

6. Talmud Bavli Bava Kama 92a.

D

Event 4 – Internal: The *Akeida* takes place.

We have already noted the approach of the Rashbam who views the *Akeida* as God's direct response to Avraham's covenant with Avimelech (see Vayeira 4, *Approaches* C).

In effect, God delivers a wakeup call to the patriarch concerning the preciousness of Avraham's own family and the balance that must be struck in his dealings with an outside world. He must pull back. Involvement is certainly essential, but it must have its boundaries.

E

Event 5 – The Result: *Ger v'toshav.*

Armed with the knowledge conveyed by the events outlined above, Avraham is able to define himself as a *ger v'toshav*, "a stranger and a citizen" in his negotiations with the Hittites. This self-definition not only succinctly outlines Avraham's place within society but the place that his descendents will occupy in the world community across the ages (see Chayei Sara 1, *Approaches* E).

Bitter experience has taught the patriarch the delicate balance that must be struck in his dealings with an outside world.

Proper study of the Torah text requires that we back up enough to view the flow of events. Nothing is ever random in the Torah and seemingly unrelated episodes often combine to create significant patterns.

In this case, God teaches Avraham through a series of seesawing episodes that his involvement with the outside world will have to be marked by the tension captured in the patriarch's own words: *ger v'toshav*, "a stranger and a citizen."

5 Between Avraham and Lot

Context

In previous studies we have examined the ways in which Avraham and Lot each interfaced with surrounding society. Lot's failure is exemplified by his assimilation into the evil society of Sodom (see Vayeira 2), while Avraham's success is marked by his negotiations with the Hittites for self-definition (see Chayei Sara 1).

Questions

What can we learn when we compare Lot's failure to Avraham's success?

Does the Torah reveal specific characteristics that set these two men apart from each other, consigning each to such different fates?

Approaches

A

While the differences between Avraham and Lot were certainly manifold, two potential distinctions emerge directly from the text. Each of these distinctions speaks with uncanny relevance to our lives.

B

Lot chooses Sodom; Avraham does not.

During his travels throughout the land of Israel the patriarch does not voluntarily interface with the people of Sodom. On the one occasion where interaction does occur, following the battle during which Avraham rescues Lot, Avraham refuses to take any of the bounty from the victory.

He tells the Sodomite king: "I lift up my hand to the Lord, God, most high, Maker of heaven and earth; if so much as a thread to a shoe strap…if

I shall take from anything that is yours! So that you shall not say, 'It is I who made Avram wealthy.'"[1]

Clearly Avraham desires absolutely no relationship with the citizens of Sodom. He is even willing to give up the rightful spoils of war in order to ensure that he will not be perceived as being in Sodom's debt.

Part of the patriarch's strength, apparently, lies in his recognition of his own limitations. Avraham is clearly a stronger individual than Lot. He nonetheless knows that no matter who you are, you must keep your distance from a city like Sodom.

Avraham recognizes what Lot, tragically, does not. Anyone under Sodom's sphere of influence is bound to change.

C

Avraham engages in self-assessment; Lot does not.

We have already noted that Avraham's life journey eventually brings him to a critical point of clear self-definition during the purchase of the Cave of Machpeila (see Chayei Sara 1). The patriarch reaches that milestone through a continual process of self-examination, reflected in his struggles with his world and with his God.

Lot, on the other hand, is blind to the changes that Sodomite culture works upon his life. Lot's transformation is gradual (see Vayeira 2). Had he been more self-aware, he could well have stopped the process before it was too late. Lot's failure to examine and assess his own behavior at critical moments of his life leads to tragic results.

Points to Ponder

The contrast between Avraham and Lot in the Torah delivers a twofold cautionary message which reverberates to our times:

The role of environment in our lives and in our children's development cannot be overestimated. There are aspects of the world around us that must be kept in distance. No matter how strong we are they will negatively affect us.

Complete severance from the outside world, however, is neither warranted nor desirable. Avraham's greatness lay in the balance that he struck

---

1. Bereishit 14:22–23.

as a *ger v'toshav*, "a stranger and a citizen," with regard to the surrounding society.

In the maintenance of that balance, self-awareness is a critical skill. We must recognize that the parameters of our lives are, in large measure, internally determined. Rabbis and teachers are often asked, for example, by students returning from a year of study in Israel: "Which is the real world? Is it the spiritual world that I experienced during my year of study? Or is it the material world to which I am returning?"

The same question is reflected, albeit less dramatically, throughout all our lives as we each try to reconcile our search for spirituality and meaning with elements of the outside world.

The proper answer is that both worlds are real. The most important world, however, is the one that we create for ourselves. How we actively negotiate complex realities and how we continually define our place within those realities determines the true world in which we live.

Toldot

CHAPTER 25:19–28:9

פרק כה:יט–כח:ט

Parsha Summary

Of parents and children…

Rivka conceives after a period of childlessness, as God responds to Yitzchak's prayers.

Experiencing an unusually difficult pregnancy, Rivka seeks out God's counsel. God informs Rivka that two nations will separate from her womb, that they will never be equal in strength and that the older will serve the younger.

Esav is born first. Yaakov follows, holding on to Esav's heel.

As the children grow, they follow different paths. Esav becomes a hunter and a man of the field while Yaakov develops into a quieter individual. Yitzchak favors his older son, Esav, while Rivka loves Yaakov.

Returning home exhausted from the field, Esav sells his birthright to Yaakov for a bowl of stew.

Faced with famine, Yitzchak and his family travel to the territory of the Philistines. God appears to Yitzchak and commands him not to descend to Egypt but to remain in the land of Canaan, wherein he will be blessed.

Friction develops between Yitzchak and the Philistines as the patriarch becomes increasingly successful and wealthy. As a result, Avimelech, the king of the Philistines, exiles Yitzchak from his territory.

Yitzchak uncovers his father's wells, which had been filled in by the Philistines. He then digs new wells, some of which serve as the source of additional conflict with the Philistines.

Yitzchak travels to Be'er Sheva, where God blesses him.

Yitzchak and Avimelech contract an agreement.

Struck by blindness as he ages, Yitzchak prepares to bless his older son, Esav. Rivka, aware of her husband's intentions, instructs Yaakov to masquerade as his older brother in order to receive the blessing. Yaakov complies, the ruse is successful and Yitzchak blesses Yaakov, believing that he is Esav.

Yaakov flees to Padan Aram, his mother's homeland, to escape the wrath of Esav and to find a wife.

1 Finding Yitzchak

Context

Yitzchak, the second of the three patriarchs, emerges as the most enigmatic. In stark contrast to the dramatic lives of both his father, Avraham, and his son, Yaakov, Yitzchak's life (aside from the *Akeida*) seems unremarkable. He is characterized in the text as a passive man, buffeted by events, who rarely seems to take the initiative.

Questions

Who was Yitzchak? What were his challenges? Above all, what were his contributions to the patriarchal era and to Jewish history in general?

Approaches

A

The Torah is not a history book, and therefore does not provide us with full biographies of the personalities who populate its pages. We are given only the information that God deems necessary for the fulfillment of the Torah's basic mission: the transmission of a Divine moral and ethical code to the Jewish people and the world.

Nonetheless, we can piece together pictures of our ancestors, based upon the information contained in the text. Incomplete as these pictures may be, they are nonetheless instructive. A better understanding of our ancestor's lives, times and trials provides us with critical lessons concerning our own challenges today.

Careful study of the terse narrative of Parshat Toldot reveals patterns and themes within Yitzchak's life. By analyzing these patterns we can catch a glimpse of the enigmatic second patriarch.

B

The first phrase of Parshat Toldot reads as follows: "These are the generations of Yitzchak, the son of Avraham; Avraham gave birth to Yitzchak..."[1]

At first glance, the text seems not only redundant but unnecessary. We already know that Yitzchak is Avraham's son. Why then, does the Torah find it necessary to repeat this fact not only once, but twice, in this introductory passage?

Clearly the text is underscoring the fundamental relationship between the two patriarchs.

Who was Yitzchak? In many ways, the answer is that he was *his father's son*. This relationship defined Yitzchak's life and behavior.

Over and over again, we find Yitzchak experiencing the same circumstances as his father and repeating his father's actions. Avraham and Sara were childless until God miraculously interceded; Yitzchak and Rivka are childless until God miraculously intercedes. Avraham had two sons, only one of whom would carry on his legacy; Yitzchak has two sons, only one of whom will carry on his legacy. Avraham confronted famine; Yitzchak confronts famine. Avraham dug wells; Yitzchak uncovers his father's wells and then digs his own. Avraham asked Sara to pretend that she was his sister upon entering the territory of the Philistines; Yitzchak asks Rivka to pretend that she is his sister upon entering the territory of the Philistines. Avraham contracted a covenant with Avimelech; Yitzchak comes to an agreement with Avimelech.

The parallels are nothing short of astounding. Avraham clearly casts a powerful shadow over the life of his son.

C

So strong is the influence of Avraham that Yitzchak's very relationship with God seems to be dependent upon his father. This fact is clearly mirrored in God's conversations with the second patriarch: "And the Lord appeared to him [Yitzchak] and said: 'Do not go down to Egypt.... Dwell in this land, and I will be with you and I will bless you.... *and I will uphold the promise that I gave to your father, Avraham.* And I will multiply your children as the

---

1. Bereishit 24:19.

stars of the heaven.... *Because your father, Avraham, listened to my voice and observed my traditions, commandments, statutes and laws.*'"[2]

Later God reprises the refrain: "And the Lord appeared to him that night and said: 'I am the God of your father, Avraham. Do not fear for I am with you and I will bless you, and multiply your children for the sake of my servant Avraham.'"[3]

God bases his promises to Yitzchak on the merit of Avraham, rather than upon Yitzchak's own merit. Is it possible that God understands that Yitzchak is unable to relate to his Creator, unless it is through the medium of his father's memory?

The rabbis poignantly describe the overwhelming influence of Avraham on Yitzchak's life in the following Midrashic passage quoted in the Talmud:[4]

"And Avraham was old, well on in years":[5] Until Avraham's day old age did not exist. Because of this fact, people who came to meet with Avraham would (in error) meet with Yitzchak, while those who came to meet with Yitzchak would (in error) meet with Avraham. Avraham, therefore, requested mercy from God, and old age was instituted.

In typical Midrashic fashion, the rabbis identify a fundamental problem facing Avraham. So identical are father and son that the patriarch is compelled to request from God the one gift essential for Yitzchak's development: the personal space needed to allow Yitzchak to define his own identity.

D

As powerful as Avraham's influence on his son may be, there are clear textual indications that Yitzchak successfully struggles to emerge from behind his father's shadow.

The Torah discusses in detail the wells of water that Yitzchak digs.[6] Some scholars accept this narrative on the level of *pashut pshat*.[7] The text, they say, is describing the difficult effort of developing actual sources of

2. Ibid., 26:2–5.
3. Ibid., 26:24.
4. Talmud Bavli Bava Metzia 87a.
5. Ibid., 24:1.
6. Bereishit 26:15–26.
7. Rashi, Bereishit 26:15; Rashbam, Bereishit 26:15–18.

water in Canaan, an effort that remains critical in the land of Israel to this very day. Others suggest that the wells be understood in Midrashic fashion. Water, they say, is often used as a symbol of Jewish tradition. The wells dug both by Avraham and Yitzchak refer to aspects of that tradition.[8]

Whatever approach we choose, it is significant that Yitzchak not only uncovers the wells that his father dug and "calls them by the names that his father called them,"[9] but also creates new sources of water and struggles with the Philistines concerning their ownership. Yitzchak certainly respects and reveres his father's accomplishments. When the second patriarch digs his own wells, however, he moves beyond his father's actions as he struggles to define his own personal historical role.

Similarly, Yitzchak's agreement with the Philistine king, Avimelech, differs in significant ways from the flawed covenant that had been contracted in Avraham's time. Yitzchak apparently learns from his father's mistakes and is much more cautious in his dealings with the Philistines. (See Toldot 2 for a full discussion of the contrast between the two agreements.)

In these and other instances we catch a glimpse of the second patriarch's efforts to move out from under the towering shadow of his powerful father and define his own unique identity.

E

Yitzchak's personal struggles for self-definition become even more significant when seen against the backdrop of his unique place in Jewish history.

Yitzchak is the first Hebrew child. He is, therefore, the first individual within our history to face the challenge of preserving the Mesora (Jewish tradition). This challenge begins with the two steps of receiving and transmitting.

Yitzchak, unlike Avraham, receives his divine instruction not only from God, but from his parents. He must respect and absorb what his parents teach, often a considerable challenge.

God, for example, tells Avraham to climb Mount Moriah on the occasion of the *Akeida*. Yitzchak, on the other hand, receives no such commandment directly from God. His instructions are received from his father,

8. Midrash Rabba Bereishit 64:8; Ramban, Bereishit 26:20.
9. Bereishit 26:18.

Avraham. Nonetheless, Yitzchak faithfully follows his father's instructions even to the point of potentially sacrificing his own life.

Upon receiving the tradition from his parents, the second patriarch must also successfully transmit that tradition to the next generation. Much of Yitzchak's story centers on this particular task as he makes the difficult journey, with the help of his wife Rivka, towards understanding the true nature of his two children, Yaakov and Esav, and the legacy appropriate for each (see Toldot 3, *Approaches* C).

We often make the mistake, however, of defining Mesora simply in terms of the receipt and transmission of tradition. There is a pivotal additional step that must take place. To fully participate in the process of Mesora, an individual must receive tradition, *make it his or her own*, and then pass it down to the next generation.

Our ritual heritage is not simply the sum total of the hard-and-fast laws of the Torah, nor only the result of rabbinic interpretation and emendation. There is a personal component that involves us all. Jewish belief and practice change in subtle but significant ways as they course through the life of each Jew in every generation. We all contribute, consciously and unconsciously, to the complexion of our tradition. As a result, the Mesora that we pass down is different from the one we received. We each leave a personal mark upon our heritage.

On a national level, this phenomenon can be seen in the changing face of Jewish tradition throughout the journeys of our people. The communities of Spain, Poland, Lithuania, Morocco, Russia and countless others have each left an indelible and individual mark on the nature of our heritage. Judaism is richer and more beautiful for all of those communal contributions.

On a personal level, many of our own memories can prove the point. Judaism is not only the laws of kashrut and Shabbat, but the experience of a family Pesach Seder, the aroma of a grandmother's gefilte fish, the kiss of a parent after the blessings on Shabbat Eve and so much more.

Yitzchak's efforts to define his own identity acquire greater urgency when seen in light of his unique place at the head of the chain of Jewish tradition. If the process of Mesora is to fully take root, the second patriarch cannot simply be a carbon copy of his father. He must actively determine and make his own contribution to the unfolding saga of his people. In this way he sets the stage for generations of Jews to follow, each of whom will be challenged to receive a tradition from their parents, make it their own, and hand it down to their children.

F

No discussion of Yitzchak's life would be complete without mention of the *Akeida* as a formative experience. Yitzchak's existence is undoubtedly shaped by the traumatic events that take place on the summit of Mount Moriah.

The rabbis point to two significant consequences of that overwhelming episode:

1. Yitzchak's blindness was caused by the tears of the angels, which fell into his eyes as he lay bound on the altar.[10]

2. Yitzchak is the only patriarch never to leave the land of Canaan. As he prepares to travel to Egypt in the face of famine, God appears and prohibits the journey. The rabbis explain that Yitzchak was considered a pure sacrifice. No other land was worthy of him.[11]

Each of these rabbinic observations may well connect to one specific aspect of Yitzchak's life that develops as a result of the *Akeida*. The dramatic events on the summit of Mount Moriah transform Yitzchak into the first "survivor" in Jewish history.

In this role the second patriarch becomes the paradigm of Jewish martyrdom across the ages. The rabbis in the Midrash refer to Yitzchak as "the first of the bound,"[12] while the Talmud quotes Chana (who witnessed the brutal murder of her seven sons at the hands of the tyrant Antiochus) as saying, "My sons, go tell your father, Avraham: 'You erected one altar; I erected seven.'"[13]

It is only natural for someone who was a powerless victim of a deeply traumatic event to gravitate to strength and power in others. This phenomenon is evidenced today in the powerful bond between survivors of the Holocaust and the State of Israel. These individuals understand better than others the price to be paid when a people stand alone and stateless in the face of danger; and they appreciate beyond measure the way that

10. Midrash Rabba Bereishit 65:10.
11. Rashi, Bereishit 26:2.
12. Midrash Rabba Esther Pesichtot 10.
13. Talmud Bavli Gittin 57b.

the State of Israel has changed the nature of Jewish experience throughout the world.

Is it possible that Yitzchak's "blindness" to the true nature of his sons, Esav and Yaakov, can be traced to the effect of the *Akeida* on the patriarch's psyche? Perhaps, as a survivor, Yitzchak gravitates so powerfully to the physical strength of his older son, Esav, that he fails to see the faults that accompany that strength. Yitzchak, the passive patriarch, sees in Esav all that he, himself, is not; while Yaakov, the quiet son, is too similar to his father to be fully appreciated.

Yitzchak, as a survivor, can also not be allowed to leave the land of Canaan, even with a promise of return.

Survivors cannot live on dreams and promises. Only the concrete allows them to persevere. This fact is, once again, reflected today in the lives and accomplishments of Holocaust survivors throughout the world. Their drive to succeed – to build families and careers – and their invaluable contributions to their own communities and to the State of Israel reflect an overwhelming desire to create a new concrete reality. Only such a reality allows them to endure in spite of the horrific memories of past trauma.

Yitzchak, who would always live with the memory of his father raising the knife above him as he lay bound on the altar, could not be asked to leave the Land of Canaan. Only the concrete reality of living on his land would enable him to succeed.

2 Another Covenant?

Context

In an episode strikingly similar to an earlier event in Avraham's time, Yitzchak is approached by Avimelech, king of the Philistines, for the purpose of contracting a covenant of non-belligerence. After throwing a celebratory party, Yitzchak apparently agrees and the two camps part in peace.[1]

Questions

How are we to explain Yitzchak's strange behavior? Confronted with the request for a peace treaty with the Philistines, he abruptly ends the conversation and throws a party which lasts through the night.

Why are the rabbis openly critical of Avraham's treaty with Avimelech (see Vayeira 4, *Approaches* C), yet strangely silent when it comes to Yitzchak's agreement with the same king?

Is it possible that these two episodes, which seem so similar, actually differ in significant ways?

Approaches

A

As is often the case, a straightforward reading of the *pashut pshat* of the text before us is extremely revealing. Such a reading brings to light a subliminal dialogue between Yitzchak and Avimelech within this passage, a dialogue that explains the patriarch's seemingly strange behavior and carries tremendous relevance for our own times.

1. Bereishit 26:26–31.

B

As soon as Yitzchak sees Avimelech and his entourage approach, he raises the following objection: "Why have you come to me? [It is obvious that] you hate me, for you exiled me from among you."[2]

Avimelech responds by insisting that he has come to contract a covenant with the patriarch: "That you shall not do evil to us, just as we did not harm you, and as we did only good to you, for we sent you away in peace."[3]

It is important to note that there is no disagreement between Yitzchak and Avimelech about the facts. They both acknowledge that during their past interaction Yitzchak was exiled from the territory of the Philistines. What they disagree about is, in fact, a much deeper issue. They are arguing about the definition of "peace."

To paraphrase the subliminal dialogue taking place between the patriarch and the king:

Yitzchak opens the conversation with the following objection: *How can you possibly suggest that we enact a peace treaty? Your intentions until now have been anything but peaceful. Did you not revile me and exile me from your land?*

Avimelech responds: *How can you say that we hate you? If we hated you, we would have killed you. Our intentions were obviously peaceful because all we did was send you away.*

The patriarch and the king are, in effect, living in two different worlds.

Avimelech defines "peace" as the absence of war and physical violence. As long as the two parties are not killing each other, in the king's eyes, they are living in peace.

To Yitzchak, however, "peace" means much more. For true peace to exist there must be both an absence of hostility and an effort towards cooperation. Anything less might be defined as mutual coexistence but cannot be considered true peace.

C

At first glance what the patriarch does next seems abundantly strange.

2. Ibid., 26:27.
3. Ibid., 26:29.

Instead of responding to Avimelech's interpretation of past events, Yitzchak abruptly ends the conversation. Without another word, suddenly, Yitzchak "made for them a party, and they ate and they drank."[4]

Armed with our understanding of the verbal interchange until this point, however, we can begin to understand Yitzchak's unfolding strategy in his continued dealings with Avimelech.

The patriarch recognizes that further conversation with Avimelech would be futile. You can negotiate with someone when you share the same reality and when the terms that you use are mutually understood. An unbridgeable chasm, however, separates Yitzchak from the Philistine king. When they each speak about "peace," they are talking about two very different concepts. If you can't agree upon the definition of peace, you certainly cannot contract a peace treaty.

Yitzchak, therefore, ends the conversation. As a smokescreen, he throws a celebratory party that lasts through the night.

Upon awakening the next morning, Yitzchak and Avimelech exchange promises with each other. The text, however, conspicuously fails to mention a *brit*, "covenant." Unlike his father, Avraham, Yitzchak does not contract a full treaty with the Philistines. He recognizes that temporary agreements with Avimelech are possible, but a lasting covenant cannot be drawn.

D

Then, finally, Yitzchak executes the coup de grace. With brilliant irony, the text states: "He [Yitzchak] sent them away; and they went from him in peace."[5]

Yitzchak turns the tables on Avimelech. In effect he says: *I will operate with you according to your definition of peace. Just as you sent me away "in peace," I now send you away from me "in peace."*

The second patriarch learns from his father's mistakes. Whereas Avraham was comfortable contracting a full covenant with Avimelech and continued to live in the territory of the Philistines "for many days,"[6] Yitzchak understands the dangers of such an agreement and insists on physical separation. He recognizes that the Philistines can only be trusted in mini-

4. Ibid., 26:30.
5. Ibid., 26:31.
6. Ibid., 21:34.

mal fashion and, even then, only from afar. The rabbis are, therefore, silent concerning Yitzchak's agreement with Avimelech although they had been critical of a similar agreement contracted by Avraham, a generation before (Vayeira 4, *Approaches* c). Their silence reflects acknowledgement of the lessons well learned by the second patriarch.

Points to Ponder

Once again, the Torah text speaks to us in eerily relevant fashion as we recognize that human experience has not changed much over the centuries. The definition of peace, which lay at the core of Yitzchak's interchange with Avimelech, continues to be at issue today as the State of Israel struggles to live in harmony with its neighbors.

The failure of the "peace process" in the Middle East is directly traceable to the limited and hypocritical definition of "peace" in the Arab world. True peace cannot take root in countries where children are raised in hate and where the daily rhetoric lauds murderers and spews venom upon the Jewish nation.

Even those Arab countries that have treaties with Israel, such as Egypt and Jordan, fall frighteningly short in their definition of what those agreements should mean. Like Avimelech, they maintain that peace is defined by the current absence of war. Cooperation, support and mutual understanding remain far from their reality.

We pray for the day when the world will embrace Yitzchak's vision of true peace.

3 A Blessing on Your Head?

Context

As Yitzchak ages and develops blindness, he arranges to bless his older and favored son, Esav. Rivka, upon overhearing her husband's plans, instructs her favorite, Yaakov, to masquerade as his older brother in order to receive his father's blessing.

Yaakov complies with his mother's instructions and is successful in deceiving his father and obtaining the blessing.

When Esav returns and discovers his brother's actions, he threatens Yaakov's life. In response, Rivka instructs Yaakov to return to her homeland, both for his own protection and to find a wife. Yaakov leaves for Padan Aram with his father's agreement and further blessings.[1]

Questions

A number of difficult and fundamental questions can be raised as we take a new look at this familiar, yet strange, biblical narrative. These questions strike to the very core of the tale and to the basic issues that it raises.

First, and foremost, how do we understand the concept of interpersonal *berachot* (blessings bestowed by man) within Jewish tradition? What, exactly, is the nature of man's power to bless? What strength do the blessings that we recite on behalf of others, such as prayers for those who are ill, really have?

Are interpersonal blessings so magical that if they are recited in error they are, nonetheless, effective? Specifically, if Yitzchak bestows a blessing upon Yaakov believing that he is really blessing Esav, does Yaakov nonetheless receive the blessing because he is standing there?

How does God fit into the picture? What is Rivka so terribly fright-

1. Bereishit 27:1–28:5.

ened of? If Esav had been blessed by his father couldn't God have countermanded that blessing? Doesn't God ultimately bless the individual who is most deserving?

Why is the entire struggle for the blessing necessary? Couldn't Yitzchak have blessed each of his children? Esav's objection upon discovering Yaakov's deceit, "Have you only one blessing, my father?"[2] seems to make a great deal of sense.

How could Yitzchak have been so unaware as to believe that Esav, and not Yaakov, should be the heir to the spiritual legacy of the family? [Note: One approach to this question has already been offered (see Toldot 1, *Approaches* F).]

How are we to approach the issue of means and ends as it applies to Yaakov and Rivka in this narrative? What moral lessons are we meant to learn? How could Rivka instruct her son to deceive his father and how could Yaakov agree? Is there any value to a blessing received through deceit? Does the end justify the means? (These questions will be addressed separately in the next study.)

Approaches

A wide variety of answers are suggested by the rabbis in response to the questions raised above. Listed below are some, although far from all, of their approaches. As will soon become clear, the pieces of the puzzle can be mixed and matched as the rabbinic comments are combined to create a cohesive picture.

A

The power of interpersonal blessing is a God-given gift so fundamental that it is included in the very first instructions given to the first Hebrew. As God commands Avraham to leave his homeland and embark upon his career, God states: "And you will be a blessing."[3]

The rabbis, in the Midrash, interpret this phrase as follows: "Blessings are given to your hand. Until now, they were in My [God's] hand. I blessed Adam and Noach. From this time on you will bless whom you wish."[4]

---

2. Ibid., 27:28.
3. Ibid., 12:2.
4. Midrash Rabba Bereishit 39:11.

By granting man the power to bless, God withdraws and deliberately limits his own power. As part of the divine partnership agreement with humanity, God will respect the words spoken by man and reckon with them when he makes his decisions. Man, thus, acquires the power of blessing and prayer.

God grants effectiveness to our prayers, both on behalf of ourselves and for the welfare of others.

In addition to the power of interpersonal blessing and prayer, there is strength in every spoken word. Words make a difference, affecting the people and the world around us for better and for worse. This strength can be seen when we speak kindly towards others and, conversely, when we attack others with our words, even indirectly. Jewish law, therefore, pays great attention to issues concerning appropriate and inappropriate speech. Speech is the domain in which our humanity is most keenly expressed; God created the world with His word, and we were created in His image, with the power to build or destroy with our words.

If God takes into account the words spoken by every individual, he pays particular attention to the words spoken by the righteous. A blessing granted by Yitzchak to Esav, therefore, would have had some effect; God would have been "forced" to reckon with the words of the righteous patriarch. Similarly, a blessing bestowed by Yitzchak, even unintentionally, upon Yaakov has significance.

B

While Yitzchak could well have blessed each of his children with individual blessings, some authorities suggest that the struggle between Yaakov and Esav takes place over a specific blessing.

The Ramban, for example, maintains that at issue was the blessing concerning the inheritance of the land of Israel and the continuing covenant with God.[5] The Abravanel agrees but adds that the *bracha* included the mission of imbuing mankind with the belief in one Deity.[6]

The sibling struggle is, therefore, understandable, for this blessing would determine the spiritual heir to the patriarchal legacy.

Another explanation as to why Yitzchak seems to have only one bless-

5. Ramban, Bereishit 27:4.
6. Abravanel, Bereishit 27:1–28:9, questions 1–2.

ing may be rooted in the prophetic vision granted to Rivka during her pregnancy.

"Two nations are in your womb...and the might shall be passed from one to the other..."[7]

The rabbis understand this prophecy to mean that Yaakov and Esav and their descendents can never be equal in strength. When one is ascendant the other will be weak.[8]

Although Yitzchak could have blessed each of his children, the one who received the primary blessing would, by definition, have ruled the other. This knowledge gives rise to the struggle between Yaakov and Esav.

C

An alternative approach to the entire narrative is suggested, with minor differences, by a number of scholars. This approach is based upon evidence within the text that, all along, Yitzchak intended to bestow two separate and very different blessings upon his children: one upon Esav, and one upon Yaakov.

The key to this approach lies at the core of the story, in the blessing that serves as the source of contention. The blessing, ultimately bestowed upon Yaakov disguised as Esav, reads as follows:[9]

> Behold the scent of my son is as the scent of a field which God has blessed – And may God give to you of the dew of the heavens and the fat of the land, and abundant grain and wine. Nations will serve you and régimes will bow down to you; those who curse you will be cursed and those who bless you will be blessed.

One can't help but be disappointed upon reading this text. Is this what the fuss is all about? Strikingly absent in this passage is any spiritual component. The blessing is totally physical in nature. Where is the spiritual heritage that is meant to lie at the center of the patriarchal legacy?

You could easily miss it, but a second blessing is found at the end of the narrative. This blessing is bestowed by Yitzchak upon Yaakov as the latter

7. Bereishit 25:23.
8. Talmud Bavli Megila 6a.
9. Bereishit 27:27–29.

prepares to leave for Padan Aram. This time, however, Yitzchak knows to whom he is speaking:

> May Keyl Shakkai (the Lord) bless you, make you fruitful and numerous, and may you be a congregation of nations. May He grant you the blessing of Avraham, to you and to your children with you, to inherit the land upon which you have dwelt, which God gave to Avraham.[10]

Here, then, is the missing content – the reference to the spiritual legacy of Avraham. This legacy appears only in the blessing given deliberately by Yitzchak to Yaakov and not in the *bracha* originally intended for Esav.

The critical differences between the two blessings lead some scholars to maintain that the text clearly reflects Yitzchak's original intention to bless each of his children differently. Contrary to popular assumption, the patriarch never intended to choose one child at the expense of the other. Instead, he planned to maximize the strengths of each. Esav, whose power lay in the physical world, would be blessed with material bounty, while Yaakov, the mild-mannered student, would be encouraged towards success in the spiritual realm.[11] Some commentaries even suggest that Yitzchak intended that there be an unequal partnership between his two sons.

Esav would rule over Yaakov and provide for his physical needs. In this way, Yaakov would be free to pursue his study of Torah.[12]

At face value, it would seem that Yitzchak, far from showing favoritism, is actually applying proper parenting skills. He recognizes the strengths and weaknesses of each of his children and encourages each child to pursue the lifestyle most appropriate for him.

Rivka, however, knows better. She recognizes the painful truth that Yaakov can neither live in partnership with nor be dependent on the likes of his brother, Esav. She also realizes something much deeper. Yaakov and his descendents will survive and thrive only if her younger son receives both blessings. Yaakov must learn to succeed not only in the tent of study but on the battlefield of life. Rivka, therefore, does the one thing she can

---

10. Ibid., 28:3–4.
11. Sforno, Bereishit 27:29; Sfat Emet, Bereishit Toldot 5637.
12. Sforno, Bereishit 27:29.

do. She pushes Yaakov out of the tent and into the arena of struggle for the physical blessing.

Rivka knows that the third patriarch cannot afford to be an innocent student who avoids the challenges of life. She also recognizes in her younger son hidden abilities of which even he is unaware. Her intuition is proven correct as, from this point on, Yaakov faces challenge after challenge, in the house of Lavan and beyond. When the patriarch successfully rises to meet those challenges, he demonstrates life skills essential not only to his own survival but to the perpetuation of his legacy across the ages.

Once again, the actions of a matriarch, in difficult circumstances at the dawn of our history, lay the groundwork for our nation's survival and success.

Points to Ponder

1. Our final interpretation of the narrative of Yitzchak's blessings serves as a challenge to current trends within the Orthodox Jewish community. The proliferation of young men who dedicate their lives solely to the study of Torah, while laudable on one level, is placing a tremendous burden upon family after family, and upon the Jewish community in Israel and throughout the world.

The concept of kollel (an institution of all-day high-level Torah study for the married man) has had a long, proud tradition within Jewish history. Kollel, however, was never meant for the masses. This institution was classically reserved for the select few who could dedicate their lives to such study and who would then give back to the community by serving as rabbis, educators and *dayanim* (judges).

Judaism places great stress upon an individual's responsibility to be self-sufficient and not dependent upon parental or communal funds. The rabbis of the Talmud were almost all self-supporting, as were Rashi, the Rambam, the Ramban and countless sages across the pages of our history.

In question, as well, is our place on the world stage. The contributions that we, as a people, have made to countless human endeavors have historically benefited world civilization in immeasurable ways. Who knows how many young men, unsuited to full-day Torah study, pushed into that world by peer and communal pressure, could actually sanctify God's name in greater fashion through accomplishments in other spheres of human activity? All this could, of course, be done while still setting time aside for regular Torah study.

A reassessment of our priorities, without a dilution of our dedication to Torah study and observance, is in order as we look towards the future. Can this system be self-perpetuating? What will be the fate of the next generation, children of "learners" who will not have wealthy parents to support them?

The time has come to re-examine Rivka's premise: To survive as a people we must be the beneficiaries of both the physical and the spiritual blessings. We must succeed both in the tent of study and on the battlefield of life.

2. An additional layer to the concept of *bracha* may be hinted at in our tradition's only formal blessing recited over a mitzva (commandment) of interpersonal blessings. As the Kohanim (priests) ascend the platform in the synagogue to bless the community they recite the following preliminary *bracha*: "Blessed art Thou, Lord, our God, Who has sanctified us in the sanctity of Aharon (the brother of Moshe and the first High Priest) and commanded us to bless your people of Israel, *with love*."

The last two words of this preliminary blessing are unique. No other blessing over a mitzva concludes with the words "with love." We do not say "to light the Sabbath candles, with love," nor "to sound the shofar, with love."

This phenomenon can be understood if we view man not only as the *conveyor* of blessing but as the *creator* of blessing. The true role of the Kohanim is then reflected in both the Priestly Blessing and the preliminary blessing before it.

The Priestly Blessing culminates with the summoning of the greatest gift God can bestow upon man: *shalom*, "peace." Peace may be a divine gift, but it is created in this world, as part of the God-man partnership, through our mortal efforts.

When the Kohanim bless the congregation "with love," therefore, they are not only bestowing God's blessing but creating it. The harmony inherent in their actions concretizes God's gift of peace and roots it in our reality. So, too, every time we recite an interpersonal blessing, underscoring the love and connection between ourselves and those around us, we play a role in bringing the blessing of God's blessings to this world.

4 Debating Means and Ends

Context

In order to ensure that her favored son Yaakov receives his father's blessing, Rivka instructs Yaakov to deceive Yitzchak by masquerading as Esav. Yaakov obeys his mother's directions and is successful in obtaining the blessing.[1]

Questions

How are we to approach the moral questions raised by this narrative? What lessons are we meant to learn? Does the end justify the means? Are there circumstances where deceit is acceptable? How could Rivka instruct her son to deceive his father and how could Yaakov agree? Does Yaakov escape unscathed after apparently lying to his father?

Approaches

A

As previously noted (see Lech Lecha 2, *Questions*), a spectrum of opinion exists within rabbinic thought concerning the potential fallibility of biblical heroes. At one end of this spectrum are those who refuse to see any possible failing on the part of the patriarchs, matriarchs and other heroes of the Torah and Tanach. At the opposite end of the spectrum stand those rabbinic authorities who insist upon seeing the heroes of the Torah as human beings, with human frailties. The narrative before us provides a perfect example of the various shades of opinion that exist along this spectrum, as the rabbis struggle to understand the actions of Rivka and Yaakov.

1. Bereishit 27:1–40.

B

Some authorities struggle vigorously to deny any possible deceit on Yaakov's part, in spite of the clear textual evidence to the contrary.

Rashi, for example, focuses on the sentence in which Yaakov seems to lie to his father by claiming: "I am Esav, your firstborn."[2]

Unable to accept the possibility that Yaakov would actually lie, Rashi solves the problem by punctuating the text creatively and splitting the passage into two: "I am [the one who brings you food]; and Esav [is your] firstborn."[3]

Rabbeinu Bachya explains this same sentence on the basis of Yaakov's purchase of the birthright from Esav earlier in the parsha. Someone who participates in an event in place of someone else, contends Rabbeinu Bachya, actually becomes that individual. When Yaakov identifies himself as Esav, he is not lying. Having purchased the birthright from Esav, he is claiming his rightful place in his brother's stead. In general, says Rabbeinu Bachya, "There is no question that all of Yaakov's words are truthful."[4]

C

Other commentaries, while admitting the fact of Yaakov's deceit, claim that the patriarch's actions were not only justified, but necessary.

Rabbi Yitzchak Arama, in his work the *Akeidat Yitzchak*, maintains that Yaakov was obligated to use all means at his disposal to prevent Esav from receiving the blessing. Under no circumstances could Esav be allowed to attain the spiritual role normally associated with the birthright.[5]

Rebbe Simcha Zissel of Kelm goes so far as to say that one who uses subterfuge to save the truth shall be blessed.[6]

Summarizing the views of these and other commentaries who take similar approaches, Rabbi Yehuda Nachshoni essentially states that "all is fair in love and war." If we are obligated to kill on the battlefield in order

2. Bereishit 27:19.
3. Rashi, Bereishit 27:19.
4. Rabbeinu Bachya, Bereishit 27:19.
5. Akeidat Yitzchak Bereishit, sha'ar 23.
6. Quoted in Yehuda Nachshoni, *Hagot B'parshiot HaTorah* (Tel Aviv: Zohar Publishing, 1979), p. 107.

to defeat evil, he says, it stands to reason that we are obligated to use subterfuge, when necessary, to accomplish the same goal.[7]

D

Whatever the potential justification, Yaakov is by no means comfortable with the task that lies before him. His deep inner conflict is revealed through subtle hints in the Torah text.

The Midrash, for example, comments on the unusually detailed description of Yaakov's actions as he responds to Rivka's instructions: "'And he went; and he took; and he brought to his mother'[8] – under force; bowed and weeping."[9]

Rabbi Yaakov Zvi Mecklenberg, on the other hand, focuses on Yaakov's initial objection to Rivka: *Ulai yemusheini avi*, "Perhaps my father will feel me (and realize who I really am)."[10]

The Torah, says Mecklenberg, is very specific in its language. The word *ulai*, "perhaps," is used when an outcome is desired, while the term *pen*, "lest," is used when a protagonist does not want something to occur.[11]

Perhaps Yaakov, through innuendo, is protesting against his mother's plan; or, perhaps, we are witnessing a "Freudian slip" on Yaakov's part (millennia before Freud). One way or the other, with the words *Ulai...*, "Perhaps my father will feel me," Yaakov reveals an inner hope that his deceit will actually be uncovered. He feels forced to follow his mother's directions, but he harbors a desire to fail.

E

The Torah text contains its own response to Yaakov's deceit. As the third patriarch's life unfolds, the clear message emerges that "what goes around comes around." Whatever the explanation or excuse for Yaakov's subterfuge, he is, nonetheless, paid back, time after time, as he becomes the victim of deceit perpetrated by those closest to him.

1. Yaakov is deceived by his father-in-law, Lavan. When Yaakov falls in love with Lavan's younger daughter, Rachel, Lavan promises him her hand

---

7. Ibid.
8. Bereishit 27:14.
9. Midrash Rabba Bereishit 65:15.
10. Bereishit 27:12.
11. Rabbi Yaakov Zvi Mecklenberg, *Haktav V'hakabala* (Germany, 1834), Bereishit 27:12.

in marriage. On the wedding night, however, Lavan secretly substitutes his older daughter Leah for her younger sister.[12] Lavan defends his actions the next morning in particularly telling fashion: "We don't do things like that in our place, to give the younger before the elder."[13]

Lavan is not only hiding behind communal norms, he is also hurling a not so veiled accusation at Yaakov: "You may do things like that; but we don't. We would never place the rights of the younger sibling over those of the elder."

2. Yaakov is deceived by Leah and Rachel. Leah's participation in the wedding night ruse is underscored in the following dramatic Midrash: "The entire night she (Leah) masqueraded as Rachel. As soon as he (Yaakov) arose in the morning, he said to her: 'Daughter of a trickster! Why have you deceived me?' She responded: 'And you – why did you deceive your father? ...You (think that you have the right to) ask: Why have you deceived me?'"[14]

Clearly the rabbis were not present in the bedroom as Yaakov awoke in surprise on that fateful morning. They were not witnesses to the conversation between Yaakov and Leah. They are, however, imagining what could well have been said. Yaakov has no right to object when he is victimized by others. He lost the moral high ground the moment he deceived his father.

Rachel's involvement in the subterfuge is defended by the rabbis who claim that she acted to preserve her sister's dignity (according to the Midrash, in order to spare her older sister humiliation and pain, she sacrificed her own happiness and gave Leah the secret password she and Yaakov had established between themselves).[15] Yaakov must nonetheless have been greatly pained by the participation of the woman whom he loved so deeply.

3. Yaakov is again deceived by Lavan. Over the course of twenty years of service to his father-in-law, Yaakov is cheated on numerous occasions as Lavan attempts to avoid paying him his due. With obvious bitterness the patriarch comments to Rachel and Leah: "You know that I served your

12. Bereishit 29:18–24.
13. Ibid., 29:26.
14. Midrash Tanchuma Bereishit Vayetzei 11.
15. Talmud Bavli Megila 13b.

father with all my strength. Yet your father mocked me and changed my wages ten times."[16]

4. Yaakov is deceived by his sons Shimon and Levi. In a violent episode chronicled in Parshat Vayishlach, Shimon and Levi exact revenge upon the inhabitants of the city of Shechem for the abduction of their sister Dina (see Vayishlach 4). Their successful plan includes an elaborate subterfuge by which they convince their enemies to undergo ritual circumcision. Shimon and Levi then take advantage of the Shechemites' weakened state and kill all of the male inhabitants of the city.

In the course of this episode, Shimon and Levi also deceive their father. Yaakov learns the truth, to his chagrin, only after the massacre has taken place.[17]

5. Yaakov is deceived by ten of his twelve sons. In the greatest and most painful act of deceit of all, Yaakov's sons kidnap and sell their brother, Yosef, into slavery. They do not reveal the truth to their father but instead lead him to believe that Yosef has been killed by a wild beast. Yaakov mourns the presumed death of his beloved son for twenty-two years, until Yosef finally reveals himself to his brothers and orchestrates the descent of his entire family to Egypt.[18]

F

It would seem that life exacts more than measure for measure from Yaakov in response to his act of deceit concerning the blessing. Whether the events that buffet his life are to be understood as punishment or as unavoidable consequence remains an open question. The Torah makes it clear, however, that no action is committed with impunity. Once Yaakov introduces deceit into his story, the Pandora's box is opened and subterfuge will continue to mark his entire life.

G

One final note is raised in the Midrash: God deals justly with all, even our enemies.

The rabbis are honest enough to recognize that the episode concerning

16. Bereishit 32:6–7.
17. Ibid., 34:1–31.
18. Ibid., 37:18–45:27.

the blessings was not a victimless event. Yaakov not only deceived his father but left Esav bereft of the *bracha*. Justice demands that Esav's claim somehow be addressed.

The Midrash, therefore states: "Anyone who maintains that God does not settle just claims – may his life be forfeit. God is long-suffering, but He ultimately collects what is due. Yaakov forced Esav to utter a cry of pain, as it is written: 'He (Esav) cried with a loud and bitter cry.'[19] When was he (Yaakov) punished for this act? In Shushan the capital (centuries later during the Purim story), as the text states: 'And he (Mordechai) cried with a loud and bitter cry.'"[20]

Basing its observation on the appearance of the same language in association with two events occurring centuries apart, the Midrash sees the hand of divine justice at work. Yaakov causes his brother pain. Esav's descendents will, therefore, threaten the Jewish people with pain on many occasions.

In a world governed by a just God, even Esav's cries do not go unanswered.

19. Ibid., 27:34.
20. Megillat Esther 4:1; Midrash Rabba Bereishit 67:5.

Vayeitzei

ויצא

CHAPTER 28:10–32:3

פרק כח:י–לב:ג

Parsha Summary

Dreams and exile…

Yaakov leaves Be'er Sheva for Charan as he flees the wrath of his brother, Esav, and prepares to search for a wife.

As the sun sets, Yaakov beds down for the night and dreams of a ladder stretching heavenward upon which angels ascend and descend. God appears to the patriarch and promises to guard him on his journey and to return him to the land of Canaan. Startled by this vision, Yaakov awakens and remarks upon the holiness of the place.

Upon arising the next morning, Yaakov names the location Beit E-l and vows fealty to God in return for continued divine protection. He then continues on his journey.

Yaakov arrives at a well where he encounters his first cousin, Rachel, and assists her in the watering of her family's flock. Rachel informs her father, Lavan (Rivka's brother), of Yaakov's arrival and Lavan rushes out to greet his nephew.

Lavan and Yaakov arrive at an agreement by which Yaakov will work for his uncle for seven years in return for Rachel's hand in marriage. When the wedding night arrives after the seven years have passed, however, Lavan deceives Yaakov by substituting his older daughter Leah for Rachel. Lavan also gives his servant, Zilpa, to Leah.

When Yaakov discovers Lavan's deceit the next morning he admonishes his uncle but agrees to work for an additional seven years in return for Rachel's hand in marriage. The second marriage takes place and Lavan gives his servant Bilha to Rachel. Yaakov works the additional seven years.

The Torah chronicles the growth of Yaakov's family as Reuven, Shimon, Levi and Yehuda are born to Leah; Dan and Naftali are born to Bilha and Gad and Asher are born to Zilpa after Yaakov takes the maidservants as con-

cubines at his wives' behest; Yissaschar, Zevulun and Dina are born to Leah; and, finally, after a long period of childlessness, Rachel gives birth to Yosef.

After Yosef's birth, Yaakov informs Lavan of his intention to return to Canaan with his family. Lavan convinces Yaakov to remain and work for wages. Six years pass, during which time Lavan continuously attempts to cheat his nephew.

At the end of the six-year period, Yaakov tells Rachel and Leah that God has commanded him in a dream to return with his family to Canaan.

The members of Yaakov's family gather their belongings and flee without Lavan's knowledge. Rachel secretly steals her father's house idols. After three days, Lavan discovers Yaakov's escape and pursues the patriarch and his family, overtaking them at Har Gilad.

Lavan and Yaakov exchange harsh words, Lavan searches unsuccessfully for his idols, and the Patriarch and his uncle finally agree to part ways. They erect a monument to commemorate their peaceful parting.

Yaakov continues on his journey and encounters angels. He names the location of the encounter Machanaim.

1 What Place?

Context

In the course of his journey from Be'er Sheva to Charan, Yaakov arrives at a location where he is forced to bed down for the night. There he dreams his famous dream of a ladder stretching from the earth heavenward.[1]

The phrase used in the Torah to describe Yaakov's initial encounter with the location of his dream is: *vayifga ba'makom*, "and he encountered the place."[2]

Questions

The text seems to be referencing a specific location of importance, already known to us. And yet the site of Yaakov's dream is later identified in the text as the town of Luz, a location that has not been mentioned previously in the Torah and which is of no inherent significance prior to Yaakov's dream.

Why then does the text read *ba'makom*, "*the* place" as opposed to *b'makom*, "*a* place"?

Approaches

A

Two distinct and very different approaches are offered by the rabbis in answer to this question.

1. The Midrashic approach:

The location of Yaakov's dream was actually Mount Moriah, later to become the Temple Mount in Jerusalem.[3]

1. Bereishit 28:10–12.
2. Ibid., 28:11.
3. Talmud Bavli Sanhedrin 95b, Chulin 91b.

Two generations earlier, when Avraham arrives at Mount Moriah, the site of *Akeidat Yitzchak*, the Torah states: *Va'ya'ar es hamakom mei'rachok*, "and he saw the place from afar."[4]

By referring to both Mount Moriah and the location of Yaakov's dream as "the place," the Torah connects the two sites and indicates that they are one and the same.[5]

The Midrashic approach encounters a serious geographical difficulty. At the time of his dream, Yaakov is actually at a location which he will identify as Beit E-l (literally "The House of God") far to the north of Jerusalem.

The Talmud addresses this difficulty by suggesting, based on textual hints, that Yaakov actually completes his entire journey and reaches Charan. The patriarch, however, then suffers remorse at having passed by Mount Moriah, "the place where his fathers prayed," without stopping for prayer. God miraculously transports Yaakov back to Mount Moriah where he dreams his dream.[6]

Rashi, in his commentary on the Talmud, explains that, according to this interpretation, when the patriarch names the site of his dream "Beit E-l," he is not referring to the location identified as Beit E-l today, but to Jerusalem, which he prophetically identifies as the "House of God."[7] In his commentary on Chumash, however, Rashi takes a different tack. He interprets the Talmudic position by maintaining that God performed the additional miracle of uprooting Mount Moriah and temporarily bringing it to Beit E-l.[8]

The Midrash Rabba quotes Rebbe Elazar in the name of Rebbi Yossi Ben Zimri who suggests that the ladder of Yaakov's dream was rooted in Be'er Sheva, stretched to Beit E-l and had its center at Jerusalem.[9]

2. The approach of *pashut pshat*:

As night fell, Yaakov arrived at a location outside the town of Luz.[10]

Some authorities suggest that this location was specifically set aside for

4. Bereishit 22:4.
5. Rashi, Bereishit 28:11.
6. Talmud Bavli Sanhedrin 95b, Chulin 91b.
7. Rashi, Chulin 91b.
8. Rashi, Bereishit 28:17.
9. Midrash Rabba Bereishit 69:7.
10. Rashbam, Bereishit 24:11; Sforno, Bereishit 24:11.

wayfarers. While it was not a site of particular significance, the Torah nonetheless refers to it as *hamakom*, "the place," because of the practical purpose that it served. Similar sites existed outside other towns at that time.[11]

B

The debate concerning the site of Yaakov's dream might, at first glance, seem to be of only passing interest. What exactly is driving this rabbinic discussion? What compels the Midrash to perform geographic calisthenics simply to allow the dream to occur on Mount Moriah? And is there any deeper meaning to the approach of *pashut pshat* and its claim that the dream occurred in a location of no special significance?

C

Yaakov's reaction, upon abruptly awakening from this dream, lends significance in retrospect to the issue at hand. Suddenly the question of the dream's location becomes very important, indeed, striking to the core of the concept of sanctity within Jewish thought.

Yaakov exclaims: "Behold the Lord is in this place and I did not know.... How awesome is this place! This is none other than the House of God and this is the gate to heaven!"[12]

On the basis of this observation, Yaakov subsequently renames the location Beit E-l, "the House of God."[13]

The interpretation of Yaakov's words is dependent upon which position one takes in the debate concerning the location of the patriarch's dream. Once again, two very different possibilities emerge:

1. According to the Midrashic approach Yaakov cries out: *Oh my God, look at where I am! I am sleeping on Mount Moriah, the very gateway to heaven! How could I have been so blind to the inherent significance and sanctity of this location? How could I have failed to act with greater deference?*

2. According to the approach of *pashut pshat*, on the other hand, Yaakov's observation is very different: *I had no idea... God is everywhere! If the Lord can appear to me in a vision of such grandeur at this unimportant spot,*

11. Sforno, ibid.
12. Bereishit 28:16–17.
13. Ibid., 28:19.

outside the city of Luz, then every place upon which I stand is potentially the house of God and any location on earth can be the gateway to heaven.

The power of this observation is multiplied a thousandfold when we recognize that, at this point, a patriarch is about to leave the land of Canaan for the first time in over a generation. Common religious belief in the patriarchal era dictated that specific gods were tied to specific lands. Yaakov could well have been concerned, therefore, at this frightening moment of his life, that his God might offer only limited or no protection outside the land of Canaan.

As we will note in the next study (see Vayeitzei 2, *Approaches* E–G) much of Yaakov's dream is tailored to disabuse the patriarch of this notion and to remind him of the all-encompassing power of the One and only God.

D

Which of the two approaches is correct? Exactly where did Yaakov dream his dream? And what is the substance of the patriarch's observation upon awakening?

As is always the case in such rabbinic disputes, both approaches are philosophically correct. Taken together, they create the balance that defines the idea of *kedushat makom*, "sanctity of place," in Jewish tradition.

On the one hand, we certainly believe in the existence of locations of inherent, overarching sanctity. The Land of Israel, Jerusalem, the Temple Mount (Mount Moriah) – these are locations which draw us with singular power, sites where our connection to God is stronger than at any other. To the mind of the authors of the Midrash it had to be the holiest of these sites, Mount Moriah, upon which Yaakov experienced his lofty vision.

On the other hand, we believe that we are partners with God in the creation of holiness wherever we may be. God is everywhere, and our ability to reach Him is not limited to a specific time or place. *Kedusha* (sanctity) can surprise us, appearing when and where it is least expected – outside the town of Luz or anywhere else – in a kind word, a loving gesture, a heartfelt prayer.

Elements of these two types of *kedusha* (sanctity) are not mutually exclusive; in fact, they clearly overlap.

Locations of inherent holiness in Jewish tradition achieve their *kedusha* only through the efforts of man in partnership with God. The Land of

Israel, for example, was first sanctified upon the entry of the Jewish nation, and that sanctity only became permanent, according to most authorities, centuries later, when our ancestors returned from Babylonian exile.[14] Even the holy Temple became sacred through the participation of man.[15]

On the other hand, while we are enjoined to create *kedusha* in partnership with God wherever we may be, there remains a fundamental distinction between sanctity created within and outside the Land of Israel. In the diaspora, we are enjoined to generate sanctity through our words and actions – through the way in which we live our lives – but we cannot bestow lasting *kedusha* upon a specific location. Outside the land, such sanctity remains temporal and fleeting; it dissipates once our efforts cease and our presence ends. Only in the Land of Israel does the possibility of permanent *kedusha* exist. Once sanctified properly, the Land of Israel retained its holiness even when our people were exiled beyond its borders.[16] In this way, once established, our holiest sites remained a continuing beacon of inspiration to a far-flung people across a turbulent history.

A Personal Reminiscence

A number of years ago I traveled with members of my congregation to Eastern Europe prior to our annual mission to Israel. Among our experiences was a visit to the Theresienstadt concentration camp, a way station for countless of our brethren on the journey to their final destination.

At one particular location in the camp, our guide took us behind a bakery and down some steps to a hidden underground room. Suddenly we found ourselves, to our astonishment, in a small synagogue which had been built by a group of Danish Jews, secretly, under the very eyes of their Nazi tormentors. We were speechless, struck by the courage and devotion of these individuals who, at the risk of their lives, had continued to worship their Creator, even at a time when God's very face was hidden from them.

As we walked around that small shul, we noticed that passages from the Torah and liturgy had been painted on the walls in a fashion common

14. Talmud Bavli Chulin 7a; Rambam, *Mishneh Torah*, Terumot 1:2.
15. Ohr Hachaim, Shmot 25:8.
16. Rambam, *Mishneh Torah*, Terumot 1:5.

to European synagogues of that time. One such passage poignantly read, "And in spite of all, we have not forgotten, [Dear Lord] do not forget us."[17]

But, then, as I continued to read, I was suddenly struck completely dumb. For on the wall before me appeared the following passage, painted through who knows how many tears: "How awesome is this place! This is none other than the House of God and this is the gate to heaven!"

I was astounded… Here in Theresienstadt, the "House of God"? In the depths of hell, the "gate to heaven"?

I gazed at the words spoken by the patriarch, Yaakov, in the darkness of the night outside the town of Luz, painstakingly painted centuries later on the walls of a secret synagogue in Theresienstadt…and I felt a fleeting sense of the sanctity which had existed in that room decades earlier. A sanctity created by a courageous group of nameless Jews who understood that even in the darkness of hell, even in the presence of their tormentors, even in the depths of pain and sorrow, holiness could somehow be achieved and God could somehow be found.

Their courage and devotion will remain with me forever.

17. *Machzor Vitri* 93, liturgy for Mondays and Thursdays.

2 Yaakov's Vow

Context

On the morning after his dream of a ladder stretching heavenward, Yaakov renames the location of the dream Beit E-l.

He then makes the following vow: "If God will be with me and will guard me on this path upon which I go; and [if he] will give me bread to eat and clothing to wear; and [if] I will return in peace to the home of my father and the Lord will be my God – then this stone which I have set up as a pillar will be a House of God and all that you give to me I will repeatedly tithe to you."[1]

Questions

How are we to understand Yaakov's vow? The patriarch seems to be making his worship of God conditional upon material gain!

Pivotal to our understanding is the interpretation of the phrase "and the Lord will be my God." Could Yaakov possibly be saying that "the Lord will be his God" only if certain conditions are met?

Compounding the problem is the fact that the very conditions which Yaakov now seems to be questioning were already promised to him by God in his dream: "And behold I will be with you; and I will guard you wherever you will go; and I will return you to this soil…."[2]

Why does Yaakov seem to be unsure of those promises now?

Approaches

A

A variety of approaches to Yaakov's vow are offered by the classical

1. Bereishit 28:20–22.
2. Ibid., 28:15.

commentaries. One authority quoted in the Midrash simply cannot accept Yaakov's vow as a response to his dream. Yaakov would not question the very assurances that he had already received from God. This scholar, therefore, makes the radical suggestion that the order of events within the biblical text must be reversed. The patriarch's vow actually preceded the dream, and God's promises were a direct response to Yaakov's concerns.[3] (Note: The rule that events in the Torah are not necessarily recorded in chronological order is used by the rabbis sparingly, often to address otherwise unsolvable issues.)

B

Numerous other commentaries maintain that Yaakov's words are not to be understood as a conditional vow at all but, instead, as a promise or a heartfelt prayer.

"If I am simply given the opportunity," the patriarch is saying, "this is what I promise to do."

Rashi, for example, directly correlates each of Yaakov's requests to God's corresponding promise in the dream. The patriarch is outlining how he will respond if the details of the dream are fulfilled.

Yaakov's statement "and the Lord will be my God," continues Rashi, relates to an earlier divine promise given to Yaakov's grandfather, Avraham: "to be a God to you and to your children after you."[4] By recalling that pledge, says Rashi, quoting the Sifrei, Yaakov prays that God's name will rest upon him and upon his children, so that he will give rise to no unfit progeny."[5]

The Rashbam interprets the phrase "and the Lord will be my God" as a prayer that God assist the patriarch in all of his future dealings,[6] while the Sforno maintains that the patriarch's entire vow should be seen as a request on Yaakov's part that God remove all impediments to spiritual growth from his path. The Sforno goes on to say that Yaakov agrees to be held to a higher standard if his request is fulfilled: "'and the Lord will be my God' – then the Lord will relate to me as a judge and determine whether or not I fulfill my obligations."[7]

3. Midrash Rabba Bereishit 70:4.
4. Bereishit 17:7.
5. Rashi, Bereishit 28:20–21.
6. Rashbam, Bereishit 28:21.
7. Sforno, Bereishit 28:20–21.

C

A totally different, fascinating approach is suggested by the Ramban. Unlike the scholars previously quoted, the Ramban interprets the phrase "and the Lord will be my God" not as part of Yaakov's requests but as a realization.

As a result of God's promise to return him to the Land of Israel, the patriarch now understands that a complete relationship with God can only be experienced within that land. He therefore says: "'And I will return in peace to the home of my father; and the Lord will be my God.' – Only once I return to this land will the Lord fully be my God."[8]

Yaakov is not placing conditions upon his belief in God. He is simply stating that he understands the truth: A Jew can only be complete with his God within the Land of Israel.

The Ramban bases his interpretation of the vow upon the rabbinic dictum "all who live outside the land of Israel are is if they have no God."[9]

The Ramban's explanation of Yaakov's vow is consistent with a global, revolutionary approach taken by this scholar concerning the relationship between Jewish observance and the Land of Israel. The Ramban maintains that all mitzvot which we fulfill outside of the Land of Israel are fundamentally incomplete. So singular is our connection to God when we are within the Land of Israel, that Shabbat, kashrut, tefillin, the holidays, and all other obligations of our tradition can only be observed in their fullness within that land.[10]

In a perfect example of practicing what you preach, the Ramban's philosophical commitment to the Land of Israel was concretely mirrored in his own life decisions. At the age of seventy-three, the Ramban embarked on the difficult and dangerous journey to the Land of Israel, thereby fulfilling his lifelong dream of settling in the Holy Land. Once in Israel, the Ramban worked diligently to restore the Jewish community in Jerusalem. He is considered by many to be the father of modern Jewish settlement in that holy city.

D

Perhaps the Ramban's approach can be taken one step further by interpreting

8. Ramban, Bereishit 28:21.
9. Talmud Bavli Ketubot 110b.
10. Ramban, Vayikra 18:25.

Yaakov's words "and I will return in peace to the home of my father" not as one of the patriarch's requests but as the first of his promises.

Yaakov's first and primary commitment was a commitment to return to the Land of Israel.

This pledge was much more complex than it sounds.

E

To understand, we must return to the scene of Yaakov's dream. Put yourself, for a moment, in Yaakov's place during the moments before his vision.

Bedding down in the darkness of the night, you are terribly fearful – fearful of the unknown, of your aloneness and of the threat posed by your brother…

You harbor, however, an even deeper fear. You live at a time when gods are considered territorial. If you leave your land, you leave your God behind.

And now you stand poised, for the first time, to run from the land that your family has not left for over a generation, the land to which your grandfather had been commanded to journey. What will become of your relationship with your God?

In response to your fears, God grants you a majestic vision of a ladder stretching heavenward upon which angels are ascending and descending. True, the angels who have watched over you until now are leaving; but other angels, other emissaries of your God, are descending to accompany you on your journey.[11]

God appears to you in your dream with promises: that the land upon which you lie will be given to you and to your children; that your children will be as numerous as the dust of the earth and will spread to the west, to the east, to the north and to the south; that the nations of the world will be blessed through you and your descendents.[12]

But then God says something truly astonishing: "And behold I will be with you and I will guard you wherever you may go."[13]

Suddenly you truly realize that your God is different – that there is only one God, Who is not tied to any land, Who is omnipresent.

---

11. Rashi, Bereishit 28:12.
12. Bereishit 28:13–14.
13. Ibid., 28:15.

You are no longer afraid…for you now know that by leaving the land you will not leave your God behind. He will be with you always.

— F —

This realization, however, potentially makes you think: If God will be with me wherever I go; if I can be successful anywhere; then, perhaps, I need no longer be tied to a specific land or place.

Further, if my task is to spread God's word, won't that be best accomplished by living in the world? Perhaps my family has developed past the need for a homeland.

But then God continues in your dream: "And I will return you to this soil; for I will not leave you until I have done all that I have promised to you."[14]

And you realize the fullness of your challenge. For while God will be with you wherever you may go; His constant presence does not release you from the obligation to return to your own land. There, and only there, will your relationship with God be complete; there and only there can you truly fulfill your destiny.

Your relationship with your Creator will be defined by a constant tension. You will live under his protection wherever you may be but you will fully relate to him only within your land. You may succeed in exile but your destiny waits for you in your homeland.

— G —

Yaakov, therefore, awakens the next morning and pledges: "Dear God: If You truly will be with me wherever I go; if I am successful in my endeavors in exile; then, I promise You I will not misunderstand. I will not assume that my success in exile means that I can remain there.

"I promise: 'And I will return in peace to the home of my father.' Given the opportunity, I will come back."

Points to Ponder

The tension delineated at the dawn of our history, in Yaakov's dream and in his subsequent vow, has marked our nation's experience across the face of history.

---

14. Ibid.

For centuries, during a long and turbulent exile, we have retained a deep belief in God's constant presence. Given the opportunity, we have succeeded greatly in land after land, contributing well beyond our numbers to the society around us.

And yet, we have always harbored the dream of a return to our homeland, of a return to Zion.

During the modern era, however, this age-old balance came under new scrutiny and challenge. The late 1800s and early 1900s saw within the world Jewish community growing dreams of real acceptance, coupled with visions of a new universal culture. Many Jews began to view the concept of a return to Zion as parochial and outdated. We had become, they felt, a global people and had, therefore, outgrown the need for a homeland. Zionism, with its practical vision of a return to Israel, was seen as an archaic throwback, to be actively opposed.

Thus, in 1885, the Pittsburgh Platform of the Reform Jewish movement stated that in light of the modern era of "universal culture of heart and intellect": "We consider ourselves no longer a nation, but a religious community, and therefore expect neither a return to Palestine, nor a sacrificial worship under the sons of Aaron, nor the restoration of any of the laws concerning the Jewish state..."[15]

By 1937, however, things had dramatically changed. Buffeted by the reality of world events, the same Reform movement affirmed in its Columbus Platform "the obligation of all Jewry to aid in [Palestine's] upbuilding as a Jewish homeland by endeavoring to make it not only a haven of refuge for the oppressed but also a center of Jewish culture and spiritual life."[16]

The Holocaust, of course, gave further lie to the vision of a harmonious universal culture; and Zionist ideology can be found today alive and well across the religious spectrum, within the Orthodox, Conservative and Reform communities.

Ideology, however, is not enough. As noted before (see Lech Lecha 1, *Points to Ponder*), we live at a time when a personal return to Zion is within our grasp.

Yaakov's vow challenges us.

What will be our response?

---

15. "Pittsburgh Platform," *Encyclopedia Judaica*, vol. 14.
16. "Columbus Platform," *Encyclopedia Judaica*, vol. 14.

3 Yaakov's Second Dream

Context

Hidden in the shadow of Yaakov's dramatic dream at Beit E-l (see Vayeitzei 1) is a second dream, experienced by the patriarch and recorded in Parshat Vayeitzei.

Unlike the first, this second dream is not recorded directly as it occurs. We learn about it only secondhand when, at the end of twenty years in the house of Lavan, Yaakov tells Rachel and Leah that the time has come to return to Canaan. In the course of the discussion the patriarch says:

> And it was at the time of the mating of the flock that I raised my eyes and saw in a dream: And behold all of the goats mounting the flocks were ringed, speckled and checkered. And an Angel of God said to me in the dream, "...Lift up your eyes and see that all the goats mounting the flocks are ringed, speckled and checkered; for I have seen all that Lavan is doing to you. I am the God of Beit E-l where you anointed a pillar and where you made me a vow; now arise, leave this land and return to the land of your birth."[1]

Questions

Yaakov's vision of sheep clearly relates to the financial agreements which he had made with Lavan and to Lavan's attempts to undermine those agreements. At the beginning of his last six years in his father-in-law's house, Yaakov arranged that his payment would consist of any unusually marked

1. Bereishit 31:10–13.

or colored animals born to the flocks under his care. Lavan attempted to manipulate the flocks to minimize the birth of such animals.[2]

What, however, is the relationship between the symbolism and substance of this second dream? There seems to be no clear connection between Yaakov's vision of sheep and the divine commandment to return to his homeland.

Why, in addition, does the angel in the dream refer to himself as the emissary of the "God of Beit E-l," and why does he makes specific reference to Yaakov's vow (see Vayeitzei 2)?

Approaches

A

Clearly bothered by the disconnect between the vision and the message of Yaakov's dream, the Ramban maintains that Yaakov is actually describing the content of two separate dreams to his wives.

The first of these dreams, which consisted of the vision of sheep, occurred towards the beginning of the six-year period during which Yaakov was to be paid through the receipt of the unusually marked animals. With this vision God was informing the patriarch that divine intervention would overcome Lavan's machinations.

The second dream, says the Ramban, occurred at the end of the six years, right before Yaakov spoke to his wives. In this dream the angel appeared and informed Yaakov that the time had come to return to Canaan.[3]

B

Other commentaries maintain that Yaakov was referring to one unified dream. They differ, however, as to the message conveyed by that vision.

Rashi, for example, sees the dream as emphasizing God's miraculous protection of Yaakov's welfare. He quotes the Midrashic tradition which pictures heavenly angels overcoming Lavan's deceit by physically returning to Yaakov sheep that Lavan had unfairly appropriated.[4] The Ralbag ex-

2. Ibid., 30:31–36; Ramban, Bereishit 30:35; Sforno, Bereishit 30:35.
3. Ramban, Bereishit 31:10–13.
4. Rashi, Bereishit 31:10.

plains the dream as underscoring the partnership between God and man. Yaakov's own efforts[5] are supplemented by God's support.[6]

Neither of these approaches, however, seems to address the apparent disconnect between the vision and the angel's message to return home.

The Malbim connects the disparate segments of the dreams by suggesting that God's message is: "Stay in this place no longer, so that you will no longer have to rely upon miracles to succeed." [7] The Rivash, on the other hand, sees the unified message as: "Don't think that because God is protecting you, you can at last relax and bask in your success. God is now commanding you to return to Canaan." [8]

C

Finally, it has been suggested that Yaakov's second dream can be connected to his first vision at Beit E-l, yielding an entirely different approach. Seen in context, the two dreams recorded in Parshat Vayeitzei emerge as contrasting end points in Yaakov's philosophical journey over his years in exile.

When Yaakov leaves the home of his parents and embarks on the path to Charan, he dreams of angels ascending and descending a ladder. Towards the end of his journey, after twenty years in the house of Lavan, when the patriarch dreams again, he dreams of sheep.

The message of that second dream may simply be: Yaakov, when you stop dreaming of angels and start dreaming of sheep, it's time to go home.

The words of the angel who appears in Yaakov's second dream are, thus, to be interpreted as follows:

"I have seen what Lavan is doing to you."[9] *I have seen how your father-in-law has changed you. You no longer set your sights upon the heavens. Your focus is, instead, upon material gain.*

"I am the God of Beit E-l where you anointed a pillar and where you offered to me a vow; now arise and leave this land and return to the land of your birth."[10] *Remember that morning at Beit El when you vowed to return?*

---

5. Bereishit 30:37–42.
6. Ralbag, Bereishit 31:11.
7. Malbim, Bereishit 31:13.
8. Rivash, Bereishit 31:12.
9. Bereishit 31:12.
10. Ibid., 31:13.

The time has come to fulfill your vow before it is too late; return to your roots before you are unalterably changed.

Points to Ponder

The frightening possibility that Yaakov needed prodding from God to return and fulfill his vow serves as a cautionary reminder of the powerful allure of material wealth and of its potential effect on our lives. Jewish tradition clearly acknowledges the value of self-sufficiency and underscores that the physical world is a gift from God, meant to be appreciated and enjoyed.[11] The attainment of material wealth, however, should never become the primary focus of our lives. When that happens, and it can easily happen without our conscious realization, wealth becomes a god, effectively supplanting lofty principles and ideals with pedestrian, limited dreams.

Simply put, when we stop dreaming of angels and we start dreaming of sheep, it's time to go home.

11. Talmud Yerushalmi Kiddushin 4:66 (Tur 2, halacha 19); Talmud Bavli Nedarim 10a.

4 Angels, Angels, Everywhere

Context

Yaakov, returning to Canaan from the house of Lavan, is met by angels. The Patriarch reacts to the encounter by exclaiming, "This is a camp of God!" He then names the location Machanaim.[1]

Questions

The encounter between Yaakov and the Angels at Machanaim remains extremely mysterious. No communication takes place between the patriarch and the heavenly beings. What, then, is the purpose of the meeting?

Why, in addition, does Yaakov name the location of the encounter Machanaim, which literally means "two camps"?

Approaches

A

Before addressing the specifics of the event at Machanaim, let us briefly consider the topic of angels within biblical literature and within Jewish tradition in general. Although, as we have seen, angels figure prominently in a number of events within the Torah, there is neither clear record in the text of their creation nor any discussion of their nature.

Who and what are angels? What is their purpose and role? What are their powers and limitations? Can they operate independently from God?

A review of rabbinic literature on the topic of angels reveals a wide spectrum of opinion on an array of issues. Even the most basic questions are subject to debate. One can find, for example, classical scholars who

1. Bereishit 32:2–3.

contend that angels are corporeal beings,[2] and others who believe them to be spiritual entities visible to man only in prophetic visions or dreams.[3] While some modern thinkers see angels in symbolic terms,[4] no less an authority than the contemporary scholar Adin Steinsaltz proclaims: "It would be quite misleading...to regard angels as abstractions, as hypothetical conceptualizations...that have no real existence. Each angel is a complete being that possesses consciousness of itself and awareness of its surroundings."[5]

In spite of these disparate views, two basic, almost universally accepted principles do emerge from the rabbinic discussion:

1. Angels have no evil inclination or free will.[6]

2. Each angel is created for one specific task.[7] Some angels, in fact, cease to exist after their job is performed,[8] while others operate in recurrent fashion and continue their work indefinitely (e.g., Rafael, whose task is *refua*, healing the ill).

Our tradition thus presents a picture of entities created by God for the sole purpose of affecting His will in the physical world. These beings, whether actual or envisioned, are manifestations and extensions of God's resolve, meant to bridge the monumental chasm between an unfathomable Creator and limited man. Angels have no choice or decision to make; their very nature obligates them to fulfill their predetermined, divinely ordained missions.

The Hebrew word for angel, *malach*, in fact, underscores this one-dimensional role as a representative of God's will. *Malach* literally means "messenger." The term, in fact, is used interchangeably in the text, dependent upon context, to refer either to human or heavenly messengers. Angels are thus completely and totally God's messengers to man. Often a second term, *hasharet*, "who serves," is appended as well to further emphasize that angels exist only as servants of God.

---

2. Talmud Bavli Hagiga 13a–b.
3. Rambam, *Moreh Nevuchim* 2:6, 2:42.
4. *Encyclopedia Judaica*, vol. 2, p. 975.
5. Adin Steinsaltz, *The Strife of the Spirit* (Northvale, NJ: Jason Aronson Inc., 1988), p. 45.
6. Midrash Rabba Bereishit 48:11.
7. Ibid., 50:2; Talmud Bavli Bava Metzia 86b; Midrash Tanchuma Vayeira 20.
8. Talmud Bavli Hagiga 14a.

In no way, therefore, does the existence of angels impinge upon the Oneness of God, which remains the cardinal principle of the Jewish faith.

Angels serve to help man relate to the complex, ultimately unfathomable network of ideas that comprises God's will. As perceived by man, God embodies seemingly conflicting streams of purpose which are difficult to comprehend. How can God, for example, be at once all merciful and all just? The rules that govern the heavens clearly remain beyond our limited frame of reference. Through the use of angels, however, each one representing a different, isolated facet of divine intent, God reveals aspects of His will to man.

Satan, for example, is not a being independent from God, but an angel who represents that part of God's will which demands strict justice upon man for his weaknesses and failings. The very concept, therefore, of Satan worship is not only anathema to Jewish thought, but an outright impossibility. There could be no purpose in worshiping an entity that has no independent free will of its own.

Finally, one last position, particularly expressed in Chassidic thought, maintains that "with every mitzva he performs, man creates an angel.... Thus, by means of the mitzvot...man extends the realm in which his activity is effective from the lower to the upper worlds."[9] These angels, different from those mentioned above, are not God's messengers to man but man's messengers to the heavens.

B

Returning specifically to the episode before us, we encounter numerous approaches among the commentaries as they struggle to explain the mysterious, silent encounter between Yaakov and the angels at Machanaim.

Rashi, basing his interpretation upon the Midrash, [10] proposes a clear connection between the angelic visitations at the beginning and at the end of Parshat Vayeitzei. The angels who appear at Beit E-l and at Machanaim represent the two separate sets of heavenly beings who accompany the patriarch at different points in his journey.

As the parsha opened at Beit E-l, the angels of the Land of Israel, who could not leave the land, ascended the ladder in Yaakov's dream, while the

9. Adin Steinsaltz, *The Strife of the Spirit*, p. 46.
10. Midrash Rabba Bereishit 68:12; Midrash Tanchuma Vayishlach 3, Vayeishev 2.

angels of exile descended. Now, years later, as Yaakov travels back to Canaan, the angels of Israel silently meet the patriarch to escort him home. Yaakov names the location of the second meeting Machanaim (two camps) to acknowledge his awareness of these two "camps" of angels who have been with him at different times. [11]

This Midrashic approach quoted by Rashi provides a perfect example of how angels are used in the text to reflect significant philosophical principles. Yaakov learns over the course of his journey that while God will relate to him and his progeny wherever they may be, a full relationship with our Creator can only be achieved within the Land of Israel. This message is first conveyed to the patriarch at Beit E-l (see Vayeitzei 2) and fully realized only when Yaakov returns home.

To symbolize the dialectic between God's omnipresence and His unique relationship to the Land of Israel, two sets of angels are created, one to accompany the patriarch within the land and another to escort him in exile.

Yaakov acknowledges his understanding of this lesson when he names the location of the second encounter Machanaim, reflecting the existence and significance of the two sets of angels.

C

The Ramban acknowledges, perhaps more than any other classical commentary, the centrality of the Land of Israel to our relationship with God (see Vayeitzei 2). He objects, however, to Rashi's specific interpretation of the episode at Machanaim. The Ramban notes that at the time of the encounter at Machanaim Yaakov is still geographically distant from the border of Israel. The angels who meet the patriarch, therefore, cannot be symbolic of the Land of Israel.

Instead, says the Ramban, the meeting takes place in foreign territory and is specifically meant to reassure the patriarch in advance of his encounter with the overwhelming military might of his brother, Esav. Through the visitation of the angels, God informs Yaakov that, in spite of appearances, Yaakov's own forces are actually greater than those of his enemies.

Although thankful for this reassuring vision, Yaakov refuses to rely

11. Rashi, Bereishit 32:2–3.

totally upon divine protection. Instead, as the next parsha records, [12] he energetically prepares on numerous levels for the fateful reunion with his brother. Yaakov's actions, continues the Ramban, are meant to serve as a model of the balance of faith and action that must be struck within our own lives.

The name Machanaim, the Ramban maintains, does not reflect Yaakov's awareness of two sets of angels but his dawning recognition of – literally – two parallel camps. Yaakov comes to the profound conclusion that his own encampment on earth is similar to the heavenly encampment of the angels. Both of these *machanot* are Godly encampments which exist for the purpose of blessing and glorifying God's name. Just as the angels sanctify God in the heavens, Yaakov realizes, man must learn to sanctify God on earth.[13]

Having successfully survived his tribulations in exile, the patriarch has become truly aware of his own capabilities and responsibilities.

D

The Rambam, for his part, views the event at Machanaim as an introductory allusion to an even more mysterious episode: the struggle recorded in Parshat Vayishlach between Yaakov and an unidentified stranger.[14] (For a fuller discussion of that event and the Rambam's approach see Vayishlach 2.)

E

Finally, a striking yet easily missed linguistic parallel at the edges of Parshat Vayeitzei grants new depth and significance to the encounter at Machanaim. Suddenly, this event becomes the key to our understanding of the entire parsha as a cohesive whole.

When Yaakov arrives at Beit E-l at the beginning of the parsha, in an unusual application of the verb *lifgoa*, "to encounter," the Torah declares: *vayifga bamakom*, "and *he encountered* the place."[15] As the parsha closes at Machanaim, the text once again uses the same term when it states *vayifge'u vo malachei Elokim*, "and angels of the Lord *encountered him*."[16]

---

12. Bereishit 32:4–22.
13. Ramban, Bereishit 32:2–3.
14. Rambam, *Moreh Nevuchim* 2:42.
15. Bereishit 28:11.
16. Ibid., 32:2.

At Beit E-l, Yaakov encounters; at Machanaim, he is encountered. He is now the object, the center of the event. A momentous transformation in the patriarch's own position has occurred during the course of his exile. Yaakov now towers over the very angels who had towered over him in the darkness of the night, as his journey began.

The Torah's message is clear. Man, when he fulfills his responsibilities here on earth, stands higher than the angels themselves. Yaakov, having survived the challenges of the house of Lavan, returns spiritually triumphant to his own home. To mark the patriarch's accomplishments, and to greet him on the way, heavenly angels welcome him. This, on one level, is the message of Machanaim.

Points to Ponder

Our analysis of the encounter at Machanaim touches upon a fascinating theological discussion that courses through rabbinic literature concerning the respective places of angels and men within God's universe. While the verdict is not unanimous, most sources indicate that when man fulfills his potential he actually towers above the celestial hosts.[17]

The Talmud suggests a dramatic three-way discussion at Mount Sinai which lends concrete significance to this theological position.[18] As God prepares to give the Torah to the Jewish nation, the angels strenuously object: "How can you give this treasure, which was hidden for countless generations…to flesh and blood?"

God orders Moshe to respond.

After initial, fear-filled reluctance, Moshe offers the following arguments:

> The Torah states: "I am the Lord God Who took you out of the land of Egypt." Did the angels descend to Egypt? Were they enslaved by Pharaoh? Why should the Torah be given to them?
>
> The Torah states: "You shall have no other gods." Do the angels live among the nations of the world who are steeped in idolatry?

17. Talmud Bavli Sanhedrin 92b–93a; Talmud Bavli Nedarim 32a; Talmud Bavli Chulin 91b; Talmud Yerushalmi Shabbat 6:8.
18. Talmud Bavli Shabbat 88b–89a.

> The Torah states: "Remember the Sabbath Day." Do angels work that they need a day of rest?
>
> The Torah states: "Do not take the name of God in vain." Are the angels involved in business (where swearing might be necessary)?
>
> The Torah states: "Honor your father and your mother." Do angels have parents?
>
> The Torah states: "Do not murder! Do not commit adultery! Do not steal!" Do angels experience jealousy? Do they possess an evil inclination?

Moshe's arguments are accepted and the Torah is given to the Jewish nation.

In typical Midrashic fashion, the rabbis are conveying a profound truth through this dialogue: More precious to God than the attainment of perfection is the pursuit of perfection. Our lives are defined less by reaching a specific goal than by the quality of the journey towards that goal.

Angels, who exist simply as an extension of a perfect God, are, by definition, themselves perfect. Only man, of his own free will, can aspire to and battle towards perfection. While he may never fully reach that goal, the very struggle, in God's eyes, raises him above the angels.

Vayishlach

CHAPTER 32:4–36:43

פרק לב:ד–לו:מג

Parsha Summary

Entering a world of ambiguity…

Yaakov's return to the land of Israel launches a series of events so complex that the final outcome of each remains uncertain.

As the patriarch approaches the border of his homeland, he initiates contact with Esav by sending emissaries with a conciliatory message. The messengers return with word that Esav is approaching with a vast military force.

Frightened by his brother's apparent belligerence, Yaakov prepares for the looming encounter in three ways:

1. *he sets up his camp for battle;*
2. *he prays to God for protection;*
3. *he sends Esav a vast array of gifts as an appeasement.*

On the eve of the confrontation with Esav, Yaakov awakens in the middle of the night and moves his family and possessions over the ford of Yabok. Suddenly, Yaakov finds himself alone, locked in mortal combat with a mysterious stranger. Injured in his thigh during the struggle, Yaakov perseveres, refusing to release his hold until the stranger blesses him. The stranger informs the patriarch that his name will no longer be spoken of as Yaakov, but as Yisrael.

As a continuing symbol of Yaakov's injury, the sciatic nerve of even a kosher animal (found in the thigh) becomes forbidden to the patriarch's progeny.

As morning arrives, Yaakov observes Esav and his forces drawing near. The patriarch makes final preparations for the encounter and then approaches Esav, bowing down seven times during his approach. Esav, in an apparent display of reconciliation, runs to his brother, embraces him, falls upon his neck and kisses him. Both brothers begin to cry.

Yaakov introduces his family to Esav, implores Esav to accept his gifts, and refuses to receive any gifts in return. Then, in spite of the apparent harmony of the meeting and in spite of Esav's arguments to the contrary, the two brothers go their separate ways.

Yaakov encamps outside the city of Shechem. When the patriarch's daughter, Dina, leaves the camp to see the women of the land, she is abducted and assaulted by Shechem the son of Chamor, the ruler of the area. Shechem asks his father, Chamor, to solicit Yaakov for Dina's hand in marriage. Chamor presents the request and also suggests that Yaakov's family settle among the Shechemites and that the two peoples intermarry. Yaakov's sons insist that, as a prerequisite to the agreement, all male inhabitants of the city undergo ritual circumcision.

On the third day following the mass circumcision, Yaakov's sons, Shimon and Levi, enter the city and, taking advantage of the weakened state of the inhabitants, slaughter all the males. They then lay waste to the entire city. Yaakov criticizes his sons, claiming that their violent and deceitful behavior has left the family vulnerable to attack from the surrounding nations. Shimon and Levi respond, "Shall our sister be treated as a harlot?"

God appears to Yaakov and commands him to his fulfill his vow (see Vayeitzei 2) by returning to Beit El and building an altar. Yaakov complies and God blesses the patriarch, again informing him that his name will be Yisrael.

As Yaakov journeys from Beit El, his beloved Rachel dies as she gives birth to Binyamin. The Matriarch is buried in Beit Lechem.

Yitzchak dies and is buried by Esav and Yaakov.

The parsha closes with a listing of Esav's descendents.

1 To Appease or Not to Appease

Context

Yaakov adopts a subservient attitude towards Esav both prior to and during their fateful reunion. The patriarch initiates communication with his brother, repeatedly refers to Esav as "my lord," plies his brother with gifts, bows down to him again and again and, in general, diminishes himself before his older brother.[1]

Questions

Was Yaakov right or wrong in assuming this subservient posture towards his brother? Should a potential enemy be met with conciliation or strength? Where does diplomacy end and self-debasement begin?

Approaches

Once again, rabbinic authorities stake out dramatically disparate positions as they consider Yaakov's actions.

Numerous commentaries are strongly critical of Yaakov's approach to his brother. One source in the Midrash, for example, contends that Yaakov's plan was flawed from the very outset: "Rav Huna applied the following verse: 'One who passes by and meddles in strife that is not his own can be compared to an individual who takes a dog by the ears'....[2] God said to Yaakov: '[Esav] was going on his way and you dispatch a delegation?'"[3]

Rav Huna maintains that Yaakov was unnecessarily asking for trouble

1. Bereishit 22:4–23:17.
2. Mishlei 26:17.
3. Midrash Rabba Bereishit 75:2.

simply by initiating communication with Esav. The patriarch should have quietly slipped back into the Land of Israel without alerting his brother.

Building on Rav Huna's observation, the Ramban claims that the destructive potential of Yaakov's behavior becomes tragically evident centuries later in Jewish history. During the period of the Second Temple, the Hasmonean kings of Judea repeat the patriarch's mistakes when they willingly initiate and enter into a covenant with the Roman Empire. This covenant, contends the Ramban, invites the Romans into our lives, opens the door to Roman domination of Judea and directly leads to the subsequent downfall of the Second Jewish Commonwealth and to our nation's exile from the Land of Israel.[4]

The Ramban's remarks acquire even greater poignancy in light of the rabbinic tradition which identifies the Roman Empire as the spiritual heir to Esav. The Talmud, Midrash and numerous other sources, including the Ramban himself, often refer to Rome as "Edom," the biblical nation descended from Esav.

Another Midrashic source goes even further in its condemnation of Yaakov's behavior.[5] Noting that, during the encounter, Yaakov refers to his brother Esav by the title "my lord" no less than eight times, the rabbis state: "At the moment when Yaakov referred to Esav by the title 'my lord,' God proclaimed: 'You have debased yourself and called Esav "my lord" eight times. By your life! I will establish from his descendants eight kings who will rule over their nation before even one king reigns over your children.' As the Torah states: 'And these are the kings who ruled in the land of Edom before a king reigned over the Children of Israel.'"[6]

Finally, the Midrash Hagadol connects Yaakov's obsequious approach to his brother to a series of disastrous losses eventually experienced by the Jewish nation. "Yaakov bowed to Esav seven times, therefore seven [cherished locations/institutions] were forcibly taken from [his children]: the Sanctuary, Gilgal, Shilo, Nov, Givon, the First Temple and the Second Temple."[7]

These sources and others not only condemn Yaakov's behavior but see within that behavior seeds of disaster and tragedy that will affect his children across the ages. [Note: For a discussion concerning the effect of the

4. Ramban, Bereishit 32:4.
5. Midrash Rabba Bereishit 75:11.
6. Bereishit 36:31.
7. Midrash Hagadol Bereishit 33:3.

actions of parents upon the lives of their children see Lech Lecha 4, *Approaches* A.]

B

At the opposite end of the spectrum are those rabbinic authorities who not only defend Yaakov's conciliatory approach to Esav but believe that the patriarch sets a skillful example of diplomacy which we are meant to follow.

Looming large in this camp is the major historical figure Rabbi Yehuda Hanasi, editor of the Mishna (the first authoritative written compilation of Jewish Oral Law) and leader of the Jewish people in the Holy Land during the second century of the Common Era. Less than two centuries after the destruction of the Second Temple at the hands of the Romans, Rabbi Yehuda developed a friendship with the Roman emperor, Antoninus. The extensive Midrashic and Talmudic record concerning this fascinating relationship includes the following interchange between Rabbi Yehuda and his secretary, Rabbi Aphes:[8]

> Rabbi Yehuda Hanasi said to Rabbi Aphes: "Write a letter in my name to his Majesty the Emperor Antoninus."
>
> He [Rabbi Aphes] arose and wrote: "From Yehuda the Prince to his Majesty the Emperor Antoninus…"
>
> Rabbi Yehuda took the letter and tore it up. He then instructed [Rabbi Aphes] to write: "From your servant, Yehuda, to his Majesty the Emperor Antoninus…"
>
> He [Rabbi Aphes] objected: "Why are you debasing your honor?"
>
> Rabbi Yehuda responded: "Am I any better than my elder, Yaakov? Did not Yaakov say [to Esav]: 'Thus says your servant, Yaakov…'[9]?"

Using Yaakov's behavior towards Esav as a model, Rabbi Yehuda eschewed his own personal honor in his dealings with the Roman monarch. Through such diplomacy and discretion, Rabbi Yehuda maintained good relations with the Roman authorities and was able to protect the interests of the Jewish population under Roman rule.

---

8. Midrash Rabba Bereishit 75:5.
9. Bereishit 32:5.

Another Midrashic authority is even more direct in his suggestion that Yaakov's approach to his older brother serve as the model of appropriate behavior towards authority: "Rabbi Yonatan said: Anyone who wishes to placate a king or ruler but is unfamiliar with his ways and tactics should place this chapter [the chapter chronicling the encounter between Yaakov and Esav] before him and learn from it the arts of conciliation and appeasement."[10]

For his part, the Sforno underscores approval of Yaakov's behavior through a brief but telling reference to two Talmudic passages. He first cites the rabbinic observation concerning the curse pronounced by the prophet Ahiya the Shilonite: "The Lord will strike Israel as the *reed* is shaken in the water."[11] This curse is preferable, claim the Talmudic Sages, to the blessing of the evil sorcerer Bilam who prophesized that the Jews would be "as the *cedars*."[12] A reed survives by bending in the wind while a cedar stands firm and is uprooted.[13] Yaakov's example teaches us, says the Sforno, that we must be flexible enough to bend – to humble ourselves, in order to escape the sword of Esav's descendents.

The Sforno goes on to quote the powerful claim of Rabbi Yochanan Ben Zakai, the architect of Jewish survival at the time of the destruction of the Second Temple:[14] "Had it not been for what the zealots did (responding to the Romans with resistance rather than negotiation), Jerusalem would not have been destroyed."[15]

Finally, the Talmud itself frames the concept of diplomacy in halachic terms by simply stating: "It is permissible to offer false flattery to evildoers in this world."[16] Reish Lakish traces the source of this legal ruling directly to Yaakov's behavior towards Esav.[17]

C

Rabbi Shimshon Raphael Hirsch adds new depth to our understanding of

10. Pesikta Zutrata, Bereishit 32:4.
11. I Kings 14:9.
12. Bamidbar 24:6.
13. Talmud Bavli Ta'anit 20a.
14. Sforno, Bereishit 33:4.
15. Talmud Bavli Gittin 56b.
16. Talmud Bavli Sota 41b.
17. Ibid.

Yaakov's behavior towards Esav by contrasting this behavior with Yaakov's earlier interactions with his father-in-law, Lavan.

Earlier, when Yaakov confronted Lavan's deceit, the patriarch responded with strength rather than subservience. The contrasting conciliatory attitude that Yaakov now exhibits towards Esav, says Hirsch, stems from his own sense of guilt over his taking of the birthright and the blessing from his older brother: "Better to endure corruption and injustice for twenty years (as did Yaakov at the hands of Lavan) than stand one moment before an individual who we know has been injured by our hands and who is incapable of understanding the circumstances which…might mitigate our guilt."[18]

Yaakov can deal with the evil that Lavan represents. He has difficulty, however, confronting his own complex feelings of guilt as the reunion with Esav approaches. Even though he may have been justified in his actions towards Esav, Yaakov knows that his brother will never really understand.

Points to Ponder

Once again, an ancient rabbinic debate concerning an even more ancient Torah text speaks to our time with uncanny relevance. As the global confrontation with terror increases in intensity – as the nations of the world confront rogue regimes armed with nuclear capability; as the State of Israel, always on the front line of civilization's struggles, wrestles with the next steps to be taken in the ongoing confrontation with implacable foes – the questions loom large.

What is the correct approach to be taken in the face of hostility? Will conciliation avoid further conflict or be interpreted as weakness on our part and lead to increased danger? How far can diplomacy go in ensuring our safety?

The rabbinic debate concerning Yaakov's actions reminds us that no single approach to an enemy is always correct. Each situation calls for its own response and, even then, we can never be certain we are on the right path. Constant ongoing assessment of the circumstances facing us, careful application of both the principles of strength and diplomacy, and a willingness to change course midstream when necessary will all be required if we are to successfully meet the challenges of our day.

18. Rabbi Shimshon Raphael Hirsch, Bereishit 32:8.

2 In the Darkness of the Night

Context

On the eve of his dramatic reunion with his brother, Esav, Yaakov awakens in the middle of the night and begins to cross his family and possessions over the Ford of Yabok. Yaakov finds himself alone and, without warning, locked in mortal combat with a mysterious stranger. The struggle, which leaves Yaakov wounded in his thigh, lasts until the break of dawn.[1]

Questions

No episode in the Torah text is more puzzling than the enigmatic mortal struggle between Yaakov and the unidentified stranger on the eve of the patriarch's reunion with Esav.

The mystery, however, actually begins earlier, when Yaakov awakens in the middle of the night and, for no clear reason, begins to move his camp across the Ford of Yabok. This maneuver apparently leaves Yaakov vulnerable to attack.

What causes Yaakov to awaken in the middle of the night?

Why, after having made detailed preparations for the forthcoming encounter with Esav, does Yaakov apparently change his mind and move his camp across the Ford of Yabok?

Why does Yaakov find himself alone?

Who is the stranger who suddenly appears and, without preamble, struggles with Yaakov?

What is the meaning of this battle in the darkness of the night between the patriarch and the mysterious stranger?

1. Bereishit 32:23–33.

Approaches

Various approaches are offered by the scholars as they strive to explain each aspect of the mysterious episode before us. Their approaches interweave to create complex pictures laden with significance and meaning.

A

"And he woke that night and he took his two wives and his two maidservants and his eleven children and he crossed over the Ford of Yabok…"[2]

The Rashbam contends that Yaakov awakens in the middle of the night because he is overcome by fear of the impending encounter with his brother. In spite of all his careful preparations, at the last moment the patriarch decides to flee with his family and avoid the meeting completely.[3]

Yaakov's attempted escape forces God to respond (see *Approaches* c below).

Most other classical commentaries are strangely silent concerning the motivation for Yaakov's night maneuvers, perhaps simply viewing these actions as additional tactical preparations for the encounter with Esav on the morrow.

B

"And Yaakov was left alone…"[4]

Both the Sforno and the Rashbam suggest that Yaakov's abrupt isolation can easily be explained within the realm of *pashut pshat*. The patriarch verbally directed his encampment over the Ford of Yabok with full intent to follow. For an instant after the others crossed, however, Yaakov stood alone on the bank of the stream. At that moment, the stranger attacked.[5]

Other commentaries, noting a redundancy in the text, suggest slight variations of the above. Yaakov first crossed together with the members of his family. He then returned and commanded the rest of the encampment to cross. Some even add an initial, preliminary crossing on the part of the patriarch to ascertain the safety of the journey before beginning to move his camp. All of these commentaries, however, agree with the Sforno and

---

2. Ibid., 32:23.
3. Rashbam, Bereishit 32:23.
4. Bereishit 32:25.
5. Rashbam, Bereishit 32:25; Sforno, Bereishit 32:24–25.

the Rashbam that Yaakov finds himself alone as a result of his directing the last section of his camp to cross before him.[6]

The Talmud, however, sees the origin of Yaakov's aloneness in an entirely different, somewhat surprising Midrashic light: "Rabbi Eliezer stated, '[Yaakov] remained behind because of some small [forgotten] jars. From this episode we learn that the righteous consider their possessions dearer than their own safety. Why is this so? So that they will never [be tempted to] stretch out their hands in theft.'"[7]

Rabbi Shimshon Raphael Hirsch, in his commentary on this passage, explains this startling attitude towards material possessions:

> A righteous man considers honestly acquired possessions to be holy, even if their value is small. He believes that he will eventually be called upon to account for the rightful use of that which he, through the grace of God, has accrued.
>
> He will, therefore, not squander or uselessly waste even a penny but will spend great sums without hesitation for God-pleasing purposes. He considers only that which he has acquired by honest toil to be his own and views his very smallest possession as a token of God's providence and, therefore, of inestimable value.[8]

Yaakov, according to the Midrash, was appalled by the possibility that he might have lost possessions that could have been used for a constructive purpose. He was therefore willing to take the risk entailed in remaining behind to find them.

Rashi goes a step further and interprets the Midrash as suggesting that Yaakov had actually safely crossed the stream together with his entire camp when he remembered the small vessels inadvertently left behind on the other side. The patriarch returned to retrieve his property and, as a result, found himself alone in the darkness of the night.

To the Midrashic mind, Yaakov's aloneness and resulting vulnerability could not have developed simply as a matter of chance. Yaakov finds himself alone because of a deliberate decision to remain on, or to return

6. Ramban, Bereishit 32:23; Rabbeinu Bachya, Bereishit 32:23.
7. Talmud Bavli Chullin 91a.
8. Rabbi Shimshon Raphael Hirsch, Bereishit 32:25.

to, the other side of the stream. This decision, while apparently laudable on one level, carries risks and leaves the patriarch vulnerable to the attack that follows. The Talmud paints a cautionary picture reflecting the need to carefully weigh the benefits and the risks inherent in all life decisions.

Whatever the origin of Yaakov's aloneness, the message of the Torah text is immediately and powerfully clear: "Yaakov was left alone, and a man wrestled with him until the break of dawn." [9]

We are vulnerable when we stand alone. Had Yaakov not been left alone on that fateful night, he would not have been endangered.

Some scholars connect this lesson to the halachic prohibition which finds its roots in Yaakov's struggle with the stranger: the Torah's ban concerning the consumption of the *gid hanasheh* (the sinew containing the sciatic nerve) of even a kosher animal.[10] The *gid hanasheh* is prohibited, these commentaries suggest, not only as a remembrance of Yaakov's wounding, but as a fine levied upon the patriarch's descendents across the ages. Yaakov's family should never have allowed him to stand alone on that fateful night. To ensure that no Jew will ever leave his brother or sister alone again, God reminds us of our responsibility by prohibiting the consumption of the sciatic nerve.[11]

C

"And a man wrestled with him until the break of dawn."[12]

Who, then, is the mysterious stranger who suddenly attacks the patriarch? What eternal lessons are to be learned from the desperate battle that unfolds in the darkness of the night?

The identity of Yaakov's mysterious adversary and the symbolism of the struggle itself are, understandably, the subject of much discussion among the biblical commentaries.

Midrashic sources identify the stranger as an angel, specifically *sar tzeva'o shel Esav*, "the representative angel of Esav."[13]

On the eve of the physical reunion with his brother, Yaakov finds himself locked in mortal combat with Esav's spiritual emissary. The patriarch

9. Bereishit 32:25
10. Ibid., 32:33.
11. Da'at Zekeinim Miba'alei Hatosafot, Bereishit 32:33.
12. Bereishit 32:35.
13. Midrash Rabba Bereishit 77:3.

emerges victorious, but at a cost (represented by the physical injury to Yaakov's thigh).

Some of the Midrashim go on to suggest that the struggle itself is a prophetic representation of the ongoing war that will be waged across the ages between the descendents of Yaakov and the descendents of Esav. Yaakov's injury, these sources claim, represents the heavy price the Jewish nation will be forced to pay, at the hands of Esav, over the course of a turbulent history.

The struggle is destined to continue, "until the break of dawn – until the moment of our redemption."[14]

Later commentaries are basically unanimous in their acceptance of the Midrashic identification of Yaakov's adversary as an angel. They differ, however, as to the fundamental lessons to be learned from the struggle. Particularly instructive as an example is the contrast between the Ramban and Rabbeinu Bachya, on the one hand, and the Rashbam, on the other, as they strive to identify the central issues around which the struggle revolves.

The Ramban and Rabbeinu Bachya are among a large group of scholars who focus, in concrete fashion, upon the prophetic dimensions of the event, first cited by the Midrash.

The battle between Yaakov and the angel, they say, foreshadows the physical persecution which will be perpetrated against the Jewish people by the progeny of Esav, specifically the Roman Empire. The wounding of the patriarch, in close proximity to his reproductive organs, corresponds to historical periods when, tragically, "Esav will overcome Yaakov almost to the point of total extinction." In spite of these tragedies, however, Yaakov will ultimately emerge victorious.[15]

An entirely different approach is taken by the Rashbam. This scholar remains consistent in his view that, at the time the struggle begins, Yaakov is attempting to flee in order to totally avoid the impending encounter with Esav (see above). God, desiring that the reunion between the brothers take place, moves swiftly to forestall Yaakov's escape. He sends an angel to force Yaakov to remain and witness the fulfillment of the divine prophecy that Esav will do him no harm. When the angel sees that he "cannot prevail"

14. Pesikta Zutrata, Bereishit 32:25.
15. Ramban, Bereishit 32:26; Rabbeinu Bachya, Bereishit 32:26.

and that Yaakov still intends to flee, he wounds Yaakov, effectively preventing the patriarch's escape.[16]

Underlying the Rashbam's approach is the sentiment expressed by King Solomon in the book of Proverbs: "Many are the thoughts in the heart of man, but the will of God will prevail."[17]

Man cannot evade his own destiny. Our free will operates within parameters determined by God. The divine message to the patriarch is clear: "The confrontation with your brother is inevitable. Your choices are limited to the manner in which you will respond to that confrontation." (For a fuller discussion of the relationship between free will, prescience and predestination see Bereishit 4, *Approaches* A.)

D

On an entirely different plane, Yaakov's struggle with the angel serves as a prototype for a foundational rabbinic debate concerning the nature of all encounters with angels recorded in the Bible.

The Rambam declares that every time the Torah discusses an encounter between an individual and an angel the event is actually an internal event, occurring on the level of prophetic vision or dream rather than on the level of physical experience. In this case, the Rambam connects the struggle between Yaakov and the angel to the end of the previous parsha and the earlier mention of angels at Machanaim (see Vayeitzei 4). In the Rambam's eyes, the encounter at Machanaim was not a separate event but, instead, a foreshadowing of the struggle with the angel which was to follow:

> And so it was with Yaakov. First the text stated: 'And angels of the Lord encountered him.'[18] Then, the text began to discuss the events which led to that encounter – that Yaakov sent messengers to Esav, what the patriarch did to prepare, how Yaakov was left alone – and finally the text described the actual encounter: the struggle and dialogue with the angel which took place entirely in the realm of prophetic vision.[19]

The Ramban argues strenuously against this approach, raising

16. Rashbam, Bereishit 32:23–25.
17. Mishlei 19:21.
18. Bereishit 32:2.
19. Rambam, *Moreh Nevuchim* 2:42.

fundamental objections from a series of encounters recorded in the text which, according to the Ramban, could simply not have occurred only in the realm of prophecy or dream.

Specifically, in our case, the Ramban asks how Yaakov could have been physically injured during the course of a vision and why the patriarch would have exclaimed, "I have seen God face to face yet my soul was spared," if he had only dreamt the event.[20]

Numerous scholars rise to the Rambam's defense, while others support the arguments of the Ramban, as this unresolved debate concerning the nature of man's interface with angels courses across the ages (For a fuller discussion of angels see Vayishlach 2, *Approaches* C).

E

"No longer will it be said that your name is Yaakov, but Yisrael, for you have striven with the divine and with man and have overcome."[21]

An additional layer to Yaakov's struggle is alluded to by Rashi in a short comment on the end of the episode. As the struggle draws to a close, Yaakov demands a blessing from his adversary. The angel responds with the name change. The root of the name Yaakov is *eikev*, "heel," which connotes subterfuge. The name Yisrael, on the other hand, is comprised of two words meaning "struggle with God" and reflects open, honest striving.

Rashi therefore explains the angel's response as follows: "No longer will it be said that the blessings have come to you through subterfuge and deceit. Rather [you have achieved the blessings] through superiority in open competition."[22]

Is it possible that Yaakov wrestles in the darkness of the night not only with the angel but with his own demons and self-doubt? Perhaps, as he prepares for the reunion with his brother, he remembers the deceit which he perpetrated upon his father, recognizes the pain he has inflicted upon Esav and questions whether or not he truly deserves the spiritual legacy he has received. Yaakov's dramatic struggle reminds us that, no matter how hard we try, we cannot escape or ignore our past. Like the patriarch in the

20. Ramban, Bereishit 18:1.
21. Bereishit 32:29.
22. Rashi, Bereishit 32:29.

darkness of the night, we must openly confront the troubling issues that haunt us, and strive to reach resolution.

In this context, the *ish* (man) with whom Yaakov wrestles is none other than Yaakov, himself. This approach is supported by the fact that in a number of other locations in the text Yaakov is referred to by the term *ish*.[23]

God responds to Yaakov's doubts through the angel's message: "Yaakov, you return from the house of Lavan a changed man. You have shown that you deserve the legacy which you have received. All will acknowledge that the blessings are truly yours, fairly and openly earned."

F

Whatever approach we ultimately take to Yaakov's mortal struggle with the angel, an overarching message is clear. Yaakov faces two powerful potential dangers as he prepares for the fateful reunion with Esav:

1. He faces the clear danger that the meeting will end in open conflict and hostility. Recognizing this possibility, Yaakov actively prepares.

2. He faces the more subtle, yet equally perilous, possibility that the meeting will end in complete harmony – that he will be overwhelmed with relief at Esav's willingness to forgive and forget, and will lose sight of the philosophical chasm that separates him from his brother.

Towards this danger, Yaakov must be educated.

God, therefore, causes Yaakov, on the very eve of the brothers' reunion, to struggle throughout the night with Esav's spiritual emissary. Through this struggle, the patriarch is meant to learn that, whatever may appear to take place on the morrow, there can be no true peace between a Yaakov and an Esav. Theirs is a philosophical enmity that will last "till the break of dawn."

Points to Ponder

There are no coincidences in Jewish experience. How appropriate, therefore, that the yearly reading of Parshat Vayishlach always takes place against the backdrop of the "Hanukkah-Christmas season" in the diaspora. For at this time of the year, a sad irony becomes acutely apparent.

Hanukkah, the holiday that most clearly celebrates the Jewish nation's

23. Bereishit 25:27, 26:31, 27:11.

ongoing historical victory against the forces of assimilation, has become, in our day, the most assimilated Jewish festival.

Hanukkah-Christmas clubs, seasonal parties, public religious displays and more all conspire to create, in the minds of many, an equality between two vastly different religious events. In many households, Hanukkah becomes a "Jewish Christmas" as, throughout the community, the spirit of the "Judeo-Christian ethic" fills the air. Theological harmony is assumed where no such harmony exists.

Monumental chasms separate Jewish philosophy from Christian philosophy. We disagree upon such basic issues as the concept of sanctity and its relationship to the physical world, the ability of man to interface with God directly, the notion of original sin, and more. If we fail to recognize and be sensitive to these differences, if we fail to teach our children about these differences, then we run the real risk of assimilating, God forbid, into a culture not our own.

The image of our forefather Yaakov struggling through the darkness of the night with the "angel of Esav" is presented to us each year at the time of the year when that image is most necessary. If we are to survive as a people, we cannot allow artificial harmony to blind us. We must certainly strive for respectful, harmonious coexistence and cooperation with our non-Jewish neighbors, we should certainly acknowledge and appreciate the specific values and goals that we share, but not at the expense of losing our uniqueness.

Ours is a philosophical struggle that is destined to last "until the break of dawn."

3 Negotiating a Severance

Context

As the apparently harmonious reunion of Yaakov and Esav draws to a close (a reunion which, according to the rabbis, is actually more discordant than appears on the surface),[1] the Torah recounts the following conversation between the brothers:

> Esav: Let us travel…and I will proceed alongside you.
>
> Yaakov: My lord knows that the children are tender and that the sheep and cattle are a burden upon me. If they are driven hard for a single day, then all the sheep will die. Let my lord travel ahead of his servant and I will make my way according to the pace dictated by the cattle…and by the children; until I come to my master at Seir.
>
> Esav: Allow me to assign to you some of the people who are with me.
>
> Yaakov: For what purpose? Simply allow me to find favor in my lord's eyes.[2]

After the conversation concludes, Esav returns to his home in Seir while Yaakov travels to Succot.[3]

Questions

Why does the Torah record this dialogue? Are the brothers' travel arrangements so significant that they need to be detailed for posterity?

How does this seemingly innocuous conversation serve as an

1. Midrash Rabba Bereishit 78:9.
2. Bereishit 32:12–15.
3. Ibid., 33:16–17.

appropriate epilogue to the dramatic reunion between Yaakov and Esav and to the powerful events that preceded it?

Why does Yaakov tell Esav that he will join him at Seir, and then travel to a totally different destination?

Approaches

A

As usual, the *pashut pshat* of the Torah text conveys volumes. What seems, at first, to be an innocuous conversation is actually, upon examination, a critical negotiation. Years of separation and the dramatic reunion have all led to this one moment. The patriarch must now carefully delineate his ongoing relationship with his brother as he cautiously treads along the path between open hostility and "too much" harmony.

We find ourselves, again, at one of those quiet moments within the patriarchal era when a misstep on the part of one man can inexorably and permanently alter the course of our nation's history.

Against the backdrop of the preceding events and with the undercurrents beneath the diplomatic language revealed, the conversation between Yaakov and Esav might well read as follows:

Esav's opening gambit: "Let us travel…and I will proceed alongside you…" *I am not going to let my brother out of my sight again. I will, therefore, suggest that we travel together towards a shared destination. If we move together through life, it will only be a matter of time before he and his family are overwhelmed by the strength of my presence and lose their uniqueness. Our camps will then coalesce and become one entity under my control.*

Yaakov's rejoinder: "My lord knows that the children are tender and that the sheep and cattle are a burden upon me. If they are driven hard for a single day, then all the sheep will die. Let my lord travel ahead of his servant and I will make my way according to the pace dictated by the cattle…and by the children; until I come to my master at Seir." *Dear God, what a dangerous moment! At all costs, I cannot allow our camps to travel together. Our lives and our priorities are totally different. I must find a way to negotiate a severance from my brother. And yet, how can I do so diplomatically, without arousing his anger? Perhaps if I remind him that I will have to travel slowly and if I let him think that I will join him in Seir, he will go on alone, ahead of me.*

Esav's second attempt: "Allow me to assign to you some of the people who are with me." *Yaakov's trying to slip away! Not so fast! All I have to do is place some of my agents in his camp and, eventually, I will still be able to control him.*

Yaakov's rejoinder: "For what purpose? Simply allow me to find favor in my lord's eyes." *Oh, no, that's all I need – a fifth column within my own camp! I will just have to politely refuse and again insist that all I want is good relations. Hopefully, my brother will then go on his way to Seir and I will go somewhere else entirely. By the time we reach our respective destinations, he'll get the message that I want to keep my distance. Hopefully he will come to accept that reality or, at least, he won't find it worth the effort to come back and find me.*

B

In the light of day, we witness that Yaakov has learned well the lessons that were conveyed to him, dramatically and perilously, in the darkness of the night.

In our previous study (see Vayishlach 2, *Approaches* C) we noted that, on the eve of Yaakov's reunion with his brother, God caused the patriarch to struggle in mortal combat with a mysterious stranger, identified by the Midrash as an angel, the spiritual representative of Esav. Clearly, on one level, this conflict was meant to warn Yaakov to see beyond appearances at the meeting with Esav the next day. In the most effective way possible, God teaches the patriarch the hard and bitter truth that, although things might seem harmonious on the surface, philosophical and even at times physical confrontation will define the relationship between the brothers until the end of days. In order to survive, Yaakov will be forced to build the relationship with his brother within clearly defined philosophical boundaries.

Now Yaakov meets his moment of truth. When all is said and done, Yaakov cautiously negotiates a severance from his brother. His successful completion of this delicate negotiation helps define the parameters for our nation's long journey across the ages.

4 Violence: Condoned or Condemned?

Context

A powerfully violent episode is set in motion when Yaakov's daughter, Dina, is abducted and assaulted by Shechem, the son of Chamor, the ruler of the city of Shechem. Following the assault, Shechem asks his father to approach Yaakov for Dina's hand in marriage.

When Chamor presents the request to Yaakov, he also proposes that the patriarch's family, as a whole, settle among the Shechemites and intermarry with the local population. Yaakov's sons insist that, as a prerequisite to this arrangement, all male inhabitants of Shechem undergo ritual circumcision.

On the third day following the mass circumcision, Yaakov's sons, Shimon and Levi, enter the city and, taking advantage of the weakened state of the inhabitants, slaughter all the males. They then lay waste to the entire city.

Yaakov criticizes his sons, claiming that their actions have made the family vulnerable to attack from the surrounding nations. Shimon and Levi respond: "Shall our sister be treated as a harlot?"[1]

Questions

The Torah opens this episode with the sentence: "And Dina, the daughter of Leah, whom she had borne to Yaakov, went out to observe the daughters of the land."[2] What is the significance of this statement and why is it included the text? Why does the text specifically identify Dina as "the daughter of Leah, whom she had borne to Yaakov"?

Are Shimon and Levi morally justified when they avenge the assault

1. Bereishit 34:1–31.
2. Ibid., 34:1.

upon their sister? Can the destruction of an entire city be condoned as a response to the crimes of its prince?

Yaakov was present when his sons outlined their conditions to Chamor and Shechem.[3] How much did the patriarch know? Was Yaakov complicit in the planned deceit of the Shechemites? If so, why does he later criticize his sons Shimon and Levi? If not, how could he have possibly agreed to a plan that would have allowed for the assimilation of his family into Shechemite society?

Yaakov only reprimands Shimon and Levi for making their family vulnerable to attack. Did Yaakov object to his sons' actions on moral grounds, as well?

The text does not record any response on Yaakov's part to his sons' counterargument: "Shall our sister be treated as a harlot?"[4] Does the patriarch accept the rationalization offered by Shimon and Levi or not?

Approaches

A

Confronted with the deceit and violence perpetrated by Yaakov's sons upon the city of Shechem, the commentaries struggle with the moral dimensions of this difficult episode. The Rambam, the classical jurist, finds legal grounds to justify both the deceit perpetrated upon the citizens of Shechem and the violent actions of Shimon and Levi.

The nations of the world, says the Rambam, are responsible to observe the seven Noachide laws upon pain of death. (See Noach 4 for a discussion of the Noachide code).

Dina's assailant clearly transgressed the Noachide law that prohibits abduction. The entire society of Shechem, however, incurred guilt as well. One of the seven Noachide laws mandates the establishment of courts of law. This injunction, claims the Rambam, obligates all non-Jewish societies to establish judicial systems designed to enforce the entire Noachide code. When the citizens of Shechem failed to maintain this legal standard by bringing their prince to justice, they, themselves, became liable to the

3. Ibid., 34:6–17.
4. Ibid., 34:31.

death penalty. Shimon and Levi were, therefore, justified in exacting punishment upon the city.[5]

B

The Ramban objects to the Rambam's interpretation of the Noachide code on two fundamental levels. Firstly, he says, the requirement to establish courts of law refers to monetary issues and not to the enforcement of the other Noachide laws. Secondly, one is guilty of a capital crime under the Noachide code only if an action is actually committed. Failure to do something, such as establish courts of law, does not carry the death penalty. Therefore, although Shechem himself was certainly guilty of a punishable offense under the Noachide code, in this instance the citizens of the city were not.

The population of the city, continues the Ramban, was certainly guilty of other ongoing capital crimes unrelated to the event before us, such as idolatry and sexual immorality. Yaakov and his sons, however, had no legal right to exact punishment for those crimes.[6]

The Ramban, therefore, suggests a radically different approach to the story of Shechem. When the patriarch's family demanded that the inhabitants of the city undergo circumcision, they fully believed that the Shechemites would not comply, that the proposed agreement would collapse and that Dina would be returned without further harm. If, by some chance, the Shechemites did agree to circumcise themselves, Yaakov's sons intended to enter the city on the third day, take advantage of the weakness of the inhabitants and free their sister without further violence. Yaakov, therefore, agreed to this proposal, seeing it as a way to rescue Dina without bloodshed. Shimon and Levi, however, took matters into their own hands, violently avenged their sister's honor and incurred their father's reprimand.[7]

C

Other scholars see hints within the text that the violent actions of Shimon

5. Rambam, *Mishneh Torah*, Hilchot Melachim 9:14.
6. Ramban, Bereishit 34:13.
7. Ibid.

and Levi were performed in self-defense against an enemy that intended Yaakov and his family serious harm.

Some suggest that the phrase "and it was on the third day, when they (the Shechemites) were in pain"[8] refers not to physical pain resulting from the circumcision but to remorse felt by the citizens of Shechem over their agreement with Yaakov's family. Shimon and Levi recognized that the Shechemites had changed their minds and acted preemptively.[9]

Others, building on a Midrashic source,[10] point to the words of Chamor as he convinces his subjects to undergo circumcision: "Their (Yaakov and his family's) livestock, their possessions, and all their animals; will they not be ours?"[11]

Clearly, these scholars maintain, the Shechemites were only going along with the agreement for personal gain at the expense of Yaakov and his family. At the first possible opportunity, Chamor and his subjects would have turned against the patriarch. Shimon and Levi acted to forestall such an eventuality.[12]

D

While the biblical commentaries struggle over the moral issues involved in this tragic event, the *pashut pshat* of the text seems to render a verdict, of sorts, of its own. The Shechem narrative opens and closes with a surprising tone of ambivalence and ambiguity. We are reminded, once again, of the overarching message of Parshat Vayishlach: Life is often painted in shades of gray rather than in black and white, and issues of right and wrong are not always clearly defined.

This ambivalent tone is struck with the very first sentence of the story: "And Dina, the daughter of Leah, whom she had borne to Yaakov, went out to view the daughters of the land."[13]

According to the Ramban, the text identifies Dina as Leah's daughter as a foreshadowing of events to come. Dina is singled out as the full sister

8. Bereishit 34:25.
9. Da'at Zekeinim Miba'alei Hatosafot, Bereishit 34:25.
10. Pesikta Zutrata, Bereishit 34:32, 33.
11. Bereishit 34:23.
12. Sforno, Bereishit 34:25.
13. Bereishit 34:1.

of Leah's sons, Shimon and Levi, the two brothers who eventually defend her honor.[14]

Rashi and other commentaries, however, take a different tack. They attribute the textual connection of Dina to Leah as a reference to Dina's character. Yaakov's daughter, says Rashi, like her mother, was excessively outgoing.[15] A daughter of Rivka, states the Ohr Hachaim, would never have gone out to "view the daughters of the land."[16]

Nothing can mitigate Shechem's guilt over his abduction and assault of Dina. By no means should we ever blame the victim of a violent crime. Nonetheless, the Torah reminds us that, at times, we contribute to our own downfall. Surrounded by a dangerous world, Dina should have been more careful. Her tragic misstep alerts us to the care that must be exercised in each era as we and our children relate to an often perilous environment.

It is only when we reach the end of the story and its aftermath, however, that the ambivalence of the text rises to full crescendo. After Shimon and Levi violently massacre the inhabitants of Shechem, their father, Yaakov, turns to them with the following criticism: "You have troubled me by making me odious in the eyes of the inhabitants of the land.... I am few in number and should they band together and attack me, I will be annihilated, I and my household."[17]

The utilitarian tenor of Yaakov's remarks is profoundly striking. The patriarch criticizes his sons for rendering their family vulnerable to attack, but offers no moral judgment over their actions. Furthermore, when Shimon and Levi respond, "Shall our sister be treated as a harlot?"[18] the Torah records no reaction on Yaakov's part. The narrative abruptly closes with Shimon and Levi's words.

Does Yaakov condone or condemn his sons' violent actions? Does he question their morality in acting as they did? The text is unclear; the jury is out.

To make matters more intriguing, Yaakov does, decades later, eventually render a clear verdict concerning Shimon and Levi's behavior. On his deathbed, blessing his sons, the patriarch turns to Shimon and Levi and

14. Ramban, Bereishit 34:1.
15. Rashi, Bereishit 34:1.
16. Ohr Hachaim, Bereishit 34:1.
17. Bereishit 34:30.
18. Ibid., 34:31.

exclaims: "Cursed be their anger, for it is fierce, and their wrath, for it is harsh. I will separate them within Yaakov, disperse them within Yisrael." [19]

Here, then, is the moral judgment that one would expect from the patriarch.

Upon closer examination, however, even here the ambiguity persists. Shimon and Levi's descendents are not, according to Yaakov's blessing, to be read out of their nation's history. They are, instead, to be dispersed throughout the tribes within the land of Israel. Is Yaakov saying that righteous indignation and strength are necessary components of our national character – just not in concentrated fashion? Does he believe that our people require the zealotry of a Shimon and a Levi, but only as necessary, and only in small doses?

As a final complication, we must briefly note how Yaakov's prophetic vision finally comes to fruition. Exactly how were Shimon and Levi's descendents eventually scattered among their brethren?

Levi becomes the progenitor of both the Kohanim (priests) and the Leviim (those who serve within the Temple). While the Kohanim and Leviim owned no land of their own and were, indeed, scattered among the tribes, they occupied positions of exceptional honor. Shimon's descendents, for their part, according to rabbinic tradition, served as scribes and teachers of young children throughout the land.[20] When properly channeled, it would seem, the zealous pride and strength of Shimon and Levi serve our people and our tradition well.

We arrive, fittingly, at a complicated close to a complicated story. Violence is neither totally condoned nor totally condemned; some acts are neither totally right nor totally wrong. Issues of good and evil are presented with all of their complexity in the Torah text. We are reminded that moral truth often lies beneath layers and layers of complicated contextual concerns.

The ambiguity and ambivalence that has marked Parshat Vayishlach from the beginning reaches its climax with the story of Shechem. The Torah paints the world, with all its shades of grey, for our examination across the ages.

---

19. Ibid., 49:7.
20. Rashi, Bereishit 49:7.

Vayeishev

CHAPTER 37:1–40:23

פרק לז:א–מ:כג

Parsha Summary

The final chapter of the patriarchal era begins…

Yaakov settles in the land of Canaan, seemingly oblivious to the emotional undercurrents that threaten the very stability of his family. The turmoil centers on Yosef, Yaakov's favored son. Yosef is hated by his brothers who, jealous of their father's favor, are further angered as Yosef brings negative reports concerning their behavior to their father. The brothers' hatred grows when Yosef shares the content of two dreams which seem to indicate his superiority over his brothers.

The brothers travel to Shechem to shepherd their father's flocks and Yaakov sends Yosef to inquire after their welfare. When the brothers see Yosef approaching from a distance they determine to kill him and throw his body into a pit. Reuven, the eldest, however, objects and convinces the others to thrust Yosef into the pit alive, rather than murder him directly. Reuven fully intends to return later, release Yosef and bring him safely back to their father.

Yosef arrives. The brothers rip off his cloak and throw him into the pit. When, however, the brothers observe an approaching caravan, Yehuda convinces his siblings of the benefit of selling Yosef as a slave rather than allowing him to die in the pit.

As the caravan passes, Yosef is pulled from the pit and sold into bondage for twenty pieces of silver. Reuven returns, finds the pit empty and bemoans the loss of Yosef. The brothers return to their father and lead him to believe that Yosef has been killed by a wild beast. Yaakov descends into mourning. Yosef is brought to Egypt and sold to Potiphar, an aide to Pharaoh, the Egyptian king.

The Torah digresses from the story of Yosef to relate the tale of Yehuda and Tamar.

After the sale of Yosef, Yehuda separates from his brothers. He marries and has three sons: Er, Onan and Shela. Er takes a wife, Tamar, but he sins and dies at the hand of God. Tamar then marries the second brother, Onan, but he also sins and dies, leaving Tamar childless. Afraid that Shela will die like his brothers, Yehuda delays giving him to Tamar in marriage.

After years pass, Tamar seduces Yehuda by masquerading as a prostitute. When Yehuda hears that Tamar is pregnant and threatens her with execution for licentious behavior, Tamar reveals that Yehuda, himself, is the father of her unborn child. Yehuda admits his error in not allowing Tamar to marry Shela, reverses the order of execution and accepts responsibility for his actions. Tamar gives birth to twins: Peretz and Zerach.

The Torah returns to the story of Yosef as he earns his master's trust and is appointed overseer over all of Potiphar's possessions.

Potiphar's wife is attracted to Yosef and attempts to seduce him. Infuriated by Yosef's repeated rejection of her advances, she twists the truth and accuses Yosef of attempting to seduce her. Angered by the apparent betrayal of his trust, Potiphar has Yosef placed in prison.

While in prison, Yosef earns the confidence of the chief officer and is placed in charge of the other prisoners.

Pharaoh's butler and baker are placed in prison by the king, and Yosef interprets their dreams. Based on the dreams, Yosef informs the butler that in three days he will be released and the baker that in three days he will be executed. Yosef's predictions prove to be accurate.

Yosef asks the butler to remember him. The butler, however, quickly forgets Yosef.

1 Yosef the Righteous?

Context

No character in the biblical text is more complex or more intriguing than Yosef, Yaakov's favored son.

The Torah, as a rule, does not provide general biographical data on the figures within its pages (see Toldot 1, *Approaches* A). In Yosef's case, however, the picture painted in the text is astoundingly complex and contradictory.

On the one hand, "handsome of form and handsome of appearance,"[1] Yosef emerges as a personally engaging and naturally successful individual, a man who certainly knows how to "win friends and influence people." No matter where Yosef is placed or under what circumstances he finds himself, he always rises to the top.

In his own home, he is his father's favorite.[2] Enslaved in the house of Potiphar, he impresses his master and is appointed head of the household, in charge of all Potiphar owns.[3] Thrust into prison as a result of the false accusations of Potiphar's wife, he makes such an impression on the chief officer that he is selected to supervise all the other prisoners.[4] Abruptly rushed out of prison for a sudden audience with Pharaoh, he interprets the king's dreams so successfully that Pharaoh appoints him to rule over the entire Egyptian Empire, second only to Pharaoh himself.[5]

On the other hand, this highly successful, engaging man is guilty of questionable behavior, specifically with regards to his own family.

Although he will later emerge as a diplomat par excellence, Yosef

1. Bereishit 39:6.
2. Ibid., 37:3.
3. Ibid., 39:2–4.
4. Ibid., 39:31–33.
5. Ibid., 41:37–44.

shows a startling lack of diplomacy in his early dealings within his home. Seemingly oblivious to his brothers' antagonism towards him, he exacerbates matters by delivering negative reports concerning their behavior to Yaakov.[6] He then further enrages his siblings by sharing with them, on two separate occasions, the content of dreams that reflect his superiority over them.[7]

Later in the story, when Yosef's brothers descend into Egypt to procure supplies in the face of famine, Yosef, who is by this time second-in-command to Pharaoh, deliberately hides his true identity. He then proceeds to put his brothers through a carefully planned series of painful and frightening experiences. Only when Yehuda rises in defense of the youngest brother, Binyamin, does Yosef finally disclose the truth (See Vayigash 1, *Approaches* B).[8]

Further complicating an already complicated picture, rabbinic tradition portrays Yosef, both in his early years[9] and later in the house of Potiphar,[10] as vain, and overly concerned about his appearance. The Midrash also finds Yosef guilty of relying too much upon the actions of man rather than trusting in God.[11]

How then, does history judge Yosef? What is the final verdict concerning this most complex biblical figure?

From a rabbinic perspective, the answer is resoundingly clear. In the Talmud, Midrash and throughout rabbinic literature, Yosef is consistently referred to by a title awarded only to a very select few. Whereas each of the patriarchs is granted the designation *Avinu*, "our father"; whereas each of the matriarchs is known as *Imeinu*, "our mother"; whereas Moshe earns the title *Rabbeinu*, "our teacher"; Yosef is simply *Yosef Hatzadik*, "Yosef the Righteous."

6. Ibid., 37:2.
7. Ibid., 37:5–11.
8. Ibid., 42:5–44:4.
9. Rashi, Bereishit 37:2.
10. Ibid., 39:6.
11. Midrash Rabba Shmot 7:1.

Questions

Given Yosef's complex, even contradictory, record, through what overarching merit does he earn the title *Hatzadik*?

What do the rabbis perceive within Yosef's life that moves them to judge him in such positive fashion?

Approaches

There certainly are moments within Yosef's life that reflect "righteousness." His repeated rejection of the advances of Potiphar's wife, in the face of the obvious threat to his own safety and freedom, for example, demonstrates deep moral commitment and tremendous courage.

No single event, however, no matter how dramatic, fully reveals the greatness of this biblical figure or captures the dimensions of his life challenge. Only when Yosef's story is viewed as a whole, against the backdrop of one critical phenomenon, does the true nature of his righteousness begin to emerge.

A momentous yet subtle change takes place in God's relationship with man when Yosef appears on the scene: for the first time since His commandment to Avraham launched the opening chapters of Jewish history, *God is silent.*

God spoke to Avraham, Yitzchak and Yaakov at critical junctures of their lives. He commanded, taught, instructed and reassured them. The patriarchs not only knew of God's existence through firsthand experience, they were also keenly aware of His personal relationship with them.

Suddenly, vis-à-vis Yosef, *God stops talking.*

When Yosef is violently thrust into the pit by his brothers, the God who reassured his father at Beit El doesn't say a word; when Yosef faces challenge in the house of Potiphar, God is nowhere to be found; when Yosef is thrown into prison, alone and in an alien country, God does not comfort him. And when Yosef has his audience with Pharaoh, God does not tell him what to do or say.

Even Yosef's dreams, and others' dreams which he interprets, are substantially different from those of his predecessors. At no point, in the dreams of the Yosef story, does God appear or even speak. Yosef finds the future hidden within symbolism and riddle, accessible only through study and interpretation.

Whereas his father, grandfather and great-grandfather had the benefit of God's clear counsel, Yosef, under the most trying of circumstances, must find his way on his own.

B

How does Yosef react to God's apparent absence and resounding silence? Astoundingly, he responds by bringing God into the picture over and over again. For example, take the following:

1. Faced with the seductive demands of Potiphar's wife, Yosef argues: "Behold, my master trusts me implicitly within the house, and all that he owns he has given to my hand. There is no one greater in this house than I, and he has denied me nothing but you, for you are his wife. How, then, shall I perpetrate this great evil, and sin against God?"[12]

Logically, Yosef's declaration should have closed with the words "and sin against my master." His arguments leading to that final clause, after all, speak of the fealty he owes to Potiphar. Seemingly out of the blue, however, Yosef switches gears. He recognizes that the challenge before him is not simply about his relationship to Potiphar. His sin would be a "sin against God." In the moral realm, Yosef answers to a higher authority.

2. In prison, confronted with the troubled dreams of the butler and the baker, Yosef states: "Do not interpretations belong to God? Please relate it (the dream) to me."[13]

Given the opportunity – in the presence of potentially powerful allies – to take personal credit for a valuable talent, Yosef instead attributes his powers to God.

3. Abruptly pulled from the prison for a sudden audience with Pharaoh, Yosef faces a king sorely troubled by dreams. Opportunity clearly knocks at Yosef's door. The most powerful ruler of the civilized world is asking him for help in an area in which Yosef has already shown great proficiency. Pharaoh himself concedes: "I have heard…that you understand a dream to interpret it."[14]

---

12. Bereishit 39:8–9.
13. Ibid., 40:8.
14. Ibid., 41:15.

Yosef, however, again refuses to accept the talent as his own. Asked by Pharaoh to interpret the dreams, Yosef emphatically declares: "It is not I! God will respond to Pharaoh's welfare."[15]

Yosef then goes on to mention God four additional times during his explanation of the dreams, attributing everything that is about to occur to Divine Providence.[16]

So deeply affected is the Egyptian monarch by Yosef's attitude, he responds: "Can we find another like him (Yosef), an individual in whom lies the spirit of God?"[17]

4. Confronting his brothers for the first time after revealing his true identity, Yosef reassures them repeatedly with references to the plans of the Almighty:

> And now do not be distressed or reproach yourselves for having sold me here, for as a provider did God send me before you....[18]
>
> And God has sent me before you to ensure your survival in the land....[19]
>
> And now you did not send me here, but God; and He has made me a father to Pharaoh, master of his entire household, and a ruler throughout the entire land of Egypt.[20]

Yosef's reassuring words reflect an astounding ability to look back upon his pain-filled years and see in them God's guiding hand. From the perspective of *Yosef Hatzadik*, nothing has happened by coincidence. His wrenching sale into bondage, his lonely years in prison, his rise to power, have all been for a higher purpose. As far as Yosef is concerned, God has been present, in silent fashion, throughout his life.

We arrive, then, not only at an understanding of Yosef's greatness, but also at an understanding of how that greatness clearly speaks to us. Yosef is a *tzadik* because he is the first of our ancestors to maintain his faith while living in a non-prophetic era – an era when God is silent.

---

15. Ibid., 41:16.
16. Ibid., 41:25–32.
17. Ibid., 41:38.
18. Ibid., 45:5.
19. Ibid., 45:7.
20. Ibid., 45:8.

Yosef emerges as the paradigm for our lives, the biblical figure whose life experience most closely mirrors our own. Like Yosef, we live and, in fact, have lived for centuries, in non-prophetic times. Our challenge, like his, is to see God's hidden hand in the world around us and to determine our role in the unfolding divine plan.

C

A striking, twofold parallel pattern emerges when the flow of Jewish history is viewed from a distance.

The patriarchal era begins with clear communication between God and man. That direct contact continues throughout the lives of the patriarchs and matriarchs as God openly directs the course of early Jewish history. A point is reached, however, when God pulls back, when his clear direction and instruction ends. Just as a parent must let go of a child's hand if the child is to learn to walk on his own, so too, God must withdraw to allow man to find his own way. That moment of severance, within the patriarchal period, occurs during the life of Yosef.

Then, however, a second era, the national era of the Jewish people, opens with the Exodus from Egypt. The beginning of this era, like the beginning of the patriarchal era, is marked by direct communication between God and man. God not only speaks to Moshe and Aharon, but also performs momentous miracles in view of the entire nation. God's contact with man continues over the centuries as He speaks to select leaders and prophets. A moment, however, is reached in the national era when God is, once again, abruptly silent. History repeats itself as, soon after the destruction of the First Temple, prophecy ends and we enter, as did Yosef centuries before, a non-prophetic world.

This recurring pattern may well serve as the basis for a strange literary phenomenon. A remarkable series of parallels can be found between the Yosef narrative and the story of Purim, which occurs centuries later at the end of our national exile in Babylon. In both stories the fates of the protagonists abruptly change at the whim of a king whose decrees are marked by the transference of his royal ring.[21] Both Yosef and Mordechai, a hero of the Purim story, are paraded publicly through the streets[22] and dressed

21. Bereishit 41:42; Megillat Esther 3:10; 8:2.
22. Bereishit 41:43; Megillat Esther 6:11.

in royal garb[23] to mark their ascension to the king's favor. Yosef and Mordechai are each appointed second-in-command to the king of their times.[24] The rabbis even see in the actions of Yosef towards Binyamin, his youngest brother, a foreshadowing of an event which will involve Mordechai, a descendent of Binyamin.[25]

At first glance, the stories of Yosef and of Purim, separated by centuries, seem totally unconnected and the parallels between them completely coincidental. Seen through the prism of Jewish history, however, a powerful correlation emerges.

The Purim story marks the onset of the non-prophetic period of the national era. Just as He was with Yosef, God is, within the Purim tale, suddenly silent. At no point does God speak directly to Esther or Mordechai, the heroes of Purim. They must, instead, determine divine will during a time of God's silence and in the face of extraordinarily trying circumstances.[26] Like the Yosef narrative, the story of the "hidden miracle"[27] of Purim serves as a paradigm of the challenges which we face in non-prophetic times.

D

When all is said and done, Yosef is truly *Yosef Hatzadik*; a man who believes in God even when God is silent; a man who steadfastly and tenaciously holds to that faith even when all seems lost and he appears to be totally abandoned. Yosef sees God's hidden hand in all that transpires as he struggles to define his divinely ordained role in a turbulent and frightening world.

How often have we, his descendents, been faced with the very same challenges? Yosef's towering example serves as a beacon across the ages.

---

23. Bereishit 41:42; Megillat Esther 8:15.
24. Bereishit 41:40; Megillat Esther 10:3.
25. Talmud Bavli Megilla 16b.
26. Megillat Esther.
27. Talmud Bavli Chulin 139b.

2 Who Sold Yosef?

Context

After thrusting Yosef into a pit, his brothers sit down to eat. When they observe an approaching caravan of Ishmaelites, Yehuda convinces his siblings to sell Yosef into bondage rather than allow him to die.[1]

The text then continues (note the pronouns and their referents): "And *Midianite* men passed by, merchants, and *they* drew Yosef up out of the pit; and *they* sold Yosef to the *Ishmaelites* for twenty pieces of silver; and *they* brought Yosef to Egypt." [2]

Later, the Torah relates: "And the *Medanites* sold him (Yosef) to Egypt, to Potiphar, a court official of Pharaoh…"[3]

Finally, even later, the text states: "And Potiphar…bought him from the hand of the *Ishmaelites* who had brought him there." [4]

Questions

The text concerning the critical event of Yosef's sale seems strangely ambiguous, even contradictory.

Who are the Midianite men who suddenly appear, as if out of nowhere, and what is their relationship, if any, to the caravan of Ishmaelites?

Who actually pulled Yosef out of the pit and sold him to the Ishmaelites: his brothers or the Midianites?

If Yosef was sold to the *Ishmaelites* why does the Torah state that the *Medanites* "sold him to Egypt, to Potiphar…"?[5]

Why does the Torah seem to contradict itself again with the state-

1. Bereishit 37:24–27.
2. Ibid., 37:28.
3. Ibid., 37:36.
4. Ibid., 39:1.
5. Ibid., 37:36.

ment "and Potiphar…bought him from the hand of the Ishmaelites who had brought him there"?[6]

Finally, why is the Torah so deliberately vague concerning the sequence of events at this critical juncture in the story of our people?

Approaches

The commentaries directly confront the ambiguity of the text in their discussions of the sale of Yosef.

A

Rashi maintains the classical position that Yosef's brothers actively sold him into slavery. Commenting on the phrase "and they drew…," Rashi simply states, "The sons of Yaakov (drew) Yosef from the pit." [7]

Rashi further explains that the appearance of the Midianites reflects the fact that Yosef was sold numerous times: "The brothers sold him to the Ishmaelites who sold him to the Midianites, and the Midianites sold him to Egypt." [8]

Yosef's grievous treatment at the hand of his brothers is further exacerbated when he is treated like chattel and sold from one hand to the next. [Rashi identifies the Medanites, mentioned later in the text, with the Midianites. He fails, however, to explain the final statement which declares that Potiphar bought Yosef from the Ishmaelites.]

B

Numerous other scholars, while agreeing with Rashi's basic premise that the brothers sold Yosef into slavery, offer their own solutions to the mention of Ishmaelites, Midianites and Medanites.

The Ramban and the Sforno both simplify the scene by suggesting that the Ishmaelites and Midianites were operating in partnership within one caravan, with the Ishmaelites serving as camel drivers for the Midianite merchants.[9] Yosef was, therefore, only sold twice: first by the brothers to the passing caravan and then by the merchants of the caravan to Potiphar. The Ramban further explains that the references in the text to

---

6. Ibid., 39:1.
7. Rashi, Bereishit 37:28.
8. Ibid.
9. Ramban, Bereishit 37:25; Sforno, Bereishit 37:28.

the Ishmaelites underscore their role as the ones who physically brought Yosef to Egypt, while the Midianites are highlighted as the merchants who actually bought and sold him.[10] The Sforno, for his part, suggests that the brothers were unwilling to speak directly to the Midianites for fear that they might be recognized. For this reason, he says, they negotiated with the Ishmaelites.[11]

The Ibn Ezra goes a step further and claims that there was only one group of merchants, at times referred to by the text as Ishmaelites and at times as Midianites.[12] To prove his position he quotes a passage from the book of Shoftim which identifies Midianite kings as Ishmaelites.[13]

At the opposite end of the spectrum, Chizkuni suggests that Yosef was actually sold four times. The brothers sold Yosef to the Midianites while he was still in the pit. The Midianites then drew Yosef out of the pit and sold him to the Ishmaelites who in turn then sold him again to the Midianites (Medanites). Finally, the Medanites sold Yosef, for the last time, to Potiphar.[14]

C

An entirely different, revolutionary approach to the sale of Yosef is first suggested by the Rashbam and then echoed by a number of subsequent commentaries including Rabbeinu Bachya,[15] Rabbi Shimshon Raphael Hirsch[16] and the Malbim.[17] Remaining true to his *pashut pshat* approach to text, the Rashbam maintains that Yosef's brothers were not actually involved in his sale. He literally interprets the passage "and Midianite men passed by, merchants, and *they* drew Yosef up out of the pit; and *they* sold Yosef to the Ishmaelites for twenty pieces of silver…"[18] as follows:

> The brothers were eating at a distance from the pit…and waiting for the arrival of the Ishmaelites whom they had observed approaching.

10. Ramban, Bereishit 37:28.
11. Sforno, ibid.
12. Ibn Ezra, ibid.
13. Shoftim 8:24.
14. Chizkuni, Bereishit 37:28.
15. Rabbeinu Bachya, Bereishit 37:28.
16. Rabbi Shimshon Raphael Hirsch, Bereishit 37:25.
17. Malbim, Bereishit 37:28
18. Bereishit 37:28.

> Before the Ishmaelites arrived, however, others, Midianites, passed by, saw [Yosef] in the pit, drew him up out of the pit – and the Midianites sold him to the Ishmaelites. It is even possible that the brothers were unaware of these events.[19]

This approach, closer to the text, changes our entire conception of the events surrounding Yosef's sale: Yosef's brothers fully intended to sell him but never actually got the chance to carry out their plans.

D

The most important question, however, yet remains. Why is the Torah, at this critical and dramatic moment in the story of our people, so deliberately vague? Why doesn't the text tell us clearly whether or not Yosef's brothers were actively involved in his sale? Why allow for conflicting interpretations?

Perhaps the text is deliberately vague to teach us that *it really doesn't matter.* It doesn't matter whether the brothers actually pulled Yosef out of the pit and sold him or whether they simply set the stage for others to do so. Their guilt, in either case, remains constant.

Centuries later the Torah text will proclaim: "Do not stand idly by the blood of your friend"[20] – If you witness danger to another, you are obligated to act.[21]

We are responsible for the pain we cause or allow to occur to others even when it is not inflicted directly by our hands.

---

19. Rashbam, Bereishit 37:28.
20. Vayikra 19:16.
21. Talmud Bavli Sanhedrin 73a.

3 Man's Plans; God's Plans

Context

Yosef's wrenching descent into Egyptian bondage begins innocuously as his father, Yaakov, sends him to inquire after the welfare of his brothers in Shechem: "And he (Yaakov) sent him (Yosef) from the valley of Hevron and he arrived at Shechem…"[1]

Strangely enough, at this critical turning point, Rashi focuses on a seemingly minor, ancillary problem in the text: "Was not Hevron on a mountain?" [2]

The answer that Rashi proposes, however, moves far beyond geography and touches upon a powerful issue, central to the story of Yosef and his brothers.

Rashi cites a Talmudic passage which explains that by referring to the "Valley of Hevron," the Torah allegorically alludes to the "deep plan" which had been revealed, decades earlier, to Yosef's great-grandfather, Avraham, who is buried in Hevron.[3]

During the Covenant between the Pieces, God told Avraham: "Know full well…your children will be strangers in a land not their own, where they will be enslaved and persecuted for four hundred years."[4] (See Lech Lecha 4.)

Avraham's prophetic vision is now about to unfold, generations later. The sale of Yosef is the mechanism which will set the initial events of the prophecy in motion. The Torah, therefore, introduces the story of Yosef's sale with a reference to the "Valley of Hevron" – the deep plan rooted in Hevron.

With his short, seemingly technical observation, therefore, Rashi alerts us to a fundamental truth concerning the story that we are

1. Bereishit 37:14.
2. Rashi, Bereishit 37:14.
3. Ibid.; Talmud Bavli Sota 11a.
4. Bereishit 15:13.

about to read. The tale of Yosef and his brothers overlays deeper currents. This is not only the painful, personal story of a family in crisis. Yosef's first steps towards Shechem are also the first steps in another journey, which will ultimately transform the patriarchal family into an eternal people.

We are about to experience the divinely guided transition from the patriarchal era to the national era of Jewish history.

Questions

While God's providence is forever present in our lives, rarely is his silent guidance as evident as in the story of Yosef and his brothers. As Yosef himself maintains, their personal saga serves the higher purpose of effectuating God's overall plans.

God's "behind the scenes" involvement, however, raises serious questions about the personal free will of the players in the story.

Considering that the descent of the Jewish nation into Egypt was preordained generations earlier, how much choice did Yosef and his brothers really have in the unfolding events? Were they simply acting out a predetermined script or can they be justifiably held accountable for their actions?

How does this narrative reflect upon the delicate balance between prescience (God's foreknowledge of events), free will and predestination; a balance which normally defines our lives? (See Bereishit 4, *Approaches* A).

Approaches

While a full discussion of these complex issues remains beyond the scope of this study, viewing the story of Yosef as a microcosm of a larger, more familiar paradigm may prove instructive.

The Jewish view of history, on a global level, mirrors the issues found in the story of Yosef and his brothers.

A

On the one hand, Jews certainly believe in a measure of preordination on a national level. A belief in such preordination is, in fact, critical to our worldview. The best known of the Rambam's Thirteen Principles of Faith emphatically states: "I believe with complete faith in the coming of the

Mashiach (Messiah), and even though he may delay, nevertheless I anticipate every day that he will come."[5]

To believe in a Messiah is to believe in a predetermined, inevitable end point to history. Rabbi Yosef Soloveitchik, in fact, maintains that our introduction of the idea of Mashiach signaled a major revolution in the way man thought about his historical journey. We brought to the world the concept of a destiny-driven history. Where others saw history governed only by causality, with each era simply the product of what came before, we saw a march towards a specific destination. Where others saw civilization only propelled by the past, we claimed to be pulled, as well, by the future.[6]

Suddenly, the world stage contained a nation which believed that there was rhyme, reason and goal to the currents of history; a nation which saw itself traveling towards a predetermined, inevitable end point: the messianic era.

On the other hand, our belief in the inevitability of the messianic era does not diminish our acceptance of the role and responsibility that individuals and communities bear in any given generation. While our nation's destination may be clear, the parameters of the journey towards that destination are not. Within the broad brushstrokes of national preordination we each freely choose the role we will play in our people's unfolding story.

B

The rabbis, however, go even further. In order to preserve the all-important concept of free will within our national journey, they presume flexibility even concerning the preordained elements of our history.

That the Mashiach will arrive, they agree, is clear. *When* he will arrive,[7] however, *how* he will arrive,[8] and, most importantly, *who among us* or among our children will be there to greet him upon his arrival – all these variables are in our hands.

Much of our people's story remains unwritten. We are the authors of that portion of the story.

---

5. Rambam, *Peirush Hamishnayot*, Sanhedrin 10.
6. *Reflections of the Rav*, vol. 2.
7. Talmud Bavli Sanhedrin 98a.
8. Ibid.

C

We can now begin to understand the interplay between free will and predestination as it unfolds in the Yosef story. For while the descent of Avraham's progeny into a foreign land was predicted by God decades before it occurred, the prophecy granted to the patriarch was general in scope. Egypt was never mentioned as the place of exile. The mode by which Avraham's descendants would be exiled was never detailed nor was the exact quality of the servitude they would experience.[9]

Even the minimal details that were clearly preordained were also potentially flexible. God predicted to Avraham, for example, that the period of servitude would last for four hundred years. Our ancestors were actually slaves in Egypt, however, for only two hundred ten years. The rabbis explain the discrepancy by maintaining that the period mentioned in Avraham's prophetic vision began with the birth of Yitzchak (who was, in a sense, an exile, never fully comfortable in his own land).[10] By beginning the count with Yitzchak's birth, God, in his mercy, diminished the pain that his people would endure.

We must accept that, one way the other, our ancestors were destined to spend a period of time as strangers persecuted in a strange land. The story, however, did not have to play out exactly as it did. If sibling hatred and jealousy had not been the catalysts for our exile, perhaps the exile itself would have been less painful.

Far from acting out a predetermined script, Yosef and his brothers wrote their own story, of their own free will, within the context of a larger tale. The story they wrote then reverberated across the years, affecting the lives of all the generations that followed. So too, we, in each era, write our own stories, as we freely determine the roles we will play in the unfolding journey of our nation. The stories we author shape the quality of our days and affect the lives of countless generations to come.

---

9. Bereishit 15:13.
10. Rashi, Bereishit 15:13.

4 Messianic Yichus (Pedigree)

Context

The ancestry of the Mashiach can be traced both to the story of Yehuda and Tamar in Parshat Vayeishev and to the story of Lot's daughters in Parshat Vayeira.

A

Yehuda fails to give his twice widowed daughter-in-law, Tamar, in marriage to his third son, Shela. In response, after years of waiting, Tamar masquerades as a prostitute and seduces her father-in-law. Twin boys, Peretz and Zerach, are born of this union.[1] In the Book of Ruth, Peretz is identified as the ancestor of Boaz, who, in turn, is identified as the ancestor of King David.[2]

According to tradition rooted in the final blessings of the patriarch Yaakov to his sons, the Mashiach is destined to be a descendent of the Davidic dynasty.[3]

B

Decades before the story of Yehuda and Tamar, the daughters of Lot survive the destruction of the evil city of Sodom together with their father. Traumatized by the devastation they have witnessed, Lot's daughters believe they and their father are the only survivors of a cataclysm that has engulfed the entire world.[4] At the suggestion of the older daughter, the two sisters cause their father to become intoxicated and seduce him on two consecutive nights. As a result of these actions, both daughters conceive. The older daughter gives birth to Moab, the

1. Bereishit 38:1–30.
2. Ruth 4:18–22.
3. Bereishit 49:10; Rashi; Targum Onkelos.
4. Midrash Rabba Bereishit 51:8.

ancestor of the Moabite nation, while her younger sister gives birth to Ben-Ammi, the ancestor of the Ammonite nation.[5]

Generations later, the righteous convert, Ruth, from the nation of Moab, marries Boaz (who, as we saw, was a descendent of Yehuda and Tamar). Ruth gives birth to Obed, the grandfather of King David.[6] The union of Boaz and Ruth thus produces the line that will lead to the birth of the Mashiach.

Questions

It seems abundantly strange that the individual destined to be the single most significant figure in our history should himself spring from such humble and even "inappropriate" origins.

What lessons can be learned from the fact that the ancestry of the Mashiach traces back both to an event of incest, on the one hand, and to a union born of a difficult family situation (to say the least), on the other?

How does this Messianic genealogy interface with the concept of *yichus* (pedigree), which seems so well entrenched within our tradition?

Approaches

An examination of the earliest sources within our tradition reveals a fascinating tension between inherited status and earned position.

In each of the three patriarchal families, for example, the eldest son loses his birthright to a younger sibling. Yishmael is overshadowed by Yitzchak,[7] Esav by Yaakov[8] and, as we will see (Vayechi 3, *Approaches* A), Reuven by Yehuda, Levi, and Yosef. The pattern continues when Moshe, as a result of his actions, is selected by God for leadership instead of his older brother, Aharon.

It was apparently self-understood even before the giving of the Torah that the firstborn son of a family inherited specific rights (rights which were later codified in Jewish law). The privilege of leadership, however,

5. Bereishit 19:30–38.
6. Ruth 4:13–17.
7. Bereishit 17:18–19.
8. Ibid., 25:31–34; 27:1–28:4.

had to be earned. If another child within the family was more deserving, he would rise to prominence.

This interplay between privilege of birth and earned position also plays out on a communal level once we enter the national era. Originally, first-born male children were to be given the privilege of serving within the Temple. That privilege, however, was lost during the sin of the golden calf and transferred to the tribe of Levi, who were not complicit in the sin.[9] Even the monarchy, clearly meant to an inherited position, is, centuries later, lost by the first occupant of the throne. When Saul, the first king of Israel, sins, the line of kingship is transferred to David and his descendents.[10] David, himself, interestingly enough, was the youngest of his father's eight sons.[11]

The fact that greatness is not necessarily inherited is dramatically evidenced in the mystery surrounding the sons of Moshe. The two sons of this great leader, Gershom and Eliezer, are mentioned briefly for the purposes of identification early in their lives and then seem to disappear completely from the scene.[12] Although Gershom is cited by the rabbis as playing a minor role in specific later events,[13] the text itself never makes mention of either son again. Compounding the mystery, centuries later the book of Shoftim identifies an individual by the name of Yehonatan the son of Gershom the son of Menashe as the patriarch of a family of idolaters.[14] The rabbis explain that this sinner was actually a descendent of Moshe Rabbeinu.[15] In order to preserve Moshe's honor and yet reflect the truth, the letter *nun* was added to Moshe's name to create the name Menashe.[16] Not only did Moshe's progeny fail to rise to leadership themselves but, according to rabbinic tradition, some of his descendents were actually guilty of the cardinal sin of idolatry.

The story of Moshe's children serves as a sobering reminder that even great personalities are not guaranteed offspring who follow in their footsteps. History is filled, in fact, with numerous examples of children who

9. Bamidbar 3:11–13; Rashi, Bamidbar 3:12.
10. Shmuel I 15:10–11; 16:1, 12–13.
11. Ibid., 16:10–11.
12. Shmot 2:22; 18:3–4.
13. Rashi, Bamidbar 11:27.
14. Shoftim 18:30.
15. Talmud Bavli Bava Batra 109b.
16. Rashi, Shoftim 18:30.

paid a serious price for their parents' communal leadership. The more involved we become in the lives of others, the more careful attention we must pay to our own families, as well.

The same tale, however, carries the encouraging reminder that Torah greatness is not inherited but open to all, regardless of background or origin. Moshe's children do not automatically inherit the mantle of leadership from their father. That mantle is given to Moshe's more deserving student, Yehoshua.

B

Perhaps the greatest proof that an individual's bloodline is no guarantee of accomplishment or contribution can be gleaned from the moment of our nation's birth. As we have noted, early Jewish history unfolds in two major stages. The introductory, patriarchal era ends with the death of Yaakov, while the national era begins with the Exodus from Egypt and the Revelation at Sinai. Revelation, in fact, becomes both the moment of the Jewish nation's birth and the defining event for individual affiliation with that nation.

Who is a Jew? The answer is rooted at Sinai.

Full descendents of Avraham and Sara, who chose not to leave Egypt at the time of the Exodus, disappeared into the mists of history. Even further, a full Hebrew who participated in the Exodus, reached Sinai, yet refused to accept God's law, was also lost to his people forever. Conversely, an individual who was not a Hebrew at all, yet was present at Revelation and accepted the Torah, became a full member of the Jewish nation. Commitment to God's law, not blood relationship, was the defining factor for individual affiliation with our nation at its birth.

Not by accident, therefore, do the rabbis identify the defining moment of Revelation as the basis for the laws of conversion to Judaism. The required steps in the conversion process, they maintain, are derived from the steps experienced by the participants in Revelation at the foot of Sinai.[17] *We are a nation of converts*, each of us, or our ancestors, having undergone the conversion process at Sinai or thereafter. The inception of our Jewishness is not genetically based. Whether we are the blood descendents of the

17. Talmud Bavli Kritot 9a.

patriarchs and matriarchs or their spiritual descendents makes no difference; we are all full members of the Jewish nation.

C

On the other hand, the place of pedigree within Jewish tradition cannot be dismissed.

Certain roles within our tradition are inherited in perpetuity. Once David becomes king, all authentic royalty descends from the Davidic dynasty.[18] All male descendents of Moshe's brother, Aharon, are automatically Kohanim (Priests), while all male descendents of the tribe of Levi are, of course, Leviim (those who serve within the Temple). Even Jewish identity itself is unalterably inherited through one's mother.[19] According to Jewish law, while someone can certainly convert to Judaism, a born or converted Jew cannot "convert out."[20]

D

Clearly, an individual's birth plays a part in determining his or her role and even status within the Jewish nation. That "birthright," however, is only a small piece of the puzzle. Just as the genetic pattern with which we are born provides us with the raw material of our lives, so, too, our birth position is the backdrop upon which we each paint a life picture. Who we ultimately are is much more the product of our own *yichus*, created of our own efforts and striving, than the *yichus* into which we are born.

E

The Mashiach's ancestry is traced to humble origins. They are, however, origins that rise to greatness. Ruth, a Moabite, distinguishes herself through her love, loyalty and kindness when she refuses to abandon her mother-in-law, Naomi, and ultimately converts to Judaism.[21] Yehuda responds to the event with Tamar by admitting his own failings and errors.[22] With this admission, Yehuda takes his first step along the path of responsibility. This

18. Rambam, *Mishneh Torah*, Hilchot Melachim 1:7–10.
19. Talmud Bavli Sanhedrin 44a.
20. Talmud Bavli Kiddushin 66b.
21. Ruth 1:16.
22. Bereishit 38:26.

path will ultimately lead Yehuda to full *tshuva* (remorse and change) for the sale of Yosef as well.[23]

The Mashiach will rise, thus, from the greatest royalty of all: the royalty of individuals who, with strength and effort, transcend difficult circumstances to "make their own *yichus*" as they leave their mark upon the history of our people.

Points to Ponder

A troubling trend within the Jewish community is evidenced by the growing number of single men and women who remain unmarried, unable to find their life partner.

This phenomenon of "singles" is the product of many different causes, some shared with secular society at large, others specific to an observant lifestyle.

One pervasive issue is the unhealthy focus upon "externals" in defining the requirements which often must be met before young men or women will even agree to go out on a first date. Physical attributes, wealth, family pedigree and more are scrutinized with great care while less obvious qualities of personal character are often given short shrift. "Horror stories" abound concerning a *shidduch* (matchmaking) system in which participants are increasingly treated as commodities rather than as whole people.

The example of the Mashiach's pedigree could well serve as a sharp reminder of the perspective which should be regained. Who we are as people goes well beyond the paper resumes that we can produce. In the current atmosphere, the Mashiach's resume would clearly be rejected out of hand.

23. Bereishit 44:18–34.

Miketz

CHAPTER 41:1–44:17

פרק מא:א–מד:יז

Parsha Summary

Cataclysmic changes of fortune…

Yosef languishes in the Egyptian prison for two years. At the end of that period, Pharaoh dreams of seven lean cows consuming seven healthy cows and of seven thin ears of grain consuming seven robust ears.

Deeply troubled by his visions, Pharaoh turns to his advisers but receives no satisfactory interpretation.

The butler, remembering Yosef and his ability to interpret dreams, mentions him to Pharaoh. At the king's command, Yosef is hurried from the dungeon to the palace, where Pharaoh recounts his dreams.

Yosef explains that Pharaoh's dreams are a divinely inspired vision, foretelling seven years of plenty to be followed by seven years of famine. Yosef suggests that the monarch appoint a wise man to supervise the storage of provisions during the years of abundance as reserves for the years of famine.

Pharaoh is so impressed by Yosef's interpretation that he immediately appoints Yosef second-in-command over Egypt with direct responsibility for the collection of food during the years of plenty and the distribution of those provisions during the famine.

Yosef's predictions prove to be accurate as Egypt enjoys seven years of bounty (during which Yosef's two sons Menashe and Ephraim are born) followed by seven years of famine. Yosef faithfully carries out his mission, storing great supplies during the years of plenty as insurance against the shortage that is to follow.

So full are the Egyptian storehouses by the time the famine arrives that people from surrounding countries descend upon Egypt to procure provisions in order to survive the devastating crisis. Among those who travel to Egypt for this purpose are Yosef's brothers (excluding Binyamin), who make the journey at their father's request.

When Yosef's brothers appear before him he immediately recognizes them. The brothers, however, fail to recognize Yosef.

Yosef deliberately conceals his identity from his brothers and begins to put them through a series of grueling experiences. He first accuses them, over their protestations, of spying upon Egypt, and imprisons them for three days. Upon their release, Yosef informs his brothers that he will keep one of them in prison while the others return to Canaan with their purchased provisions. He instructs them only to return with their missing brother, Binyamin, in tow. Binyamin's presence will serve as proof of their veracity. Yosef then imprisons Shimon and surreptitiously places the money that the brothers used towards the purchase of provisions back in their bags. As they travel towards Canaan, the brothers discover the money in their bags and are struck by the fear that Yosef will accuse them of theft when they return to Egypt.

Upon their arrival in Canaan, the brothers relate their experiences to Yaakov. In spite of Reuven's attempts to convince him, the patriarch refuses to allow Binyamin to descend to Egypt. When the famine worsens, however, Yehuda is successful in persuading his father to relent. Accompanied by their youngest brother, Binyamin, and armed with gifts and double payment for provisions, the brothers nervously make their way back to Egypt.

The brothers are shocked when, upon their return to Egypt, they are escorted to Yosef's home and treated with great honor. When they express their concerns, Yosef's servant tells them not to worry about the money that they had found in their bags after their first visit to Egypt. Yosef arrives and treats them to a feast.

Yosef instructs his servants to fill his brother's bags with provisions and to, once again, return their money by placing it in their bags. He also instructs his servants to surreptitiously place his silver goblet in Binyamin's bag.

The next morning the brothers begin their journey back to Canaan. No sooner do they exit the city, however, than Yosef instructs his servants to chase them down and accuse them of theft. When the brothers protest their innocence, a search of their possessions reveals Yosef's goblet in Binyamin's bag. In shock, the brothers are led back to Yosef, where Yehuda offers all the brothers as slaves. Yosef, however, responds that Binyamin alone will remain as a slave while the others will return in peace to their father.

1 What Frightens a King?

Context

After dreaming of seven lean cows consuming seven healthy cows and of seven thin ears of grain consuming seven robust ears, Pharaoh awakens deeply troubled. He commands "all of the sorcerers of Egypt and all of its wise men"[1] to interpret his visions but receives no satisfactory response.

The butler recalls Yosef's ability to interpret dreams and mentions him to the king. Pharaoh orders Yosef released from prison and brought to the palace. Pharaoh then repeats the content of his dreams to Yosef.[2]

Questions

Why is Pharaoh so deeply troubled by his dreams?

Does the text offer any hint as to the source of Pharaoh's fears?

Approaches

A

The narrative before us is strangely repetitive. First the text describes Pharaoh's dreams in detail as they occur. Then the dreams are described, again in detail, when the king recounts them for Yosef. The Torah could simply have stated, "And Pharaoh told the content of his dreams to Yosef." Why the redundancy?

The Torah, as noted before (see Bereishit 3 and Chayei Sara 3), never repeats a conversation or an event without reason. In this case, the repetition within the text provides a glimpse into Pharaoh's mind. When Pharaoh

1. Bereishit 41:8.
2. Ibid., 41:1–24.

speaks to Yosef, he conveys not only his dreams but his *perception* of those dreams.

Specifically, two addenda appended by Pharaoh to his first vision may provide the key to the fears of this mighty king.

1. The king dreams: "And behold out of the river emerged seven cows, of beautiful appearance and healthy flesh.... And behold seven other cows emerged out of the river after them, poor of appearance and gaunt of flesh..."[3]

The king recounts: "And behold out of the river emerged seven cows, of healthy flesh and beautiful form.... And behold seven other cows emerged after them, scrawny, and of very poor form and emaciated flesh. *Never have I seen such in all the land of Egypt for badness.*"[4]

Pharaoh is clearly disturbed by the possibility that "scrawny, emaciated cows" could even appear in Egypt at all. Like so many monarchs before and after him, Pharaoh prefers to live in a fantasy world of absolute power and success. There is no place in the king's lush, rich empire for "weak cows." Pharaoh, therefore, emphatically declares that no such cows have ever before appeared in his land, as he desperately attempts to avoid the ramifications of his vision.

2. The king dreams: "And the seven cows of poor appearance and gaunt flesh consumed the seven cows of beautiful appearance and good health, and Pharaoh awoke."[5]

The king recounts: "And the emaciated, inferior cows consumed the first seven healthy cows. *And they came inside them and it was not apparent that they came inside them – for their appearance was as inferior as before; and I awoke.*"[6]

The world in which Pharaoh lives is governed by clear rules. In this world nations conquer other nations with regularity. Through subterfuge and cunning, the seemingly weak can even defeat the seemingly strong. The king can therefore accept the possibility of lean cows eating healthy cows.

What Pharaoh cannot accept, however, is the possibility that the victor in a battle should remain unchanged. In the king's world, conquest invariably bestows upon the victor increased physical power and strength.

3. Ibid., 41:2–3.
4. Ibid., 41:18–19.
5. Ibid., 41:4.
6. Ibid., 41:20–21.

This rule is the basis of Pharaoh's own supremacy. When, in his vision, the lean cows remain visibly unaffected after consuming the healthy cows, Pharaoh's world is threatened and he awakens abruptly, sorely troubled and distraught.

B

Yosef sets the king's mind at ease by explaining both the existence of the lean cows and their unchanged status in symbolic terms. Pharaoh's visions, he asserts, represent natural challenges which can be overcome through proper planning.

Little does Pharaoh know, however, that his fears are actually well-founded. There is, unbeknownst to Pharaoh and perhaps even to Yosef, a hidden subtext to these visions. Pharaoh is about to be threatened in ways he could scarcely begin to imagine.

The king's dreams set in motion a series of events which eventually give rise to the birth of a unique nation within his very realm. This eternal Jewish nation will not be bound by the rules governing Pharaoh's world. Spiritual fortitude will overcome physical strength as this seemingly weak people outlasts the most powerful empires in the history of mankind. Pharaoh's kingdom will be only the first to fall in the face of the Jews' march across the face of history.

The victorious Jewish nation, however, will not change overtly for generations. We will measure our success, not in terms of increased physical strength, but in the unbroken maintenance and development of our enduring spiritual heritage.

"Lean cows" will consume "robust cows." The seemingly weak will overcome the strong, yet remain unchanged.

Pharaoh's world is about to crumble; he has good reason to be troubled by his dreams.

2 One Dream, Two Dreams

Context

Pharaoh is so impressed by Yosef's interpretation of his dreams that he immediately appoints him second-in-command over the Egyptian Empire with special responsibility for the collection of food during the years of plenty and the distribution of those provisions during the years of famine.[1]

Questions

Why does Pharaoh believe Yosef?

What convinces the king that the interpretations offered by this lowly Hebrew slave are accurate – so accurate that he acts upon them with startling decisiveness, abruptly assigning Yosef to a position of almost unimaginable authority?

These questions are compounded by the rabbinic assertion that Pharaoh was actually presented with other options. The rabbis explain the phrase "but none could interpret them *for Pharaoh*"[2] to mean that numerous interpretations were initially suggested by the Egyptian sorcerers and wise men, but Pharaoh rejected them all.[3]

In what ways were Yosef's suggestions different?

Approaches

A

Among the answers offered by classical sources are two approaches first found within the Midrash:

1. Bereishit 41:37–43.
2. Ibid., 41:8.
3. Rashi, Bereishit 41:8.

1. *Pharaoh actually witnessed, in his vision, both dream and interpretation.*

Upon awakening, the king deliberately withheld the true interpretation from his advisers in order to test them by determining the veracity of their explanations. He therefore rejected all the interpretations offered until he recognized Yosef's as correct.[4]

Alternatively, Pharaoh forgot the meaning of his dream upon awakening. Subliminally, however, Pharaoh remembered the truth and was able to recognize it when he heard it.[5]

2. *Pharaoh gravitated towards an explanation that offered positive, concrete suggestions for the future.*[6]

The Midrash maintains that each interpretation initially offered by Pharaoh's advisers was extremely bleak in tone. Some predicted, for example, that the king would father seven daughters who would subsequently die. Others maintained that Pharaoh would conquer seven provinces that would then rebel against his rule. Pharaoh was unwilling to accept any of these pessimistic predictions.[7]

We can only imagine the king's relief, therefore, when Yosef presented him with a scenario which could be controlled.

B

Many later scholars build upon these original Midrashic proposals. Others offer their own explanations for Pharaoh's unhesitating acceptance of Yosef's words.

Surprisingly, however, all of these explanations may be unnecessary. The text of the Torah actually offers a solution of its own. A consistent pattern in the narrative reveals a tantalizing and puzzling *pashut pshat* possibility: Pharaoh believed Yosef because *only Yosef was willing to validate the king's conviction* that his two dreams were really one.

Consider the textual interplay:

"And Pharaoh awoke and behold it was *a dream*."[8]

---

4. Midrash Hagadol Bereishit 41:37.
5. Midrash Sechel Tov Bereishit 41:37.
6. Ibid.
7. Midrash Rabba Bereishit 89:6.
8. Bereishit 41:7.

"And Pharaoh related *his dream* to them (his advisers) but none could *interpret them* to Pharaoh."[9]

"And Pharaoh said to Yosef: 'I have dreamt *a dream*, but no one can *interpret it.*'"[10]

"And Pharaoh said to Yosef, '*In my dream* I am standing…'"[11]

"And I (Pharaoh) saw *in my dream*…"[12]

"And Yosef said to Pharaoh, '*Pharaoh's dream is one*…'"[13]

The pattern is too obvious to ignore. For some reason, Pharaoh desperately insists upon clinging to a belief in a unified, single dream. When his advisers suggest otherwise, he rejects their interpretations out of hand. Only Yosef's explanation, which correlates to the king's own version of the events, is accepted.

C

The obvious question, however, remains. Why was the king so intent upon seeing his dream as a unified whole? What was so frightening about the possibility of two dreams? While the text clearly points to Pharaoh's stubborn insistence on a single vision, no reason is given for his point of view.

The Torah is telling us something important, but we are not quite sure what.

D

The answer may lie in the mindset of powerful despots from the time of Pharaoh onward. Deliberately isolated and insulated from surrounding reality, these rulers each insist upon living in a world of their own design.

Within these buffered worlds, nothing is more threatening than complexity.

To the king, existence is painted in black and white: straightforward problems, simple solutions. Whatever Pharaoh desires rules the day. Issues are disposed of through the thrust of the sword, enemies dispatched without much deliberation or hesitation.

9. Ibid., 41:8.
10. Ibid., 41:15.
11. Ibid., 41:17.
12. Ibid., 41:22.
13. Ibid., 41:25.

[Note: The paradigm of such a despot emerges centuries later in the person of King Ahashverosh of the Purim story. This monarch builds his corrupt reign upon conscious indifference to the pain and turbulence surrounding his palace.[14] Once again, an intriguing connection can be drawn between the story of Yosef and the Purim narrative (see Vayeishev 1, *Approaches* c).]

Pharaoh is content when he dreams simple, uncluttered dreams in which the challenges and necessary responses are straightforward and clear.

Suddenly, however, into Pharaoh's fantasy world intrudes the possibility of two conflicting dreams. Perhaps the combined message of these dreams is complicated, belying the possibility of easy solution. The king is beside himself with worry; his carefully constructed existence may now be facing challenges beyond his control. He turns to his advisers for reassurance, only to find his worst fears underscored. "Two dreams," they say, "the king has experienced two dreams."

Increasingly troubled, Pharaoh clings at straws. He releases an unknown Hebrew slave from prison on the small chance that perhaps, just perhaps, this slave will provide an answer.

Pharaoh conveys his dreams to Yosef; Yosef begins to speak…

"Pharaoh's dream is one…"[15] Right from the start, Yosef tells the king exactly what the king wants to hear.

What enables this brilliant young diplomat to respond so clearly and immediately to Pharaoh's concerns? Is his recognition of the dreams as one vision powered by divine spirit – the same divine spirit that allows him to perceive their prophetic content? Or, is Yosef simply so personally talented and astute that he naturally recognizes the king's fears and capitalizes upon them?

We may never know where Yosef's natural ability ends and God's supernatural assistance begins. Yosef's successes, throughout his life, are clearly produced through a marriage of these two forces. One thing, however, seems clear: Yosef's uncanny ability to respond to Pharaoh's deep-seated fears of complexity helps this slave earn a position of almost unlimited power in an abrupt leap from servitude to supremacy.

---

14. Megillat Esther 3:15, 4:2, 4:11, 8:3.
15. Bereishit 41:25.

E

One final, beautifully ironic point can be made. Pharaoh is not the only player in the Yosef story to dream two similar dreams.

The Torah relates that Yosef himself, while still in his father's home, dreams of gleaning wheat in the field with his brothers. Abruptly, Yosef's sheaf stands and his brother's sheaves bow. Yosef then dreams again. In this vision, the sun, moon and stars all bow down directly to him.[16]

Separated by years, two sets of similar dreams are experienced, one set by Yosef and one set by Pharaoh. There is, however, a critical difference. In contrast to Pharaoh, whose insistence upon a single, unified vision seems almost pathological, Yosef readily accepts the reality of two visions.

Evidence of this acceptance is clearly reflected in the text.

The second of Yosef's visions is introduced by the phrase "and he [Yosef] dreamt *another dream*."[17] Additionally, Yosef himself tells his brothers, "Behold, I dreamt *another dream*..."[18]

Yosef embraces the very complexity that Pharaoh later eschews. This scion of the patriarchal era fully understands that the world is not painted in black and white, but in shades of grey. Yosef's early acceptance of multiple dreams foreshadows his approach to the challenges soon to come. In short order, he will begin his wrenching journey from servitude to power – a journey that will be understood by Yosef as unfolding on multiple levels of meaning at once (see Vayeishev 1, *Approaches* 4).

The centuries since Yosef and Pharaoh have seen innumerable world powers rise and fall, victims of their own inability to adapt to complex, changing circumstances. These powers shone brightly in one-dimensional worlds of their own creation, only to falter and fail when those worlds collided with the ever-shifting forces of reality.

Through it all, the Jewish people, the spiritual heirs of Yosef, have endured against all odds. Our halachic tradition, with its unique blend of constancy and adaptability, has allowed us to embrace and sanctify a complex world while meeting its challenges head on.

The world of Pharaoh is no more; the world of Yosef endures.

---

16. Ibid., 37:5–11.
17. Ibid., 37:9.
18. Ibid.

3 What Gives Yosef the Right?

Context

At their father's request, Yosef's brothers descend to Egypt to procure food in the face of the famine that has affected the entire region. Together with other foreigners, they appear before Yosef, who is in charge of the sale and distribution of stored provisions.

Yosef immediately recognizes his brothers. They, however, fail to recognize him.

Deliberately concealing his true identity, Yosef proceeds to put his brothers through a series of grueling experiences.

Creating a sequence of manipulations clearly designed to keep his brothers off balance, Yosef accuses his brothers of being spies; allows them to return home with provisions but insists that they are not to reappear in Egypt unless they bring their younger brother, Binyamin, with them; imprisons his brother, Shimon, pending the brothers' return; surreptitiously returns the money that the brothers had used to buy provisions (causing them to fear that they will be accused of theft as soon as they reappear in Egypt); wines and dines his brothers in royal fashion the moment they return from Canaan; orders his servants to hide his silver goblet in Binyamin's sack; allows the brothers to begin the journey back to Canaan only to immediately order their pursuit; instructs his officers to accuse Binyamin of theft upon the "discovery" of the goblet in Binyamin's sack and, finally, threatens to imprison Binyamin while allowing the other brothers to return home.[1]

Questions

What gives Yosef the right to torment his brothers?

1. Bereishit 42:1–44:17.

Is Yosef simply seeking revenge against his brothers for their role in his sale into slavery? If so, could he not have exacted that revenge in a much simpler, more straightforward fashion?

Even if Yosef wishes to punish those brothers culpable in his sale, why involve Binyamin, who did not participate in that tragic event at all? Why, in addition, torment his father, Yaakov, by imprisoning Shimon and by forcing Yaakov to allow Binyamin to travel to Egypt?

Finally, how do these apparently vengeful acts correlate with our view of Yosef as *Yosef Hatzadik*, "Yosef the Righteous" (see Vayeishev 1)?

Approaches

A

Two distinct approaches are suggested by the classical commentaries.

1. *Yosef feels compelled to bring his dreams to fruition.*

The Ramban, among others, claims that Yosef, at this point in his life, does not see himself as a free agent. Instead, he is motivated by what he believes to be a divinely ordained mission.

Remembering his early dreams in the home of his father (see Vayeishev 1, *Context*; Miketz 2, *Approaches* E), Yosef understands those visions as predicting his ascension to leadership over the members of his own family. He further believes that to secure his family's future he must now orchestrate the realization of God's will as indicated within the dreams.

Yosef, therefore, sets out upon a course of action which unfolds in two stages:

First, he manipulates events so that all his brothers (including Binyamin) descend to Egypt, where they are forced to acknowledge Yosef's supremacy. This acknowledgment marks the fulfillment of Yosef's first dream, in which his brothers' sheaves of wheat bowed down to his.[2] Yosef then arranges for the descent of his father's entire family to Egypt, bringing about the realization of his second dream, in which the sun, moon and stars bowed down directly to Yosef.[3]

As proof of Yosef's motivation, the Ramban points to the textual description of Yosef's automatic internal reaction when he first sees his broth-

2. Bereishit 37:7.
3. Ibid., 37:9.

ers: "And Yosef recognized his brothers but they did not recognize him. *And Yosef remembered the dreams that he had dreamt of them*, and he said to them: 'You are spies! To see the land's nakedness have you come!'"[4]

The text seems abundantly strange. Yosef is suddenly and unexpectedly reunited with his brothers and all he can think about are his dreams? Surely, if Yosef's mind was on vengeance, his brothers' appearance would inspire other memories – of his torment at their hands, of their callous cruelty towards him. Why then does the Torah instead state that Yosef remembers "the dreams that he dreamt of them"?

The text proves, claims the Ramban, that from the moment he meets his brothers, Yosef's actions are motivated by his desperate desire to bring his dreams to fruition. Yosef sees himself as God's emissary, put in place to effect his family's salvation.[5] Within the context of that divinely ordained role, he feels obligated to bring God's plan, as mapped out within his own early dreams, to completion.[6]

2. Other commentaries suggest that Yosef deliberately punishes his brothers, measure for measure, for their crimes against him. These punishments enable his brothers to properly atone and eventually repent for their earlier transgressions.[7]

Certainly, by the time all of Yosef's manipulations reach their climax, the brothers are placed in the only situation where complete repentance for their crime against Yosef is possible. As the Rambam explains in his discussion on the laws of repentance: "What constitutes complete repentance? If an individual is confronted by a situation in which he sinned before, but this time does not sin…"[8]

By the end of Parshat Miketz, Yosef threatens his brother Binyamin with imprisonment while allowing the others to return to Canaan. The scene is clearly constructed to re-create the moment of Yosef's sale into servitude. Of all the brothers, Binyamin is most like Yosef in that he, too, is the son of Yaakov's beloved Rachel. In addition, Binyamin has become, in Yosef's absence, his father's favored son.[9] Once again, the brothers have

---

4. Ibid., 42:8–9.
5. Bereishit 45:5.
6. Ramban, Bereishit 42:9,
7. Abravanel, Bereishit 42:7; Kli Yakar, Bereishit 42:7.
8. Rambam, *Mishneh Torah*, Hilchot Tshuva 2:1.
9. Bereishit 42:4.

the opportunity to turn their back on one of their own, consigning him to the terrible fate of slavery.

When Yehuda, the very man who had suggested Yosef's sale, courageously refuses to allow Binyamin to remain behind, the transformation in the brothers becomes complete. Yosef recognizes that they have fully atoned for their crime and he is moved to reveal his true identity.[10]

B

A significant objection can be raised, however, to both approaches suggested above. Simply put, who appointed Yosef God? Who assigned him either the task of bringing his dreams to fruition or of orchestrating his brothers' repentance?

Countless prophets were granted heavenly visions yet remained content to allow the fulfillment of those visions to come about at God's hands. Punishment, atonement and repentance are issues between a man and his Maker. By what right does Yosef assume the prerogative of manipulating events so that his brothers will repent?

C

A fascinating twist on the classical approaches is suggested by the nineteenth-century German scholar Rabbi Shimshon Raphael Hirsch. Hirsch maintains that Yosef's true motivation is a desire to create a new relationship with his brothers.

Yosef, however, recognizes that: "Their inner feelings towards one another would have to become quite different from what they formerly were. Otherwise, an intimate relationship would never be able to be reestablished, and even if outwardly the family were to be reunited, the family would be lost to him [Yosef], and he to the family."[11]

Yosef knew that, were he to reveal himself immediately to his brothers, their shared past would haunt them all forever. Yosef would always see his brothers as the callous criminals who facilitated his sale into slavery. The brothers, on the other hand, whenever they saw Yosef, would remember his cries from the pit. They would never fully trust his feelings towards them, nor would they move past their own overwhelming sense of guilt.

---

10. Bereishit 44:18–45:3.
11. Rabbi Shimshon Raphael Hirsch, Bereishit 42:9.

Something dramatic had to cause a change.

Yosef, therefore, sets about creating a new reality, a foundation upon which a future relationship can be built. He manipulates events so that his brothers are faced with the same circumstances they faced at the time of his sale. When the brothers risk their own freedom to save Binyamin, they prove to Yosef and to themselves that they have changed; they no longer could cause or even allow a brother's pain. Yosef realizes that the time has come to begin anew, for now he and his brothers will be able to view themselves and each other differently.

Yosef finally reveals his true identity and Yaakov's sons begin their long journey towards healing.

Points to Ponder

Often, Jews are criticized for failing to move past the trauma of past tragedies and suffering. With a seeming sense of paranoia, we tend to greet each world event with the parochial questions: "Is it good for the Jews? How will these events affect us?"

Our posture can be well understood, however, in light of the Yosef story.

How can we trust a world that seems unchanged? The rising tide of anti-Semitism sweeping across Europe, bringing in its wake propaganda and physical attacks eerily reminiscent of the years before the Holocaust; the fanatic hatred of Islamic fundamentalists towards the State of Israel and the Jewish people in general; the readiness of nations to appease tyrannical regimes such as Iran rather than face them down; the inability of the world to halt clear cases of genocide such as those which took place in Rwanda, in Bosnia-Herzegovina, and, more recently, in Darfur all drive home the clear message that the world community is yet willing to tolerate the demonization and destruction of entire peoples.

The Jewish nation would be pleased to move past the pain and suspicion that has, for centuries, characterized our relationship with the peoples around us. There must, however, be a foundation for a new relationship. Tragically, to this day, that foundation remains conspicuously absent.

Vayigash
CHAPTER 44:18–47:27

ויגש
פרק מד:יח–מז:כז

Parsha Summary

A pretense ends and a journey begins…

Faced with the impending imprisonment of Binyamin, Yehuda confronts Yosef in defense of their youngest brother. Arguing eloquently, Yehuda again stresses that he has assumed personal responsibility for Binyamin's safety.

Yosef, moved by Yehuda's heartfelt pleas, is unable to maintain his masquerade. He tearfully reveals himself to his brothers and inquires after his father's welfare. Yosef reassures his stunned brothers, telling them that it was God's will that he descend to Egypt to act as provider for the entire family.

Yosef instructs his brothers to return to their father with news of Yosef's survival and success. He further urges them, with Pharaoh's approval, to bring Yaakov and his entire household to Egypt. If the extended family settles nearby in the region of Goshen, Yosef argues, he will be able to provide for its members during the years of continuing famine.

The brothers return to Yaakov laden with wagons bearing gifts and with the news that Yosef is still alive. After initial disbelief, and upon seeing the wealth that Pharaoh and Yosef have sent back with the brothers, Yaakov comes to the realization that his beloved son has indeed survived. Excitedly, the patriarch gathers his household and begins the descent to Egypt. God appears to Yaakov in the midst of the journey with a message of reassurance.

Yaakov arrives in Goshen for an emotional reunion with Yosef. Yosef prepares a delegation of his brothers for an interview with Pharaoh and, following that meeting, also brings his father for an audience with the king.

Yosef continues to provide for the citizens of Egypt in the face of the ongoing famine. At the same time, he acts to increase Pharaoh's wealth and power.

Yaakov and his entire family settle and thrive in the region of Goshen.

1 Why Didn't Yosef "Phone Home"?

Context

After thirteen years of slavery, Yosef experiences a dramatic transformation when he interprets Pharaoh's dreams and is appointed viceroy over Egypt. Yosef serves in this position through the seven years of plenty and into the years of famine before being reunited with his family.

Questions

Why doesn't Yosef contact his father and family after his rise to prominence in Egypt? As the Ramban asks: "One can only wonder.... After Yosef's multi-year sojourn in Egypt, how could he not have sent even one letter to his father to inform him and to comfort him? After all, Egypt is only a six-day journey from Hevron. Respect for his father would have justified even a year's journey!"[1]

Yosef's failure to contact his father may well be the most difficult issue arising out of the entire Yosef story. Surely Yosef must have known that his father had been mourning his loss over the years. How could he, then, have been so callous as to neglect to communicate with Yaakov concerning his survival and unimaginable success in Egypt?

Approaches

A

The Ramban offers a consistent approach to Yosef's seemingly strange behavior: the same forces that shape Yosef's actions towards his brothers after they appear before him in Egypt (see Miketz 3) also prevent Yosef from contacting his father.

1. Ramban, Bereishit 42:9.

Yosef believes that he is not a free agent, but rather the divinely chosen instrument for his family's salvation. He further believes that his early dreams in his father's home were a reflection of God's plan and that he is now obligated to bring that plan to fruition. He cannot, therefore, contact his father prematurely. He must wait until the time comes when the dreams can be fulfilled.[2]

The same objections that were raised, however, to the Ramban's explanation of Yosef's treatment of his brothers (see Miketz 3, *Approaches* A) can be raised here, as well. Who appointed Yosef as God's agent concerning the fulfillment of the dreams? As Rabbi Yitzchak Arama maintains: "As for the dreams…leave it to He Who sends them to make them come true!"[3]

B

The contemporary Israeli biblical scholar Rabbi Yoel Bin-Nun offers a bold, original and detailed explanation for Yosef's silence towards his father. Building upon hints in the text, Rabbi Bin-Nun postulates that Yosef had no way of knowing that his brothers had deceived his father with the lie that Yosef had been devoured by a wild beast. *For all Yosef knew, Yaakov never believed him to be dead.*

Yosef was therefore plagued for years with the question: "Where is my father? Why has no one come to look for me?"

The close distance between Egypt and Canaan now works in the opposite direction. Certainly Yaakov had the wherewithal to search for his son. Why then, Yosef wonders, has no search taken place? Eventually Yosef's questions concerning his father's silence lead to deeper suspicions. Why, he wonders, did his father send him to seek his brothers in the first place? Wasn't he aware of the hatred that the brothers harbored towards Yosef and the resultant potential danger?

Yosef comes to the erroneous, yet, to him, inescapable, conclusion that Yaakov was somehow complicit in the brothers' actions. In Yosef's mind, someone – perhaps the brothers, perhaps Leah, perhaps God himself – had clearly persuaded Yaakov to cast Yosef off from the family, as Yishmael and Esav had been cast off in earlier generations.

After years of torment, Yosef arrives at a grudging acceptance of his

2. Ibid.
3. Akeidat Yitzchak 29:9.

fate. He determines to live according to the traditions of his family even while he accepts his severance from them. This sentiment is expressed in the name he gives to his oldest son: "And Yosef called the name of his firstborn Menashe, for 'God has made me forget all my hardship and my father's entire household.'"[4]

When Yosef's brothers suddenly and unknowingly appear before him, he is driven by a desire to determine the truth. All of his actions from this point on are designed to obtain information concerning his father's apparent rejection of him. Finally, Yehuda, rising in defense of Binyamin, inadvertently proclaims what Yosef has, for years, desperately desired to hear: "Your servant, my father, said to us: 'You know that my wife [Rachel] bore me two [sons]. One has left me and I presumed – alas – *he has surely been torn to pieces* and I have not seen him since.'"[5]

Suddenly Yosef realizes that, all these years, his father has assumed him dead; he has not been rejected, after all. Moved by uncontrollable emotion, he reveals himself to his brothers.[6]

C

Finally, a careful reading of the text may reveal a totally different explanation for Yosef's silence towards his father.

Yosef does not contact his father, after ascending to the position of Egyptian viceroy, *simply because he cannot.* Any attempt at such contact would have endangered not only his newfound status, but his life.

In fact, a clear case can be made that Yosef's most dangerous period in Egypt actually begins when Pharaoh appoints him viceroy over the Egyptian Empire. At that point, Yosef enters a court of intrigue, a palace that has already seen the king's butler and baker imprisoned, each accused of trying to undermine the king.

Yosef is suddenly surrounded by powerful figures who resent his authority, even as they pine for their own advancement. He finds himself in a world where he can trust no one, where any messenger he sends to Canaan

4. Bereishit 41:51.
5. Ibid., 44:27–28.
6. Rabbi Yoel Bin-Nun, "A Tragic Misunderstanding: Why Did Joseph Not Send Word to His Father?" translated by Dov Lappin (Ein Tzurim: Yeshivat Hakibbutz Hadati, 2002).

might simply turn around and report him to a member of the court or even to the king, raising accusations of dual loyalty against the new viceroy.

A series of hints in the text serves to underscore Yosef's emergent vulnerability:

1. The first indication of potential trouble emerges at the moment of Yosef's appointment to the position of viceroy. After hearing Yosef's interpretation of his dream, Pharaoh immediately turns to those present and exclaims: "Could we find another such as him – a man in whom there is the spirit of God?"[7]

Pharaoh's public reaction shows remarkable cunning. This is an extremely delicate moment for the king. He is about to leapfrog a lowly Hebrew slave above all of his officers and advisers. Pharaoh therefore turns to all those present in the palace and effectively says to them: *You have seen what I have seen and heard what I have heard. Is there any among us more talented or capable than this Hebrew slave? Were any of you, other than he, able to interpret my dream correctly? Speak up now – "could we find another man such as him…?" Speak up now or forever hold your peace.*

In a brilliant tactical move, Pharaoh involves his own officers in Yosef's selection so that it will not come back to haunt him. We can be certain, however, that Yosef's appointment did not sit well with the many advisers present who desired their own advancement.

2. Yosef's isolation from those around him, even after his ascension to power, is driven home in a powerfully poignant scene as the narrative continues. When Yosef's brothers return to Egypt a second time, Yosef surprises them by inviting them to a meal in his palace. The Torah describes the seating arrangement at this state dinner: "And they served him [Yosef] separately, and them [the brothers] separately, and the Egyptians who ate with him separately, for the Egyptians could not bear to eat food with the Hebrews, it being an abomination to the Egyptians."[8]

The Egyptians, apparently, are not only unwilling to eat with Yosef's brothers, the foreigners, but *they are unwilling to eat with Yosef, as well.* In their eyes, Yosef remains a "Hebrew."

In this wrenching scene which seems to mirror his life, Yosef sits alone.

7. Bereishit 41:37.
8. Ibid., 43:32.

He is neither one with his brothers nor one with his Egyptian neighbors; he remains, as always, the ultimate outsider (See Vayechi 2, *Approaches* B).

3. Later, when Yosef finally reveals himself to his brothers the Torah offers a startling observation: "And the news was heard in the house of Pharaoh: 'Yosef's brothers have come!' *And it was pleasing in the eyes of Pharaoh and in the eyes of his servants.*"[9]

Why would Yosef's reunion with his brothers be a source of satisfaction to Pharaoh and to the Egyptians?

The Ramban and the Sforno each suggest an answer.

According to the Ramban, Yosef's presumed lowly origins were a continuing source of embarrassment to the Egyptians. "Now, however, with the arrival of these distinguished brothers it became clear that he [Yosef] was fit to serve kings."[10]

The Sforno, on the other hand, maintains that the Egyptians regarded Yosef as a foreigner whose loyalty to Egypt was in doubt. Reassured by the prospect of Yosef's family remaining in Egypt, they now believed that Yosef would "govern not as a foreign leader but as a citizen who intends to settle in the land together with his children."[11]

The common denominator between these two interpretations is the recognition of inherent weakness in Yosef's position in Egypt before the appearance of his brothers.

4. The full extent of Yosef's vulnerability is only revealed, however, in the negotiations surrounding his father's request to be buried in the Cave of Machpeila in Israel. As we will see in our discussions of Parshat Vayechi (see Vayechi 1), Yaakov's seemingly simple deathbed request puts Yosef, for all of his power, in a position of great danger. The Egyptian viceroy will have to call upon all of his diplomatic skills in order to safely negotiate the fulfillment of his father's wishes.

D

Life was not simple for Yosef even after his rise to authority in Egypt. His vulnerability may well have constrained him from contacting Yaakov for years. Only once his brothers descend to Egypt, and the opportunity to

9. Ibid., 45:16.
10. Ramban, Bereishit 45:16.
11. Sforno, Bereishit 45:16.

safely move his family presents itself, can Yosef finally reach out to his beloved father.

Points to Ponder

We are reminded, once again, that the stories in the Torah are not to be seen as "fairy tales" but as complex narratives concerning complex people. Yosef's tenuous position in Egypt stands as a clear reminder of our own diaspora experience. No matter how successful we may be in any given society, no matter how high we may rise, our position is never certain. Outside the Land of Israel, we remain, like Yosef, strangers in a strange land.

2 What's in a Name?

Context

Although Yaakov's name is "changed" to Yisrael twice in Parshat Vayishlach – once by a mysterious adversary (see Vayishlach 2, *Approaches* D) and once by God himself – the name Yaakov remains in use. The Torah refers to the last patriarch at times as Yaakov and at times as Yisrael.

A particularly glaring example of this name fluctuation is found in Parshat Vayigash when Yaakov receives word of Yosef's survival and begins his descent to Egypt. Within the span of eleven sentences the patriarch is referred to as Yaakov twice, then as Yisrael three times and then again as Yaakov four times.

Questions

Other divinely ordained name changes of the patriarchal era (Avram to Avraham, Sarai to Sara) are permanent; why not Yaakov's?

The etymology of the names indicates that "Yaakov" connotes struggle while "Yisrael" reflects supremacy. Is there any pattern, however, to the name fluctuation in the text? Under what conditions will the Torah refer to the last patriarch as Yaakov and under what conditions as Yisrael?

Can the name variation add to our understanding of specific biblical passages such as the section in Parshat Vayigash dealing with Yaakov's descent to Egypt?

Approaches

A number of classical scholars weigh in concerning Yaakov's "impermanent" name change.

A

Some authorities claim that the altering of Yaakov's name remains unfinished because, in his case, the phenomenon is not personal but prophetic. The name fluctuation reflects the impending historical journey of his descendents, a journey that will be marked by times of struggle (Yaakov) as well as periods of triumph (Yisrael).

The Sforno, for example, suggests that Yaakov's full transformation to Yisrael must wait until the end of days. This scholar interprets God's proclamation to the patriarch in Parshat Vayishlach as follows:

"Your name is Yaakov. No longer will your name be called Yaakov but Yisrael will be your name."[1] *For now your name remains Yaakov as you continue to live a life marked by struggle with those around you. The time will come, however, at the end of man's historical passage, when you will truly be Yisrael; when you will lead the remnants of the nations towards an understanding of the Lord....*

"And he [God] called his name Yisrael."[2] *I bless you, however, with a glimmer of supremacy in your lifetime; as the name Yisrael takes hold, on some level, even now.*[3]

B

The Chizkuni offers a different explanation for the retention of the name Yaakov. He explains that the total uprooting of that name would have lent credence to Esav's accusation against his brother: "Is he not rightly called Yaakov? For he has deceived me twice."[4]

Through a play on words, Esav suggests that the very root of the name Yaakov means deceit. To counter that claim, and to show that no shame is to be attached to Yaakov's name or actions, God leaves the name in place even after the introduction of the name Yisrael.[5]

C

The Ohr Hachaim maintains that the earlier name changes of Avram to Avraham and Sarai to Sara were not really "name changes" at all, but enhancements. In these cases only one letter of each name was changed and the original titles remained embedded in the new ones. Names mystically

1. Bereishit 35: 10.
2. Ibid.
3. Sforno, Bereishit 35:10.
4. Bereishit 27:36.
5. Chizkuni, Bereishit 35:10.

reflect the souls of their owners. The enhancement of Avram's name to Avraham and Sarai's to Sara, therefore, marked the spiritual growth and development of the first patriarch and matriarch.

In Yaakov's case, however, the total name transformation from Yaakov to Yisrael would have entailed the eradication of his first name. Such an act would have symbolized the rejection of Yaakov's spiritual development to this point. To negate this rejection, the name Yaakov remains partially in use.[6]

D

Perhaps the most powerful and poignant explanation for Yaakov's incomplete name change, however, is the one closest to *pashut pshat*:

The names Yaakov and Yisrael are used interchangeably to distinguish between the vastly different emotions and experiences that course through the life of the third patriarch.

In his turbulent life, buffeted by events so often beyond his control, the last patriarch is, at times, Yaakov, struggling and downtrodden, and, at times, Yisrael, triumphant and victorious.

E

Nowhere is this distinction more clearly reflected than in Parshat Vayigash as Yaakov reacts to the news of Yosef's survival and begins his descent to Egypt:

> And they [Yosef's brothers] ascended from Egypt and they came to the land of Canaan, to their father Yaakov.
>
> And they told him, saying, "Yosef is still alive and he is the ruler over all the land of Egypt"…and the spirit of Yaakov, their father, was revived.
>
> And Yisrael said, "It is too much! Yosef my son is yet alive! I will go and see him before I die."
>
> And Yisrael journeyed with all that he had….[7]

Until this point, the use of interchanging names in the text is clear and

6. Ohr Hachaim, Bereishit 35:10.
7. Bereishit 45:25–46:1.

powerful. As the section opens, we find *Yaakov* still immersed in sorrow over the loss of Yosef. Once convinced of his son's survival, however, it is *Yisrael* who begins the joyous journey towards a reunion with his son.

At this moment, however, things get complicated:

> And God spoke to Yisrael in the visions of the night and he said: "Yaakov, Yaakov." And he said: "Here I am."
>
> And [God] said, "I am the God – God of your father. Have no fear of descending to Egypt for I shall establish you as a great nation there. I will descend with you to Egypt and I will also surely bring you up again, and Yosef shall put his hand upon your eyes."
>
> And Yaakov rose up from Be'er Sheva. And the sons of Yisrael carried their father, Yaakov, and their young children and their wives in the wagons that Pharaoh had sent to carry them…and they came to Egypt, Yaakov and all his offspring with him.[8]

Why does God suddenly appear to *Yisrael* in "visions of the night" and address him twice as *Yaakov*? Why, in addition, does God tell Yaakov not to be afraid? At this point the patriarch shows no fear at all as he joyously travels to Egypt and the reunion with his beloved son. Why does God reassure Yaakov when he evidences no need for divine reassurance?

Perhaps that is precisely the point of God's message. The patriarch, overwhelmed with emotion, has been blinded to the dark dimensions of the journey upon which he now embarks. In "visions of the night," therefore, God reminds the patriarch that *he should be afraid.*

Yaakov, Yaakov, God calls, *this is not a simple moment. For as you travel to a joyous reunion with your beloved son, you leave the land of Israel for the last time. Your footsteps will mark the beginning of your nation's descent into darkness and slavery. Be afraid… but then be reassured that all will not be lost. I will eventually bring your descendents out of Egypt.*

The patriarch awakens from this vision, once again, a changed man. It is *Yaakov*, not *Yisrael*, who rises from Be'er Sheva to continue the journey to Egypt. The traveler who previously welcomed the expedition must now be "carried" by his sons or he will go no further.

Yaakov now knows that he is leaving the Land of Israel for the last time

---

8. Ibid., 46:2–6.

and that his children will return only after years of torment and slavery. In contrast, the patriarch's sons, unconflicted and blissfully unaware of the reasons for their father's sudden hesitation, remain "the sons of *Yisrael*."[9]

Our understanding of this critical section of text is enhanced immeasurably once we note the poignant wisdom behind the variations of the name of the last patriarch. We are amazed, once again, as, through every textual nuance, the Torah conveys lessons of monumental significance.

9. Ibid., 46:5.

3 The First Ghetto

Context

After the descent of Yaakov's family to Egypt, Yosef prepares a delegation of his brothers for an interview with the Egyptian king.

He counsels them to specify that they are shepherds so that Pharaoh will settle them separately in the region of Goshen, "since all shepherds are abhorrent to the Egyptians."[1]

Questions

Why does Yosef specifically counsel his brothers to identify themselves with a profession that the Egyptians find repulsive?

Approaches

A

Some commentaries believe that Yosef is simply trying to ensure that his brothers will be able to continue practicing a beneficial profession.

The Abravanel, for example, maintains that Yosef could well have appointed his brothers to positions of authority and power. He desires, however, that they eschew such leadership in favor of a simple, humble, "sacred" livelihood.[2]

According to Rabbeinu Bachya, shepherding was an intrinsically advantageous profession with clear physical and spiritual benefits. Producing a number of profitable materials (meat, milk and wool) for relatively little physical effort, shepherding also provided the opportunity for periodic isolation from civilization and its influence. Through seclusion the shepherd found time for self-examination and spiritual growth. Not coin-

1. Bereishit 46:31–34.
2. Abravanel, Bereishit 46:28–34.

cidentally, continues Rabbeinu Bachya, many great figures of Jewish history, including Moshe, Shmuel, Shaul and David, were shepherds at some point in their lives.[3]

B

Numerous other commentaries, however, see Yosef's efforts in a totally different light.

Yosef, they claim, deliberately instructs his brothers to identify with a profession that will distance them from Egyptian society. Forced to live separately, the members of Yosef's family and their progeny will have a greater chance of maintaining their own identity.

In the words of the Netziv: "Yosef's intent was to ensure that his family would dwell apart from the Egyptians. Although [Yosef's plan] would cause his father and brothers to be degraded in Pharaoh's eyes, nonetheless, all was worth sacrificing to guarantee the preservation of Israel's sanctity."[4]

Rabbi Shimshon Raphael Hirsch adds: "The disgust of the Egyptians for their [the brothers'] profession…was the first means of preservation of that race which was destined for an isolated path through the ages…. That is why Joseph acted with the express purpose of obtaining a separate province within which his family would settle."[5]

Yosef, the cosmopolitan Hebrew, the paradigm of success in an alien culture, becomes the architect of our people's first ghetto.

C

Why is Yosef, viceroy of all of Egypt, accomplished beyond measure in a foreign world, so determined that the members of his family not follow his winning path?

What motivates him to personally construct a plan for their isolation?

Perhaps he is driven by the recognition of the price that he has had to pay for his own success. The years in Egypt have taken their toll. By the time he meets his brothers after their long separation, the Torah states: "Yosef recognized his brothers but they did not recognize him."[6] *Yosef is no*

---

3. Rabbeinu Bachya, Bereishit 46:32.
4. Ha'amek Davar, Bereishit 46:34.
5. Rabbi Shimshon Raphael Hirsch, Bereishit 46:33.
6. Bereishit 42:8.

longer recognizable as a Hebrew, even to his family. Moved by this knowledge, and apprehending the devastation that would be caused if generation after generation of Hebrews paid this same price, Yosef acts to preserve his family's identity.

Or, perhaps, Yosef is motivated by the pain of his personal isolation in the face of his rise to power (see Vayechi 2, *Approaches* B) and tries to spare his family from similar disappointment and loneliness.

Or, finally, perhaps this cosmopolitan Hebrew simply understands that what he has accomplished as an individual cannot be duplicated by his family as a whole. Talents are not uniform. Yosef's enormous success could only be paralleled by a select few. Fewer still would be able to maintain the spiritual balance that had sustained him throughout his turbulent personal odyssey.

One way or the other, as Yosef orchestrates the descent of his family to Egypt, he clearly does everything he can to ensure their separation from the Egyptians. As will be the case throughout Jewish history, the delicate balance struck during Avraham's lifetime (see Chayei Sara 1) is front and center, decades later, in the thoughts and planning of his great-grandson. Yosef realizes that for the members of his family to retain their status as "strangers and citizens" over generations and in the face of an overwhelming Egyptian culture, they will have to live in our people's first ghetto.

D

Yosef's careful plans are ultimately put to the test.

While the sojourn in Egypt should have been viewed by Yaakov's family as temporary, the Torah testifies that: "Israel *settled* in the land of Egypt, in the region of Goshen, and they *secured a permanent foothold* and they were fruitful and multiplied greatly."[7]

And, although the Jews were meant to remain in Goshen, the text continues: "And the children of Israel were fruitful, multiplied, increased, and became strong…*and the land became filled with them.*"[8]

Building upon an earlier Midrashic tradition,[9] the Netziv comments: "They filled not only the land of Goshen which had been especially as-

7. Ibid., 47:27.
8. Shmot 1:7.
9. Yalkut Shimoni, Shmot 1.

signed to them, *but the whole land of Egypt*.... Wherever they could purchase a dwelling, there the Israelites went.... They wished to be like the Egyptians."[10]

Given the opportunity, in spite of Yosef's careful planning, the Israelites begin to assimilate into Egyptian culture and society. A tragic pattern, however, emerges – a pattern that is destined to be repeated over and over again across our long national journey. The harder the Israelites try to fit in, the more assiduously they try to be like those around them, the more they incur the enmity of their neighbors and set the stage for their own persecution. They are soon enslaved and pushed back into Goshen.

Yosef's implicit urgings are ignored by later generations. His efforts, however, may well have saved his people from oblivion. First by choice, than by force, the Israelites remain a population separate within Egypt. Within the "ghetto" of Goshen they remain identifiable and, therefore, redeemable when the moment of the Exodus arrives.

10. Ha'amek Davar, Bereishit 1:7.

4 A Disappointing Encounter?

Context

After orchestrating his family's descent to Egypt, Yosef brings his father before the Egyptian king. The patriarch blesses Pharaoh and the king asks, "How many are the days of the years of your life?"[1]

Yaakov responds, "The days of the years of my sojourning are one hundred thirty years. Few and difficult were the days of the years of my life and they did not reach the days of the years of the lives of my fathers, in the days of their sojourning."[2]

Yaakov blesses Pharaoh again, and the encounter ends.[3]

Questions

The conversation between Yaakov and Pharaoh can only be described as deeply disappointing. The setting, after all, is momentous. This is not only an encounter between two great world leaders, but a confrontation between two vastly different, powerful cultures. Meeting for the first and only recorded time are the monarch of the world's greatest empire and the last patriarch, the progenitor of an eternal nation which will outlast countless empires beyond Egypt.

We wait with bated breath as two worlds collide, only to finally ask in frustration: Is this all these great leaders had to say to each other?

Why is Pharaoh so concerned with Yaakov's age?

What is the real meaning of Yaakov's elliptical response to the king? Why the diplomatic doublespeak? Why not answer simply and directly?

Above all, if the conversation between Yaakov and Pharaoh was so banal, why does the Torah bother to record it at all?

1. Bereishit 47:8.
2. Bereishit 47:9.
3. Ibid., 47:10.

Approaches

A

Clearly there is much more to this brief encounter than meets the eye. Carefully read, the dialogue actually reflects a vast philosophical divide between the participants. This rift becomes clear when Yaakov, responding to Pharaoh's inquiry, distinguishes between two concepts: *chaim* (life) and *megurim* (sojourning).

Once this distinction is noted, the conversation unfolds with evident subtext. Pharaoh, king of an empire preoccupied with life, death and life beyond death, turns to the patriarch and, seeing a man apparently older than any he has met before, exclaims:

"How many are the days of the years of your life?" *My God, how old are you? How have you managed to attain the longevity we all seek? What is your secret?*

Yaakov replies:

"The days of the years of my sojourning are one hundred thirty years."[4] *Do not be impressed with my chronological age. Living long is, in and of itself, no accomplishment at all. There is a vast difference between life and sojourning, between living and existing. I have existed, but not lived, for one hundred thirty years.*

"Few and difficult were the days of the years of my life and they did not reach the days of the years of the lives of my fathers in the days of their sojourning."[5] *Do not envy me. My days of true life, of peace, comfort and ease, have been few and far between. Do not aspire to simple sojourning, to longevity alone. Be impressed, instead, by life – years of meaning. Chronological age is of little value when your days and years have been as difficult as mine.*

In subtle yet emphatic fashion, Yaakov reprimands Pharaoh for his preoccupation with prolonged existence. The patriarch has learned a difficult lesson through his years of struggle with external foes and internal family strife. What counts, says Yaakov, are years of *chaim* – life – meaningful years of peace, comfort and ease.

---

4. Bereishit 47:9.
5. Ibid.

B

One final, powerful twist to the substance of this conversation, however, emerges from a lesson possibly learned by the patriarch later in his life.

The last parsha in Sefer Bereishit, Parshat Vayechi, opens with the statement "*Vayechi Yaakov b'eretz Mitzraim shva esrei shana* (*And Yaakov lived* in the land of Egypt for seventeen years)."[6]

The Torah rarely records the exact length of periods in the lives of its heroes. Computations concerning the passage of time are usually made by the rabbis, based upon hints within the text. Why, then, does the Torah go out of its way to specify the length of time that Yaakov lived in Egypt?

Because, some commentaries explain, *these were the only years that Yaakov truly lived* (aside, perhaps, from the years between Yosef's birth and his sale into servitude). Finally, after a lifetime of struggle, reunited with his beloved Yosef, surrounded by a harmonious family, Yaakov earns the peace of mind and spirit which has eluded him for so long. He ultimately experiences years of *chaim* – seventeen years of life.[7]

The truth, however, is more complicated than it seems.

While Yaakov's last years may very well have been his only years of peace and quiet, they were also *the only years of Yaakov's life that we know nothing about.* In stark contrast to the rest of his existence, Yaakov's years in Egypt produced no great contribution.

As Rabbi Shimshon Raphael Hirsch notes, "The troubled years of his life, in which the test had to be gone through…were those in which Yaakov won his everlasting national importance."[8]

Perhaps Yaakov learns, in his final days, that Pharaoh was not the only one mistaken in his apprehension of life's goals. For while the quality of life cannot be measured by longevity alone, neither can it be measured by the attainment of comfort or ease. The very struggle of living, with all its pain and challenge, creates the cauldron from which growth and contribution can emerge.

Points to Ponder

How is the quality of our lives ultimately to be judged? Is our purpose the

6. Ibid., 47:28.
7. Ba'al HaTurim, Bereishit 47:28; Rabbi Shimshon Raphael Hirsch, Bereishit 47:28.
8. Rabbi Shimshon Raphael Hirsch, ibid.

pursuit of happiness, comfort, peace, tranquility? Is success to be measured by the attainment of those goals?

One of the most creative scholars of our day, Rabbi Adin Steinsaltz, bemoans the fact that "peace of mind" has become in our time "a spiritual ideal and significant life goal, the final achievement to which various schools of thought and meditation aspire."[9]

"Peace with no content," continues Steinsaltz, "meaningless tranquility, rest without sanctity – all are empty vessels.... There are goals that cannot be attained except through struggle waged within the soul."[10]

For his part, Rabbi Yosef Soloveitchik, considered by many the foremost teacher of our era, proclaims that religion does not provide a solution to life's problems but, instead, "*deepens* the problem."[11]

"The beauty of religion with its grandiose vistas," maintains Rabbi Soloveitchik, "reveals itself to man not in solutions, but in problems, not in harmony, but in the constant conflict of diversified forces and trends."[12]

In a society where so many have achieved a level of physical comfort and ease undreamt of in previous years, we ironically witness an extraordinary measure of existential sadness and spiritual disquiet. The more "happiness" is pursued as a goal, the more elusive it becomes. Man is built to struggle with himself, his surroundings, his fate, even with his Creator – to never be satisfied with the world as it is, but to strive to make it better. The more we try to retreat from this struggle of life, the emptier our lives become.

Significance will be found not in the futile search for "peace of mind" but in the embrace of what Steinsaltz calls the "strife of the spirit."[13] From the battlefield of that effort, value, purpose, accomplishment and true happiness emerge.

---

9. Adin Steinsaltz, *The Strife of the Spirit* (Northvale, NJ: Jason Aronson, 1988), 3.
10. Ibid., 5.
11. Joseph Soloveitchik, "Sacred and Profane, Kodesh and Chol in World Perspective," quoted in Zvi Kolitz, *Confrontation: The Existential Thought of Rabbi J.B. Soloveitchik* (Hoboken, NJ: KTAV Publishing House, 1993), p.13.
12. Ibid.
13. Steinsaltz, *The Strife of the Spirit*, 3.

Vayechi

ויחי

CHAPTER 47:28–50:26

פרק מז:כח–נ:כו

Parsha Summary

An era closes…

As the end of Yaakov's life draws near, the patriarch asks Yosef to personally ensure that he will be buried in Canaan. Yosef agrees and, upon his father's insistence, swears to accomplish this task.

Upon hearing that Yaakov has fallen ill, Yosef gathers his sons, Menashe and Ephraim, and rushes to his father's side. Yaakov informs Yosef that Menashe and Ephraim will be counted among the patriarch's own children. Yaakov then blesses his two grandsons, deliberately placing his right hand upon the head of the younger child, Ephraim.

Yaakov calls his sons to his deathbed and blesses each with an individual, uniquely tailored blessing. The patriarch then repeats his request that he be buried in Canaan, specifically in the Cave of Machpeila.

Yaakov dies and is mourned by Egypt for seventy days. Pharaoh agrees to Yosef's request that his father be buried in Canaan. Yosef, his brothers and a great Egyptian entourage travel to Canaan for the patriarch's burial.

Upon their return to Egypt, Yosef's brothers becomes fearful that, given their father's death, Yosef will now exact revenge upon them for his sale into slavery. In an emotional exchange, Yosef reassures them that he intends them no harm.

Before he dies, Yosef elicits a vow from his brothers that his remains will be brought out of Egypt when the moment of the Exodus arrives.

1 A Simple Request?

Context

As Yaakov's life nears its end, the patriarch turns to his son Yosef with the following request: "Do not bury me in Egypt. For I will lie with my fathers, and you shall carry me out of Egypt and bury me in their tomb."[1]

Although Yosef immediately agrees to his father's appeal, Yaakov insists that his son swear to fulfill the task. Yosef complies.

Yaakov later expands upon his request in the presence of all his sons when he delineates, in detail, the provenance of the Cave of Machpeila, the patriarchal burial site in Hevron:

> Bury me with my fathers in the cave which is in the field of Ephron the Hittite; in the cave which is in the field of Machpeila, which faces Mamre in the land of Canaan; the field which Avraham bought from Ephron the Hittite as a burial holding. There they buried Avraham and Sara his wife, there they buried Yitzchak and Rivka his wife and there I buried Leah. The purchase of the field and the cave within it were from the Hittites.[2]

After Yaakov's death, Yosef moves to fulfill his father's wishes. He approaches Pharaoh's household and beseeches:

> Please, if I have found favor in your eyes, please speak to the ears of Pharaoh saying: "My father made me swear as follows, 'Behold I am about to die. In my grave which I have hewn for myself in

1. Bereishit 47:29–30.
2. Ibid., 49:29–32.

the land of Canaan – there you will bury me.' And now allow me to go up and bury my father. Then I will return."[3]

Pharaoh replies, "Go up and bury your father as he has made you swear."[4]

Questions

Why does the Torah devote so much text to Yaakov's request to be buried in Israel, first outlining his initial appeal to Yosef and then detailing his more elaborate request of all his sons?

Why does Yaakov insist upon a vow from Yosef even after Yosef has already agreed to fulfill his father's wishes? Doesn't the patriarch trust his beloved son?

Why doesn't Yosef approach Pharaoh directly with his father's request, instead imploring the "king's household" to speak on his behalf?

Why does the Torah detail verbatim both Yosef's message to Pharaoh and Pharaoh's response? The text could simply have stated that Yosef forwarded his father's request to the king and that the king consented.

Approaches

In beautiful yet sorrowful fashion the patriarchal era comes full circle with Yaakov's request. The era that optimistically began with Avraham's passage to Canaan now ends with a very different journey on the part of his grandson, Yaakov, to the very same land. In death, Yaakov points the way for his children. His desire to rest in his homeland is clearly meant to serve as a cautionary message to his children: *Egypt is not your home.*

Yaakov's poignant wish, however, confronts the hard reality of diaspora existence. The nuanced details of the narrative before us all point to one

3. Ibid., 50:4–5.
4. Ibid., 50:6.

essential fact: *Yaakov's request to be buried in Israel was fraught with tremendous danger.*

The patriarch was essentially rejecting Egypt and all that it represented. Pharaoh could easily have questioned Yosef's loyalty with the blunt accusation: "Isn't Egypt good enough for your father? Why must he be buried in Canaan?"

Because of this danger the entire matter is handled with several unusual precautions.

1. Yaakov demands a vow from Yosef, although he certainly trusts his beloved son. With this vow the patriarch preemptively shows Yosef how to navigate the difficult path ahead.

Yaakov knows that, to have any chance of success at all, the appeal to the king must be based upon the concept of ancestral respect. Egypt is, after all, the empire of the mummies and pyramids, a kingdom preoccupied with the afterlife. *How could Pharaoh ignore a vow taken to fulfill a dying father's wishes?*

Yaakov's prediction proves to be accurate. Yosef, ever the diplomat, consciously opens his request to the king with the words "My father *made me swear* as follows…"[5]

And the king, tellingly, responds: "Go up and bury your father *as he has made you swear*."[6]

2. Yosef does not approach Pharaoh directly with his father's request. He instead lobbies "Pharaoh's household" to approach the king on his behalf.[7] Yosef, viceroy of Egypt, second in command only to the king himself, must enlist the aid of others in order to fulfill his father's sensitive request. If the king sees that his royal household does not object to Yaakov's burial in Canaan, he will feel politically secure and be more inclined to agree himself.

3. Yosef, in his message to Pharaoh, changes the very nature of his father's request. He omits specific critical details mentioned by Yaakov and puts other words in his father's mouth.

Gone is any mention of Yaakov's desire to be buried with his fathers, of the existence of an ancestral tomb, of the specific location of the Cave of

5. Ibid., 50:5.
6. Ibid., 50:6.
7. Ibid., 50:4.

Machpeila and of its provenance. Yosef realizes that any mention of these concepts would alert the king to the deep philosophical currents coursing beneath Yaakov's request and would guarantee its immediate rejection.

Instead, Yosef couches his father's request as follows: "In the grave that I have hewn for myself in the land of Canaan – there you will bury me."[8] The issue is simple and uncomplicated: *My father prepared a burial plot for himself. I must respect his wishes.*

4. Yosef closes his appeal to the king with the words "And now allow me to go up and bury my father. Then I will return."[9] Yosef recognizes that he must reassure Pharaoh of his own intention to return to Egypt. The king cannot risk Yosef's defection to a foreign land.

In spite of this reassurance, when Pharaoh does allow Yosef to travel to Canaan the king takes no chances. He sends with his viceroy: "all the king's servants and all the elders of his household and all the elders of the land of Egypt…also chariots and horsemen."[10] In addition, the Torah clearly states that Yosef and his brothers leave behind "their flocks, their cattle and their young children…in the land of Goshen."[11] Families and possessions remain in Egypt to ensure Yosef and his brothers' return.

C

The era that began with the promise of Avraham's journey to Canaan ends with the encroaching darkness of exile, as Yosef risks all to fulfill his father's simple request to be buried in the Promised Land. That very request, however, kindles hope for the future. With his final wish, the last patriarch reminds his family of their eternal ties to their homeland – a land to which they are destined to return.

---

8. Ibid., 50:5.
9. Ibid., 50:6.
10. Ibid., 50:7.
11. Ibid., 50:8.

2 Menashe and Ephraim: Tying up Loose Ends

Context

Upon hearing that Yaakov has fallen ill, Yosef gathers his sons, Menashe and Ephraim, and rushes to his father's bedside.

During the ensuing conversation Yaakov takes two dramatic steps that carry powerful practical implications for the future.

1. Yaakov proclaims that Menashe and Ephraim will be considered on par with his own children in the determination of his legacy.[1] Through this statement, Yaakov creates the tribes of Ephraim and Menashe in place of the single tribe of Yosef.[2]

2. The patriarch blesses his grandchildren as follows: "Through you will Israel bless, by saying: 'May God make you like Ephraim and like Menashe…'"[3] To this day, Jewish parents bless their sons with the formula "May God make you like Ephraim and like Menashe," while daughters are blessed with the prayer "May God make you like Sara, Rivka, Rachel and Leah."

Questions

Why are Ephraim and Menashe counted among the tribes of Israel? No other grandchild of Yaakov is accorded this singular honor.

Why are Ephraim and Menashe chosen as the paradigms for our sons to emulate rather than the patriarchs, Avraham, Yitzchak and Yaakov? Do the oldest sons of Yosef possess specific character traits that we wish upon our own children or are we arbitrarily fulfilling Yaakov's prophetic prediction: "Through you [Ephraim and Menashe] will Israel bless…"?

---

1. Bereishit 48:5.
2. Rashi, Bereishit 48:5.
3. Bereishit 48:20.

Approaches

Ephraim and Menashe's central place in both the legacy and blessing of Yaakov reflects a number of critical ideas. The selection of Yosef's children to this position, in fact, brings closure to a series of interlocking themes that have coursed through the Yosef story, and, in some cases, the entire book of Bereishit.

A

The tribal legacy: Yosef's reward.

We will see that Reuven, Yaakov's eldest son, loses the firstborn's leadership role as a result of his personal failings. In his place, Yehuda earns and assumes those responsibilities of leadership (see Vayechi 3).

There are two other privileges of the birthright, however, which Reuven loses, as well. The honor of religious stewardship is reassigned to Levi while the double inheritance normally accorded to the firstborn is transferred to Yosef.

The creation of the tribes of Ephraim and Menashe can thus be attributed to Yosef's merit. As a reward for his righteousness and in acknowledgment of his achievements, Yosef receives his "double portion" as the progenitor of these two tribes.

B

Emphasizing Yosef's aloneness.

While the creation of two tribes bearing the names of Yosef's sons can certainly be seen as a reward for Yosef's righteousness, this same phenomenon, in ironic fashion, underscores a tragic dimension of his life. Yosef's name does not appear in the list of tribes along with his brothers. Yosef's lonely position as the ultimate outsider is thus cemented and preserved for posterity.

Yosef never succeeds in becoming part of any society in which he finds himself. Although wildly successful in Egypt, he never earns the full trust of the Egyptians (see Vayigash 1, *Approaches* C). Even more significantly, he is never fully accepted into the company of his brothers, who do not have confidence in his intentions right through the end.[4]

A delicate balance, mirroring Yosef's complex life, is thus struck in the

4. Bereishit 50:15.

tribal system. Yosef's material success will be reflected in the double portion he receives through his sons. His isolation, however, is also mirrored in Yosef's own conspicuous and now eternal absence from the company of his brothers.

C

Reaching across the generations.

Yaakov is the first personality in the Torah and the only patriarch to openly relate not only to his children, but to his grandchildren, as well.

The last patriarch, however, goes a major step further. He concretizes his relationship with Ephraim and Menashe through the creation of tribes bearing their names, thereby ensuring that the tribal system of Israel will span the generations. With great foresight, he consciously weaves the concepts of the extended family and of intergenerational relationships into the very fabric of our national structure. (Note that building upon this phenomenon, Yaakov's son Yosef is the first individual in the Torah to interact with his great grandchildren.[5]) These relationships will remain indispensable to the transmission and development of Jewish tradition across the ages.

D

The blessing: sibling harmony.

Ephraim and Menashe succeed in reversing a tragic trend which characterizes sibling relationships from the time of Kayin and Hevel through the patriarchal period. They are the first major set of brothers, recorded in the Torah, whose relationship is not marked by jealousy, rivalry and strife. The love between Ephraim and Menashe apparently endures even when Ephraim is given precedence by Yaakov over his older brother, Menashe.

When we pray that God will make our sons "like Ephraim and like Menashe," we pray that our progeny succeed in maintaining the harmony that marked the relationship of Yosef's sons.

E

A world apart.

Yaakov reacts with wonder when he reflects upon meeting his grandchildren towards the end of his life. This reaction mirrors the unexpected

5. Ibid., 50:23.

nature of Ephraim and Menashe's success. These two children grew up in exile, separated from their extended family since birth, yet remained identifying members of their family.

The patriarch, therefore, selects his two grandchildren as the paradigm for blessings across the ages. Their selection sends a powerful message across the turbulent history of our often scattered people.

"May God make you like Ephraim and Menashe," we bless our sons. *May you always be spiritually connected to your family and people, no matter where you live, no matter how physically distant you may be.*

3 Rising to Leadership

Context

A hidden struggle courses beneath the surface of the Yosef story as, unknowingly, each of Yaakov's sons strives for a prize of overwhelming responsibility and inestimable value.

By the time the narrative reaches its conclusion a fundamental question is answered: Who, from among the sons of Yaakov, will rise to leadership within the Jewish nation?

Three possible candidates emerge from a crowded field, each a complex figure with strong positive credentials.

1. Reuven – firstborn to Yaakov; the leadership role is Reuven's birthright and, thus, his to lose. He, alone among the brothers, attempts to save Yosef and return him to his father's home.[1]

2. Yosef – a born leader; Yosef rises to the top of any environment into which he is placed (see Vayeishev 1). He becomes a powerful figure who is able to manipulate circumstances and the behavior of others in order to achieve his goals.[2]

3. Yehuda – powerfully persuasive; Yehuda convinces his brothers to sell Yosef into slavery, rather than allow him to perish in the pit.[3] Yehuda rises to protect his youngest brother, Binyamin, when Binyamin is threatened by Yosef with imprisonment.[4]

When Yaakov blesses his sons from his deathbed in Parshat Vayechi, the patriarch clearly indicates God's verdict. *Yehuda* is to be the progenitor of leadership within the people of Israel: "The scepter shall not pass from Yehuda nor legislation from among his descendents

---

1. Bereishit 37:21–22.
2. Ibid., 39:1–47:27.
3. Ibid., 37:26–27.
4. Ibid., 44:18–34.

until Shilo (the Mashiach) arrives and his will be a gathering of nations."[5]

Questions

By what criteria is Yehuda selected for leadership over his brothers?

Are there any specific characteristics or qualities that disqualify Reuven and Yosef from this leadership role?

Approaches

A

At first glance, Reuven seems to merit the leadership role which, by birthright, is naturally his.

When the brothers openly plot to murder Yosef, Reuven alone rises to his younger brother's defense. He convinces the others to throw Yosef into a pit rather than kill him directly. The Torah clearly testifies that Reuven intended to later return and "rescue him [Yosef] from their hands, to return him to his father."[6]

Why, then, is Reuven passed over in favor of Yehuda?

A clue emerges from the message that Yaakov, on his deathbed, delivers to Reuven in Parshat Vayechi: "*Unstable as water*, you shall not lead…"[7]

A careful review of Reuven's behavior at critical moments reveals that while Yaakov's firstborn often has the best of intentions, he "rushes like water," reacting impetuously, without thought for the ramifications of his actions. Three episodes clearly underscore this point.

1. After the death of Rachel, the Torah states that Reuven has relations with Bilha, his father's concubine (and the mother of two of Yaakov's children).[8]

The rabbis debate the actual details of this event.

Some suggest that Reuven felt that Bilha was permitted to him because he viewed her only as his father's concubine.[9]

---

5. Ibid., 49:10.
6. Ibid., 39:22.
7. Ibid., 49:4.
8. Ibid., 35:22.
9. Radak, Bereishit 35:22.

The Talmud, however, maintains that Reuven did not actually sleep with Bilha at all. Instead, the rabbis say, Reuven acted to protect the honor of his mother, Leah. After Rachel died, Yaakov established his primary residence in the tent of Bilha, who had been Rachel's maidservant. Reuven interpreted this act as an affront to his mother. Without his father's knowledge, he took matters in his own hands and moved his father's bed to his mother, Leah's, tent.[10] While Reuven's motives were understandable, his actions were precipitous and impulsive, earning him the reprimand from his father's deathbed, in which Yaakov rebukes him for this incident: "Unstable as water, you shall not lead, for you mounted your father's bed…"[11]

2. At the scene of Yosef's sale into slavery Reuven does attempt to save his brother. His efforts, however, fall painfully short. Instead of openly challenging his brothers' horrific plan, Yaakov's oldest son convinces his siblings that their own design can be more easily achieved by throwing Yosef into a pit.[12] Reuven, however, apparently gives no thought to the dangers potentially lurking in the darkness of that pit, which, according to rabbinic tradition, was actually filled with "snakes and scorpions."[13]

Reuven then mysteriously disappears from the scene, only to return after Yosef's sale is complete.[14] Whatever the cause for Reuven's departure (the rabbis offer numerous suggestions as to why he left), nothing should have been more important than remaining and ensuring his brother's safety.

The text, in brilliant yet indirect fashion, hints at the incompleteness of Reuven's attempts to save Yosef by openly stating that Reuven acts "in order to save him [Yosef], to return him to his father."[15]

The Torah does not generally comment on the intentions of characters in the narrative, but rather, allows people's actions to speak for them. In this case, however, Reuven's actions are so inconclusive that we would have no way of knowing that he planned to save his brother. The text must, therefore, openly testify as to Reuven's good intentions.

3. Years later, the brothers return to Canaan after their journey to Egypt

10. Talmud Bavli Shabbat 55b.
11. Bereishit 49:4.
12. Ibid., 37:22.
13. Talmud Bavli Shabbat 22a.
14. Bereishit 37:29.
15. Ibid., 37:22.

to procure food in the face of famine. Yosef, who is by now the Egyptian viceroy, has imprisoned Shimon and declared that the brothers may not return to Egypt unless they bring their youngest brother, Binyamin, with them.

Reuven attempts to convince his reluctant father to allow Binyamin to make the journey to Egypt by offering the following bargain: "You may slay my two sons if I fail to bring him [Binyamin] back to you. Put him in my care and I will return him to you."[16]

Yaakov, understandably, remains adamant in his refusal. What grandfather, after all, would trust the judgment of a son who, even in an attempt to do what is right, impulsively offers the lives of his own children as collateral for his success or failure?

While a leader certainly must be able to act decisively at a moment's notice, he cannot afford to be reckless or blind to the consequences of his actions. Reuven, while well-meaning, is simply too impulsive to inherit the critical mantle of leadership.

B

Yosef seems to possess all of the traits necessary for successful leadership. Personally attractive, naturally adept, politically savvy, he rises to the top of each and every environment into which he is placed, often against great odds. By the end of the narrative Yosef is viceroy in Egypt, second-in-command only to Pharaoh and the architect of his family's survival and descent to Egypt.

Yosef also possesses a deep, abiding faith in God and in Divine Providence. (See Vayeishev 1 for a fuller discussion of Yosef's leadership skills and personal belief system.)

Why then is Yosef not chosen for leadership within the Jewish nation?

The answer lies, perhaps, in a fundamental flaw in the nature of Yosef's leadership. Yosef always seems to lead from "without." There is no group to which he fully belongs: he remains throughout his life the ultimate outsider. Yosef never gains the trust of his brothers, who suspect his intentions until the end.[17] In Egypt, he is regarded with suspicion and is considered a

---

16. Ibid., 42:37.
17. Ibid., 50:15.

foreigner even after his rise to power (See Vayigash 1, *Approaches* c). Yosef certainly leads but his leadership is that of a puppeteer, who remains at a distance, manipulating events and people to achieve his ends.

The true Jewish leader emerges from "within" the nation and remains connected always to the people he leads.

Moshe's journey to prominence begins when he "goes out to his brethren to observe their burdens."[18] David begins life as a common shepherd and remains, even after ascending to the monarchy, a poet whose songs resonate to the chords of universal personal struggle.

In contrast, Yosef, the ultimate outsider, cannot be chosen for permanent leadership of the Jewish nation.

C

From the outset, Yehuda seems an unlikely candidate for lasting leadership.

He is fully implicated by the text in the sale of Yosef and is, in fact, the one who suggests the sale.[19] Immediately after that tragic episode, Yehuda fails to fulfill his responsibilities to his daughter-in-law, Tamar, and only corrects his errors when she openly confronts him.[20]

Closer study, however, reveals two powerful currents coursing through Yehuda's life and development, as he overcomes his own shortcomings and avoids the mistakes of his other brothers.

1. *Yehuda remains one with his brothers.* Unlike Yosef, Yehuda rises from within. A persuasive leader at the time of Yosef's sale into slavery, Yehuda separates temporarily from his brothers,[21] only to return to their company. His leadership is cemented when he convinces his father to allow Binyamin's journey to Egypt[22] and when he rises to argue with Yosef on Binyamin's behalf.[23]

Immediately before Yehuda's defense of Binyamin, the text subtly foreshadows Yehuda's rise to prominence from among his brothers by singling

18. Shmot 2:11.
19. Bereishit 37:26.
20. Ibid., 38:26.
21. Ibid., 38:1.
22. Ibid., 43:3–14.
23. Ibid., 44:18–34.

him out with the phrase "and *Yehuda and his brothers* arrived to Joseph's house."[24]

Finally, Yaakov, on his deathbed, acknowledges Yehuda's journey to popular leadership: "Yehuda – you, *your brothers shall acknowledge*."[25]

2. *Yehuda learns to take full responsibility for his actions.* The incident with Tamar marks the beginning of Yehuda's journey towards personal responsibility. Confronted with Tamar's claim that he is the father of her unborn child, Yehuda openly states, "She [Tamar] is right; it [the child] is from me."[26]

Years later, Yehuda's successful attempt to convince his father to allow Binyamin to travel to Egypt stands in stark contrast to Reuven's earlier, clumsy effort (see *Approaches* A, above). Yehuda declares: "*Anochi e'ervenu*, I will personally guarantee him; of my own hand you can demand him. If I do not bring him back to you and stand him before you, then I would have sinned to you for all time."[27]

Finally, Yehuda emerges as the prototype for the process of *tshuva* (personal repentance and change) when he rises to fight for Binyamin's safe return. The very individual who suggested the sale of Yosef now stands before Yosef arguing on behalf of their youngest brother!

There are no coincidences in Jewish history. Yehuda's journey has brought him to this point, recorded at the beginning of Parshat Vayigash. Faced with the same circumstances which previously led to failure, Yehuda courageously rises to leadership as he addresses the past and accepts full responsibility for his brother's fate.

Yaakov's deathbed blessing to Yehuda, within which he assigns leadership to Yehuda and his descendents, is specific as to the criteria by which God's choice is made:

"Yehuda – you your brothers shall acknowledge...your father's sons will bow down to you."[28] *Yehuda, you have risen from within. You serve as a model to your brothers and have earned, through their acclaim, the mantle of leadership.*

"A lion cub is Yehuda; from the prey, my son, you have elevated your-

24. Ibid., 44:14.
25. Ibid., 49:8.
26. Bereishit 38:26; Rashi, Bereishit 38:26.
27. Bereishit 43:9.
28. Ibid., 49:8.

self."[29] *You have moved past your earlier tragic failures, elevating yourself through the full acceptance of personal responsibility for your actions and deeds.*

"The scepter shall not depart from Yehuda nor legislation from among his descendents until Shiloh (the Mashiach) arrives and his will be a gathering of nations."[30] *Leadership is yours and will continue, across the ages, among your descendents. Your wrenching personal journey has earned you this honor and responsibility.*

Points to Ponder

During his journey towards personal responsibility, Yehuda makes powerful use of one of the most picturesque words in the Hebrew language: "*Anochi e'ervenu*," he says, as he convinces his father to allow Binyamin to travel to Egypt, "I will personally guarantee him."[31]

And, again, as he confronts Yosef concerning the safety of Binyamin, Yehuda declares: "*Ki avdecha arav et hana'ar*, for your servant took responsibility for the youth."[32]

The root word *arev*, which lies at the heart of Yehuda's statements, literally means *mixture* and enjoys a wide variety of applications throughout Jewish thought:

1. *Erev*, evening. Evening is a mixture of day and night.

2. *Ta'arovet*, a physical mixture. This term is often used in the halachic delineation of permitted and prohibited mixtures of food.

3. *Eruv*, a legal concept with numerous applications. For example: an *eruv chatzeirot* allows members of a community to carry on Shabbat from a private to a public area and within a public area. Contrary to popular opinion, the term does not refer to the physical enclosure built around the community (technically that enclosure is known as a *mechitza*) but to a portion of food which is set aside as communally owned. The *eruv* thus symbolically joins the community together.

4. *Arov*, the plague of a mixture of wild beasts. This is one of the plagues that afflicted Egypt.

5. *Arev*, a guarantor. This is the most important meaning, for it

---

29. Ibid., 49:9.
30. Ibid., 49:10.
31. Ibid., 43:9.
32. Ibid., 44:32.

encompasses the obligation to be responsible for another. When Yehuda "guarantees" Binyamin's safety, he declares his connection to his brother. "*We are bound together*," he effectively argues, "*with a tie that cannot be broken*."

Similarly, the rabbinic proclamation "*Kol Yisrael areivim zeh ba'zeh*,"[33] usually translated to mean "All within Israel are responsible one for the other," actually means much more. On a deeper level, the phrase indicates that we are inextricably bound to one another, connected heart to heart.

Yehuda introduces the concept of *areivut* into Jewish history. He rises to leadership when he truly grasps the ties that bind the family of Israel, ties which join us to each other to this day.

---

33. Yalkut Shimoni, Yitro 294.

4 A Retrospective: Was All This Really Necessary?

Context

Jewish history effectively begins twice. An introductory, pre-national era is launched when Avraham journeys to Canaan at God's command. This period, the patriarchal era, comes to an end with Yaakov's death.

Our story then begins again with the birth of the Jewish nation – as we journey from the cauldron of slavery, through the wrenching Exodus, to the dramatic Revelation at Sinai.

Questions

Why does the Torah include the stories of the patriarchal era? Why not begin, as the first Rashi on Bereishit suggests,[1] with the national period of Jewish history?

At first glance, this question is clearly rhetorical. We have, in our studies, only scratched the surface of the monumental lessons to be learned from the lives of the patriarchs, matriarchs and their families. The Torah would be incomplete without these lessons, which remain as relevant today as the day the events occurred.

And yet, one can't help but wonder if there isn't, perhaps, something more – lessons to be learned not only from the specific stories of the patriarchal era but from the very existence of this introductory period itself. One can't help but wonder why God would choose to begin Jewish history twice.

Approaches

At least three foundations essential to our national character are laid during

1. Rashi, Bereishit 1:1.

the patriarchal era. These underpinnings serve as the best arguments of all for the inclusion of this seminal period in the chronicle of Jewish history.

A

The patriarchal era establishes the significance of the *yachid* (the individual).

The patriarchal era is a time when there is literally no one else, when the sum total of Jewish experience is defined by the lives and dreams of individuals: Avraham, Sara, Yitzchak, Rivka, Yaakov, Rachel and Leah. Their stories are recorded to remind us, even after the dawn of the national era, of the continuing, inestimable importance of each individual.

We are meant to feel, in every era and in every generation, that the survival of our people depends upon each of us alone, as certainly as our existence depended upon Avraham in his day. Each of us has something unique to offer. The loss, God forbid, of one person's contribution leaves our entire people irreparably diminished.

The *tzibur* (community) could not be allowed to overwhelm the individual or stifle individuality. Our nation's birth, therefore, had to wait until personal value was fully established.

B

The patriarchal era establishes the importance of the Jewish family and home.

In a very real sense, this introductory period of Jewish history can be seen as a journey towards one specific moment, the moment when Yaakov lies on his deathbed surrounded by his children. Unlike Avraham and Yitzchak, each of whom had progeny who were lost to Jewish history, Yaakov now knows that all of his children intend to follow his ways. After three generations of struggle with outside influences and internal turmoil, the Hebrew family is finally whole. The patriarchal era can now safely end.

The journey of the patriarchal households to that moment teaches us that *before we could become a nation we had to be a family.*

The primacy of the home, so clearly established in the patriarchal era, is underscored centuries later, during the events which mark our nation's birth.

On the very eve of the Exodus, God commands the Hebrew slaves to mark the impending birth of their nation in a very strange way. In place of participating in constitutional conventions, mass rallies or declarations of independence, each Israelite is instructed to return to his home. There, together with his extended family unit, he is to mark the dawning of freedom through the consumption of the Pesach sacrifice, essentially a family meal.[2]

By insisting upon a retreat to the home as a prelude to our nation's birth, God delivers a simple yet powerful message: *As you begin your journey, remember that your survival will depend upon the health of the family unit. If the family is strong, if the home fulfills its educational role, your people will be strong and your nation will endure.*

This message is underscored again at Sinai as God opens his instructions to Moshe preparatory to revelation:

"Thus shall you say to the House of Yaakov and speak to the People of Yisrael…" *Do not assume that, since you are now the "People of Yisrael," you can, therefore, set the "House of Yaakov" aside. The family unit remains of primary importance.*

The Jewish home is and always has been the single most important educational unit in the perpetuation of our people. What our children learn at home, through example and word, shapes both their knowledge of and their attitude towards Jewish tradition and practice. The home's centrality finds its roots in the earliest moments of our people's story, in the journey of the patriarchal families, centuries before our nation is created.

C

The patriarchal era establishes a preexisting national legacy.

The value of our possessions, whether material or spiritual, increases exponentially when those possessions are perceived as a legacy from previous generations. A beautiful pearl necklace is infinitely more precious if it is an heirloom which belonged to a beloved mother or grandmother.

Because of the patriarchal era, our nation is born with a preexisting legacy. By the time the Exodus and Revelation launch the national era, we already possess a history. Our dreams reflect the dreams of our forefathers and our goals represent the fulfillment of their hopes. The Land of Israel is not an unknown destination, but a cherished land of which we have already heard countless tales, a land promised to our ancestors centuries

2. Shmot 12:3–11.

before. The Torah and its commandments are not foreign concepts but the expected realization of covenants already contracted between God and those who preceded us.

The phenomenon of a pre-existing legacy lends a richness and depth to the moment of our nation's birth that could not have been created in any other way. Even more, however, this phenomenon sets the initial paradigm for the ongoing process of *mesora*, the transmission of tradition from one generation to the next (see Toldot 1, *Approaches* E). From the very beginning, our mission is personal, a mission shaped not only by God's will but also by the memories of people and ages gone by. Those warm memories, together with countless others created across the years, form the ever-growing human dimension of our heritage, a dimension essential to the *mesora* process, a dimension originating in the patriarchal era.

Points to Ponder

As our examination of the patriarchal era draws to a close, we gain a real appreciation of the formative nature of this pre-national period. The foundations that are built during the lives of the patriarchs and matriarchs remain essential to our survival. Sadly, these foundations face serious challenge in our day as the one institution most critical to the cultivation of individual development and to the transmission of personal *mesora* falls short in the fulfillment of its obligations.

One can argue that the single greatest failing of today's diaspora Jewish community is not assimilation. Assimilation is, after all, a symptom, not a cause. The single greatest failing of our community is *the abdication by the family unit of its educational responsibility.*

Countless young Jews are now raised in homes devoid of concrete observance of Jewish law or custom. These youngsters never have the opportunity to experience the beauty and depth of their people's tradition. Judaism becomes for them, at best, a curiosity, and, at worst, an unwanted burden to be discarded at the first possible opportunity.

Even many affiliated families relegate, in large measure, the training of their children to the synagogue, school and Jewish community center. In the Conservative and Reform communities, after-school programs are frequently a child's main exposure to Jewish tradition. No matter how successful these programs may be, they can never be a substitute for home observance.

Within much of today's Orthodox community, as well, compromise often marks the level of personal family practice. The expectation is that children will learn the beauty of Torah study, the power of prayer, the centrality of ethics, somewhere else. If children never see their parents study, however, they will grow up believing that Torah study is important for children but not for adults. If they sit next to parents who talk in synagogue, rather than pray, they will never learn that prayer has any real importance. If they observe their parents cheating on income taxes or engaging in questionable business practices, they will learn to cut corners in the ethical realm. If the everyday behavior modeled by their elders is self-centered and aggressive, they will never learn true regard for the sensibilities of others. And if Shabbat in their home is observed in rote, unthinking fashion, they will never see Shabbat as a day of beauty.

Finally, many of our children today are denied the lessons traditionally taught through exposure to the extended family. The work of the Nazis continues to yield bitter fruit as countless youngsters grow up never knowing their grandparents. Other young people, fortunate enough to have living relatives, nonetheless experience limited exposure to them, due to our mobile, geographically fragmented society.

So many of the experiential elements of our heritage, from Shabbat and the holidays to ethical behavior, can only be properly taught through the example set within the home. The home, and only the home, provides the environment essential for each generation's personal introduction into religious tradition and observance.

From time immemorial, we have survived and thrived because of the life examples set by parents, grandparents and extended family. Those individuals, from Avraham and Sara onward, beckon us to set examples of our own.

Sources

Abravanel – Rabbi Don Yitzchak Abravanel; biblical commentator, philosopher, statesman, diplomat (Portugal, Spain, Italy, 1437–1508).

The last great figure of Spanish Jewry, the Abravanel served during his lifetime as finance minister to the kings of Portugal, Spain and Italy. The Abravanel used his high position and great wealth to benefit his brethren and spared no effort in petitioning the Spanish king and queen, at the time of the Spanish Inquisition, to reverse the edict banishing the Jews from Spain. Failing in that effort, the Abravanel himself suffered expulsion in 1492 with the rest of the exiles.

The Abravanel authored many works including major commentaries on the Torah, other books of Tanach, *Pirkei Avot*, the Hagada and the Rambam's *Guide to the Perplexed*. His commentaries are divided into chapters, each of which is introduced by the list of questions and problems which he intends to address in the chapter. The Abravanel often applied the lessons learned from Scripture to issues confronting the Jewish society of his day.

Aviezer, Dr. Nathan – Physicist, author (Israel, contemporary).

Dr. Nathan Aviezer, a Ph.D. in physics from the University of Chicago, emigrated to Israel in 1967. The author of more than a hundred scientific articles on solid-state physics, Aviezer is professor of physics and former chairman of the Department of Physics of Bar-Ilan University in Tel Aviv. Aviezer's long-standing interest in the relationship between Torah and science is reflected in his best-selling books, *In the Beginning: Biblical Creation and Science* (Hoboken, NJ: Ktav, 1990) and *Fossils and Faith: Understanding Torah and Science* (Hoboken, NJ: Ktav, 2001).

Ba'al HaAkeida – Rabbi Yitzchak ben Moshe Arama; biblical commentator, Talmudic scholar, rabbi (Spain, 1420–1494).

Yitzchak ben Moshe Arama served as the principal of a rabbinical academy at Zamosa and as rabbi of the communities of Tarragon, Fraya and Calatayud. He is most well known for his lengthy philosophical commentary on the Torah, *Akeidat Yitzchak*, which earned him the title Ba'al Ha'Akeida (author of the Akeida). This work consists of 105 "portals," each of which contains two sections: *derisha* (investigation) and *perisha* (exposition). In the first of these two sections, Arama examines a philosophical idea reflected in his chosen text. He then, in the second section, uses this philosophical idea to address and solve problems in the text itself.

The skillful manner in which Arama joins these two sections creates the template for Jewish preaching across the ages.

Ba'al Haturim – Rabbi Yaakov ben Asher; halachist, Talmudic scholar, biblical commentator (Spain, 1270–1340).

Third son of the major Talmudic commentator Rabbi Asher ben Yechiel (the Rosh), the Ba'al Haturim emerged to make towering contributions of his own to Jewish scholarship. His greatest work was the *Arba Turim* (Four Rows), a pivotal codification of practical Jewish law that continues to serve a basic text for the study of halacha to this day. This code was divided into four basic sections and was the precursor of Rabbi Yosef Caro's *Shulchan Aruch*.

The Ba'al Haturim wrote a comprehensive commentary to the Torah in which he included explanations from the works of previous scholars such as Rashi, Ramban, Radak, Ibn Ezra and others. To whet the reader's interest, he prefaced each section of this commentary with an "appetizer" – a segment featuring *gematria* (observations based on the assignment of numerical value to the letters of the text), acronyms and other symbolic references. In an ironic twist of fate, these "appetizers" captured popular attention and have been preserved and published to this day as a separate commentary in the Ba'al Haturim's name.

Bin Nun, Rabbi Yoel – Biblical scholar, educator, religious Zionist leader (Israel, contemporary).

Born in Haifa, Bin Nun studied in Yeshivat Mercaz Harav Kook and served in the paratroop division of the Israel Defense Forces.

A renowned biblical scholar and one of the world's leading experts in the field of Torah education, Bin Nun has taught in Yeshivat Har Etzion and in the Kfar Etzion and Ofra field schools where he specialized in experiential tours based on the Tanach, history and archaeology. He founded and ran the women's seminary in Ofra and also partnered in the establishment of Yi'ud, a seminary which trains young women towards the teaching of Jewish studies in scores of schools throughout Israel.

A prominent, articulate figure in Israeli public life, Bin Nun has served as the rosh yeshiva (dean) of Yeshivat Hakibbutz Hadati (the Yeshiva of the Religious Kibbutz Movement) in Ein Tzurim since September 2000.

Reb Chaim Volozhiner – Rabbi Chaim ben Yitzchak of Volozhin; rabbi, talmudic scholar, rosh yeshiva (dean of a yeshiva) (Lithuania, 1749–1821).

One of the most prominent disciples of the Vilna Gaon (the "genius of Vilna," Rabbi Eliyahu ben Shlomo Zalman), Reb Chaim Volozhiner established the yeshiva in Volozhin, Lithuania.. This renowned institution, which endured for one hundred years, became the model for all Lithuanian yeshivot after it. Reb Chaim perpetuated the Vilna Gaon's study methods: incisive analysis of Talmudic text coupled with deep study of the Rishonim (pre-1550 Talmudic commentators).

Reb Chaim's major work was the *Nefesh Hachaim,* which he wrote "to implant the fear of God, Torah, and pure worship into the hearts of the upright who are seeking the ways of God."

Chatam Sofer – Rabbi Moshe ben Shmuel Sofer; rabbinic leader, Talmudic scholar, halachist, biblical commentator (Germany, Hungary, 1762–1839).

A child prodigy, the Chatam Sofer entered yeshiva at the age of nine and was delivering public lectures by the age of thirteen. After years of intensive study, he assumed rabbinic and teaching positions in several communities before accepting, in 1807, his primary position in Pressburg, Hungary. There he established a major yeshiva which housed, at its height, five hundred students, many of whom went on to become influential leaders in their own right.

Reacting to the newly developing Reform movement, the Chatam Sofer vehemently opposed any changes or innovations in Jewish practice. He is considered by many to be one of the most influential figures in the development of Chareidi Judaism (the most theologically conservative form of Orthodox Judaism today). The Chatam Sofer authored numerous important responsa (answers to halachic questions) as well as oft-studied commentaries on the Torah and Talmud.

Chizkuni – Rabbi Chizkiya ben Manoach Chizkuni; biblical commentator (France, thirteenth century).

Almost nothing is known about the personal life of the Chizkuni, a classical biblical commentator who lived in Provence around the year 1250. The Chizkuni's commentary, which focuses on the *pshat* (simple meaning) of the text, is based, according to the author, upon a number of earlier sources. In particular, the Chizkuni often elaborates upon the observations of Rashi.

The commentary of the Chizkuni first appeared in print in Venice in 1524.

Da'at Zekeinim Miba'alei Hatosafot – A compilation of Torah commentary authored by the Tosafists (a large group of twelfth- to thirteenth-century medieval rabbis whose critical and explanatory glosses are basic to the study of Talmud).

The period of the Tosafists began after the completion of Rashi's commentaries; the first Tosafists were actually Rashi's sons-in-law and grandsons. The Talmudic commentaries of the Tosafists are characterized by lengthy analyses of difficult passages and by a willingness to critically review the positions of their predecessors, particularly Rashi.

Preserved in manuscript for centuries, the *Da'at Zekeinim Miba'alei Hatosafot* was first formally published in 1783.

Hirsch, Rabbi Shimshon Raphael – Biblical commentator, rabbinic leader, philosopher (Germany, 1808–1888).

In the wake of the emancipation, traditional Judaism was desperately in need of a powerful leader to guide the transition of Orthodoxy into a new world marked by greater freedom. Rabbi Shimshon Raphael Hirsch successfully filled that role.

In 1851, Hirsch relinquished a prominent rabbinic post to become the rabbi of eleven individuals who had separated from the general community of Frankfurt-on-the-Main in response to that community's shift towards Reform Judaism. From those humble beginnings, Hirsch built a model Orthodox community of five hundred members.

Hirsch developed a philosophy of *Torah im Derech Eretz* (lit.: Torah and the way of the land) which envisioned a relationship between traditional observant Judaism and the modern world. Much controversy exists today as to the exact dimensions of the relationship envisioned by Hirsch. There is no question, however, that Hirsch's contributions were instrumental in the development of German Orthodox Jewry and paved the way for the development of today's Modern Orthodox community throughout the Jewish world. Hirsch published many works including *Nineteen Letters*, in which he brilliantly responds to the major philosophical questions of his day; *Horeb*, a text outlining his approach to Jewish belief and practice; and an extensive, thought provoking, commentary on the Torah.

Ibn Ezra – Rabbi Avraham ben Meier Ibn Ezra; biblical commentator, philosopher, poet, grammarian, physician, astronomer/astrologer (Spain, Egypt, North Africa, Italy, France, England, Israel, 1092–1167).

Over the course of an impoverished and itinerant life, the Ibn Ezra made a profound contribution to Jewish scholarship. A prolific poet, the Ibn Ezra produced treatises on Hebrew grammar, mathematics, astronomy/astrology and philosophy.

The Ibn Ezra's greatest contribution, however, was made through his renowned commentary on the Torah and other books of Tanach (an acronym for the biblical canon – Torah, Nevi'im, Ketuvim: the five books of Moses, the Prophets and the Writings). This work, which inspired numerous super-commentaries, is singular for its strong use of grammatical principles to uncover the *pshat* of the text. While the Ibn Ezra's commentary included a great deal of exegetical material authored by his predecessors, he did not shy away from offering his own original observations.

Leibowitz, Dr. Nehama – Biblical scholar and commentator, teacher (Israel, 1905–1997).

Born in Riga, Latvia, Nehama Leibowitz was awarded a doctorate from the University of Berlin in 1930 and emigrated that same year to the British Mandate of Palestine. Over the course of her career, Leibowitz taught for decades at a religious Zionist teachers seminary, lectured at Tel Aviv University, where she was appointed full professor, delivered regular radio addresses on Voice of Israel radio and lectured in a multitude of settings throughout the country.

Leibowitz is best known for her *gilyonot* (lit.: pages), stencils on the weekly Torah reading which she distributed to all interested. Her incisive analytical approach to text made these *gilyonot* immensely popular and through their distribution she rekindled intense interest in the study of biblical text and commentary throughout the Jewish world. Later Leibowitz produced formal studies, which were eventually collected into books on the Torah. Leibowitz was awarded the Israel Prize for education in 1957.

Malbim – Rabbi Meier Leib ben Yechiel Michael; biblical commentator, community rabbi (Poland, Romania, Russia, 1809–1879).

The Malbim served as the rabbi of a series of prominent communities including Bucharest, where, for a time, he assumed the position of chief rabbi of Romania. The Malbim's strong defense of traditional Judaism and his unwavering opposition to the new rites and practices promulgated by the Reform movement provoked the resentment of many wealthy German Jews. Repeatedly, the Malbim's persecutors managed to instigate his removal from rabbinic positions and, on one occasion, their accusations actually led to his imprisonment.

The Malbim's incisive commentary on the Torah, *Hatorah V'hamitzva*, is noteworthy for projecting the unity of the Written and Oral Law and for its strong foundation in linguistic analysis.

Machzor Vitri – Halachic-liturgical work compiled in the late eleventh to early twelfth century.

The Machzor Vitri, an important source for the historical study of halacha and liturgy, was compiled by Rabbi Simcha ben Shmuel (d. 1105), one of Rashi's outstanding students. Designed to give the halachic rulings concerning the liturgical cycle of the year, the text includes information concerning the weekday, Shabbat and festival prayers. The Machzor Vitri also contains laws pertaining to other areas of Jewish observance including Shabbat, marriage and *shechita* (ritual slaughter).

Later editions of the Machzor Vitri were produced over the years with additional material added.

Mecklenberg, Rabbi Yaakov Tzvi – Rabbi, biblical commentator (East Prussia, 1785–1865).

Mecklenberg began his rabbinic career in 1829 when he became the assistant to the rabbi of Koenigsberg, the capital of the German province of East Prussia. In 1831, he graduated to the role of rabbi and remained in that position until the day he died.

Mecklenberg's major work was *Haktav V'hakabala*, a commentary on the Torah which stressed the indivisibility of the Written and Oral Law. Responding to the emerging claims of the Haskala (Enlightenment) movement that the traditional explanations of the Torah were outdated and far-fetched, Mecklenberg demonstrated the authentic textual and linguistic basis for traditional interpretation.

Midrash Hagadol – Collection of Midrashim compiled in the late thirteenth century by the Yemenite scholar Rabbi David Ben Avraham Adani.

This work, culled from ancient Tannaitic (Mishnaic) sources, was preserved in manuscript for centuries and studied primarily within the Yemenite community. European scholars, within the last 150 years, have printed carefully edited versions of the text. The Midrash Hagadol serves as a significant record of many teachings from the Mishnaic and Talmudic period which are found in no other source.

Midrash Lekach Tov – A Midrashic commentary on the Torah and the five Megilla scrolls.

Also known by the title *Psikta Zutarta*, this work was compiled by the Bulgarian rabbinic scholar Tuvia Ben Eliezer in the late eleventh century.

Midrash Rabba – A collection of Midrashic anthologies on various books of Tanach.

Although the title "Rabba" is shared by all of these anthologies, they are not a cohesive work but a series of Midrashic texts edited in different centuries and in various locales. Bereishit Rabba (Midrash Rabba Bereishit) was compiled in the sixth century and consists of wide-ranging ethical teachings, homilies, maxims, parables and metaphors all connected (albeit sometimes loosely) to the text of Bereishit.

Midrash Sechel Tov – A Midrashic anthology compiled in the twelfth century by Rabbi Menachem ben Shlomo.

While this Midrashic work originally covered all the books of the Torah, only the portions relating to Bereishit and Shmot have been preserved. The text reflects the author's comprehensive knowledge of halacha as well as his great interest in linguistic topics and Hebrew grammar.

Midrash Tanchuma – A compilation of Midrashim, many of which are ascribed to the Talmudic sage Tanchuma Bar Abba.

Rav Tanchuma Bar Abba, who lived in Israel during the second half of the fourth century CE, was a student of the renowned sage Rav Huna and a major author of *aggadot* (Midrashic tales). The text ascribed to his name has appeared over the centuries in various versions.

Mishna – First official written summary of the Oral Law.

The editing of the Mishna by Rabbi Yehuda Hanasi at the end of the second century CE marked a major transformation in the mode of transmission of Jewish tradition. Until this time, the distinction between Written Law (Torah Shebichtav) and Oral Law (Torah Sheb'al Peh) had been studiously maintained, the latter memorized and transmitted verbally across the centuries. Driven by the fear, however, that the Oral Law would be lost if not recorded in writing, Rabbi Yehuda developed the six "orders" of the Mishna. This pioneering sage, however, preserved the character of the Oral Law by recording the Mishnaic edicts in short, cryptic style which requires immediate further oral explication.

The sages of the Mishna are known as the Tannaim.

Netziv – Rabbi Naftali Tzvi Yehuda Berlin; Talmudic scholar, rosh yeshiva, biblical commentator (Poland, Russia, 1817–1893).

For forty years beginning in 1854, the Netziv served as the rosh yeshiva of the Yeshiva of Volozhin. The Netziv's scholarship, coupled with a deep personal love for all of his students, transformed the yeshiva into the largest such institution of its time and a major spiritual center for the Russian Jewish community. His opposition to the secularization of the yeshiva eventually brought him into conflict with government authorities and, according to some versions, led to the yeshiva's closing in 1892 (others suggest that the closure was due to internal upheaval). The Netziv was one of the early supporters of Jewish settlement in the Land of Israel.

Among the Netziv's publications was his popular biblical commentary, the *Ha'ameik Davar*, in which he emphasized the consonance between Talmudic interpretation and the *pshat* of the Torah text.

A son of the Netziv's first marriage was Rabbi Chaim Berlin, who became chief rabbi of Moscow and subsequently chief rabbi of the Ashkenazic community in Yerushalayim; a son of his second marriage was Rabbi Meir Berlin (later Bar-Ilan), a leader of the religious Zionist Mizrachi movement who inspired the creation of Bar-Ilan University (named in his memory).

Ohr Hachaim – Rabbi Chaim Ibn Attar; biblical commentator, Talmudic scholar, kabbalist (Morocco, Israel, 1696–1743).

One of the most prominent rabbis in his native land of Morocco, the Ohr Hachaim decided in 1733 to resettle in the Land of Israel. He was, however, detained along the way in Livorno, Italy, by leading members of the Jewish community who established a Talmudic Academy for him. Finally arriving in Jerusalem in 1742, the Ohr Hachaim served as the head of the Beit Midrash Knesset Yisrael until his death.

The Ohr Hachaim's commentary on the Torah combines textual analysis with Talmudic and kabbalistic insights. Over the years, this commentary has become particularly popular within the Sephardic and Chassidic communities.

Onkelos – Convert to Judaism, scholar and author of the seminal Aramaic translation of the Torah, *Targum Onkelos* (Rome, Israel, 35–120 CE).

According to tradition, Onkelos was the nephew of the Roman emperor Titus (who, as a general, was responsible for the destruction of the Second Temple).

After his conversion, Onkelos authored *Targum Onkelos*, a monumental interpretive translation of the Torah into Aramaic. This translation, which received the approbation of Onkelos' teachers, the Mishnaic scholars Rabbi Eliezer and Rabbi Yehoshua, offers striking insights into the text. So authoritative did this work become that the rabbis of the Talmud decreed that the weekly reading of the Torah portion should include the reading of the *Targum*, as well. *Targum Onkelos* is included in almost all published editions of the Torah today.

Pirkei D'Rabi Eliezer – Midrashic work on Bereishit, Shmot and portions of Bamidbar.

Pirkei D'Rabi Eliezer is ascribed to the Tannaitic (Mishnaic) sage Rabbi Eliezer ben Hyrcanus (first century CE). In spite of its early roots, the first authoritative version of this text apparently appeared in the ninth century.

Rabbeinu Bachya – Rabbi Bachya ben Asher; biblical commentator, rabbinic judge, preacher (Spain, 1263–1340).

A disciple of the renowned Talmudist Rabbi Shlomo ben Aderet (the Rashba), Rabbeinu Bachya served as a preacher and a *dayan* (rabbinical judge) in Saragossa, Spain. Rabbeinu Bachya is best known for his commentary on the Torah, which combines *pshat*, Midrash, philosophy and Kabbala. Each weekly parsha is introduced by an ethical discussion citing a verse from Proverbs.

Radak – Rabbi David Kimchi; biblical commentator, philosopher, grammarian (France, 1160–1235).

Best known for his commentary on the books of the Prophets, the Radak also wrote commentaries on Psalms, Proverbs and Chronicles. His commentary on Bereishit stresses the ethical underpinnings of the narrative and includes mystical interpretations of specific biblical stories.

The Radak's works, in general, are noteworthy for their stress on grammar, language and literal meanings of words in the text. He distinguished between interpretations which conformed to the *pshat* and homiletical *drashot* (which he often included for added interest).

Ralbag – Rabbi Levi ben Gershon; Talmudic scholar, commentator, philosopher, mathematician, astronomer/astrologer (France, 1288–1344).

Little is known about the life of this revolutionary Jewish philosopher who authored works ranging from biblical commentary to acclaimed philosophical and mathematical treatises. His major philosophical text, *Sefer Milchamot Hashem* (The Wars of the Lord), was composed over a twelve-year period and earned the Ralbag renown well beyond the Jewish community.

In opposition to the generally accepted position of classical Judaism, the Ralbag maintained that God deliberately limits his own omniscience with regard to his foreknowledge of human acts. By stating that God knows the choices available to us but consciously chooses not to know the specific decisions that we will make, the Ralbag addressed the age-old dilemma of how man's free will can exist in the face of God's omniscience.

Rambam – Rabbi Moshe ben Maimon, also known as Maimonides; widely recognized as the greatest post-Talmudic authority on Jewish law and thought (Spain, Morocco, Egypt, 1135–1204).

The Rambam's works include *The Guide to the Perplexed*, a philosophical work on Jewish theology; *Sefer Hamitzvot*, a compendium of the 613 commandments of the Torah; a commentary on the Mishna; and his magnum opus, the *Mishneh Torah*, a masterful, comprehensive code of Jewish law. In his commentary on the Mishna, the Rambam delineated thirteen principles still considered to be the cornerstones of Jewish belief. His *Mishneh Torah* launched the course for halachic codification across the ages and served as the forerunner of other essential texts such as the *Arba Turim* and the *Shulchan Aruch*.

A royal physician and world-class philosopher, the Rambam made a monumental impact upon the development of Jewish tradition and law, reflected in the well-known dictum inscribed on his tomb: "From Moshe (Moses) to Moshe (Rambam) no one arose like Moshe."

Ramban – Rabbi Shlomo ben Nachman, also known as Nachmanides; biblical and Talmudic commentator, scholar, physician (Spain, Israel, 1194–1270).

The Ramban's commentary on the Torah combines *pshat*, Midrash and kabbalistic insights. A towering figure in the history of Jewish scholarship, the Ramban authored numerous works on the Talmud as well as Jewish law and thought. His vigorous defense of Judaism in the face of Christian attack culminated in a public disputation with the Jewish apostate Pablo Christiano, in the presence of King James of Spain in 1263.

The Ramban's deep love for the Land of Israel is manifest in his writings and in his philosophy of Jewish law. In 1267, at the age of seventy-two, the Ramban settled in the Land of Israel and worked vigorously to rebuild Jerusalem's Jewish community.

Ran – Rabbi Nissim ben Reuven; Talmudic scholar, halachist, philosopher, physician (Spain, 1290–1380).

Widely recognized as the greatest rabbinic authority of his time, the Ran served as rabbi of Barcelona and responded to thousands of halachic inquiries from across the Jewish diaspora. The Ran is best known for his practical commentary on the halachic work of Rabbi Yitzchak ben Yaakov Alfasi (the Rif). Through this commentary, the Ran achieved a revered position in the world of Talmudic scholarship. The Ran's compendium of sermons, *Drashot HaRan,* provides insight into many of the basic tenets of Jewish faith.

Rashbam – Rabbi Shmuel ben Meier; biblical commentator, Talmudic scholar (France, 1080–1158).

The Rashbam, Rashi's grandson, was a leading member of the Tosafists (a large group of medieval rabbis whose critical and explanatory glosses are basic to the study of the Talmud). The Rashbam's commentary on the Torah is remarkable for its bold adherence to *pashut pshat* even when the *pshat* leads to controversial conclusions. The Rashbam took issue with his renowned grandfather's periodic Midrashic interpretation of the text and, in fact, claimed, "I debated with him [Rashi] and he admitted to me that, if he had the time, he would be obligated to author other commentaries based upon the straightforward explanations of the text…."

So great was the storm concerning some of the Rashbam's views that his commentary on the first chapters of Bereishit was omitted in many earlier editions of the Bible.

Rashi – Rabbi Shlomo Yitzchaki; arguably the greatest of all biblical and Talmudic commentators (France, 1040–1105).

Rashi's commentary on the Torah, considered an essential companion to the study of the text, combines *pshat* with the periodic referencing of Midrash (when he feels such referencing is necessary for textual comprehension).

In addition to commentaries on the Prophets and Writings, Rashi also authored an indispensable running commentary on the Talmud, known for its brevity and clarity.

No course of study in the Torah or Talmud is considered complete without the accompanying study of Rashi's commentary.

Reischer, Rabbi Yaakov ben Yosef – Rabbi, halachist, rabbinical judge (Czechoslovakia, Bavaria, Germany, 1670–1733).

Rabbi Yaakov Reischer served as rabbi, *dayan* (judge) and *av beit din* (head of the Jewish court) in various locations including Prague, Ansbach, Worms and Metz. While his strong leadership periodically engendered controversy, he became accepted by many of his contemporaries as the preeminent halachic authority of his day. His collection of responsa, *Shevut Yaakov*, contains queries addressed to him from the whole Jewish diaspora as well as from Israel.

Rivash – Rabbi Isaac ben Sehshet Perfet; Talmudic scholar, halachist, rabbi (Spain, Algiers, 1326–1408).

A student of renowned scholars, including Rabbi Nissim ben Reuven (the Ran), the Rivash earned his own scholarly reputation at an early age. Nonetheless, he led a private life, assuming his first rabbinic position approximately at the age of fifty. His communal career was marked by controversy and false accusation resulting, in one instance, in imprisonment for several months. The anti-Jewish riots of 1391 forced the Rivash to leave Spain and to finally settle in Algiers where, after some initial difficulty, he eventually enjoyed the deep affection and respect of the Jewish community.

The greatest contribution of the Rivash lay in his responsa, which greatly influenced the subsequent development of halacha.

Sfat Emet – Rabbi Yehuda Aryeh Leib Alter; Chassidic leader, Talmudic scholar, biblical commentator(Poland, 1847–1905).

One of the greatest Talmudic scholars of his generation, the Sfat Emet assumed the leadership of the Ger Chassidic movement in 1870. His works on the Talmud became renowned well beyond his own Chassidic community and are studied today by serious students throughout the Jewish world. His monumental commentary on the Torah, based on homilies delivered over the course of his life, was published posthumously and is arranged according to the weekly Torah readings and festivals. The Sfat Emet stresses the moral and ethical lessons to be derived from the text.

Sforno – Rabbi Ovadia Sforno; biblical commentator, Talmudic scholar, philosopher, physician (Italy, 1470–1550).

The Sforno's broad-based education earned him recognition in many fields including law, philosophy, mathematics, medicine, Hebrew language and Hebrew literature. When the famous German humanist Johan Reuchlin desired to perfect his knowledge of Hebrew literature, Cardinal Domenico Grimani advised him to approach the Sforno. A prolific writer, the Sforno is best known for his clear commentary on the Torah and many books of Tanach. These works reflect great respect for the *pshat* of the text and are written in a beautiful, almost lyrical style.

Soloveitchik, Rabbi Yosef Dov – The Rav; pioneering spiritual leader of the Modern Orthodox movement in America and throughout the Jewish world (Lithuania, America, 1903–1993).

Scion of a two-hundred-year-old rabbinic dynasty, the Rav arrived in America in 1932 armed with an education that combined traditional Lithuanian Talmudic studies and a Ph.D. in philosophy from the University of Berlin. He assumed a rabbinic position in Boston where he established the Maimonides School and played a major role in many facets of the community's development. In 1941, he succeeded his father, Rabbi Moshe Soloveitchik, as the head of the Rabbi Isaac Elchanan Theological Seminary rabbinic school of Yeshiva University. For decades thereafter he commuted weekly between Boston and New York.

The Rav combined vast Torah and secular knowledge, a deeply analytical mind, powerful teaching ability and majestic oratorical skill with a magnetic leadership personality. Through his classes, widely attended public lectures, writings and policy decisions he furthered the philosophy of encounter between the highest form of Torah knowledge and the best secular scholarship of Western civilization. Adviser and teacher to tens of thousands, the Rav shaped the course of Modern Orthodox philosophy through the twentieth century and beyond.

Steinsaltz, Rabbi Adin – Talmudic scholar, philosopher, social critic and author (Israel, contemporary).

Cited in 1988 by *Time* magazine as "a once in a millennium scholar," Rabbi Adin Steinsaltz is renowned for his innovative, even daring attempts to open the study of Talmud and other areas of Jewish thought to the masses. In 1965, he founded the Israel Institute for Talmudic Publications and began to produce translations of the Babylonian Talmud from the original Aramaic into Hebrew, English, Russian and various other languages. The

Steinsaltz edition of the Talmud also includes his own running explanation of and commentary on the text.

In addition to his edition of the Talmud, Steinsaltz has authored roughly sixty books and hundreds of articles on topics including Talmud, Jewish mysticism, historical biography, sociology and philosophy. The founder of a network of schools in Israel and in the former Soviet Union, Steinsaltz has lectured extensively in prestigious settings throughout the world. In 1988, Rabbi Steinsaltz was awarded the Israel Prize for his accomplishments in the field of Torah and education.

Talmud Bavli – Babylonian Talmud; foundational compilation of the halachic (legal) and aggadic (ethical-homiletical) discussions of the sages of the Babylonian academies from the second through the fifth centuries CE.

The scholars of the Talmud, known as the Amoraim, expound at great length upon the concise teachings of the Mishna, often digressing to discuss loosely related issues and ideas. Structurally, the style of the Talmud Bavli can best be described as "conversation in suspended animation," reflecting the origin of its subject matter, which was memorized and transmitted orally for centuries before its eventual written recordation.

Together with the Mishna, the Talmud Bavli serves as the basic source for the continually developing Oral Law.

Talmud Yerushalmi – Jerusalem Talmud; collection of the teachings of the sages of the Israeli academies from 200 to 350 CE.

Like the Talmud Bavli, the Talmud Yerushalmi centers on the discussions of the Amoraim (Talmudic scholars) concerning the Mishna. The Talmud Yerushalmi, however, is smaller in scope, more fragmented, and more difficult to study than its Babylonian counterpart; consequently, over the centuries, the Yerushalmi has exerted less influence upon the development of Jewish law. The return to the land of Israel in recent years has given birth to a renewed interest in the Talmud Yerushalmi and the laws it contains pertaining to the land.

Targum Yonatan – Interpretive Aramaic translation of the Torah commonly attributed to Yonatan ben Uziel.

The correct name of this translation, according to most biblical scholars, is Targum Yerushalmi (Jerusalem Targum [translation]). Probably due to a printer's error (in Hebrew, as in English, the first letters of Targum Yerushalmi and Targum Yonatan are the same) the work was mistakenly labeled Targum Yonatan and attributed erroneously to Yonatan ben Uziel, an outstanding pupil of the renowned Mishnaic sage Hillel. Yonatan ben Uziel did produce a famous translation of the Books of the Prophets which, according to the Talmud, reflects the interpretation of the prophets Chagai, Zacharia and Malachi. The Talmud makes no mention, however, of a Targum on the Torah produced by this sage. The erroneous attribution is perpetuated in many current Chumashim. To address the issue, scholars refer to this biblical translation as the Targum Pseudo-Yonatan.

The Targum Pseudo-Yonatan contains much aggadic material from various sources and is both translation and commentary. The actual date of its composition remains a matter of dispute.

Yaffe, Rabbi Mordechai ben Avraham – Rabbi, halachist, commentator (Czechoslovakia, Poland, 1530–1612).

A student of the great halachic authorities Rabbi Moshe Isserles (the Rema) and Rabbi Shlomo Luria (the Maharshal), Yaffe served in rabbinic positions in Prague, Grodno, Kemenetz and Posen. He earned renown as the "Baal Halevushim," author of the *Levushim*, ten commentaries on various aspects of Jewish knowledge including halacha, astronomy, philosophy and Kabbala. His work on Rashi's biblical commentary was called the *Levush Haora*.

Index

H

I

J

Z

Praise for *Unlocking the Torah Text*

"Rabbi Goldin's superb collection of essays in *Unlocking the Torah Text* illuminates basic themes in Vayikra. Through careful reading of the Torah text, especially through the prism of Chazal, he interprets what to some might seem philosophically remote. His scholarship and pedagogy make the Torah text…easily accessible and alive. It is a wonderful and inspiring read."

– **Rabbi Menachem Genack**
General Editor, OU Press

"I have found in Rabbi Goldin's volumes a fascinating mix: his thoughts are refreshingly original, while being well grounded in the classic commentaries; his conclusions are profoundly relevant to the contemporary scene, while remaining true to our age-old traditions."

– **Rabbi Dovid Miller**
Rosh Yeshiva and Associate Director
Yeshiva University's Joseph S. and Caroline Gruss Institute, Jerusalem

"Rabbi Goldin performs his task with consummate skill and in a style of writing that will appeal both to the scholar and to the ordinary reader interested in gaining an insight into the Torah text. The result is a grand tapestry of *pshat* and *drash*, classic exegesis and original thought, biblical narrative and issues facing our own society today."

– Moshe Aumann
Former Israeli Consul General to the United States
Counselor for Relations with the Christian Churches, *Jewish Press*

"[A] challenge to the reader, a challenge well worth taking. Rabbi Goldin is both a skillful teacher and writer.… [T]he book will serve as a valued resource in better understanding all the events of the Exodus, Matan Torah (Giving of the Torah) and the Mishkan's construction, as well as the incident of the Golden Calf."

– Alan Jay Gerber
"Kosher Bookworm," *Jewish Star*

"Rabbi Shmuel Goldin demonstrates in his volumes of *Unlocking the Torah Text* a remarkable knack for identifying [compelling] topics. He surveys the classic approaches to the issues addressed and then adds a new and often surprising layer of interpretation that addresses contemporary concerns and sensibilities. Many of Rabbi Goldin's novel insights serve as a springboard to vigorous classroom discussion and debate. The combination of the old and the new provides for an enriching and vigorous learning experience for a wide range of audiences.... [A] major contribution to serious study of Chumash in our day."

– Rabbi Chaim (Howard) Jachter
Rebbe, Torah Academy of Bergen County
Co-rabbi, Shaarei Orah, the Sephardic Congregation of Teaneck
Dayan, Beth Din of Elizabeth; author, three volumes of *Gray Matter*

"Rare is a study of the weekly parsha which speaks to all the generations. Rabbi Goldin's *Unlocking the Torah Text* breaks new ground not only in its clear, fascinating insights into the Torah text but in its compelling appeal to young and old alike. Many of our school's parents use Rabbi Goldin's books as the basis of their Shabbat dinner Torah discussions and have shared with me how much their children look forward each week to the challenging and dramatically presented questions which Rabbi Goldin explores. For any parent and Jewish educator seeking to inspire their children with the love of Torah, *Unlocking the Torah Text* is essential."

– Dr. Elliot Prager
Principal, The Moriah School, Englewood, NJ